MINNEAPOLIS
REHEARSALS

Tyrone Guthrie Directs Hamlet

MINNEAPOLIS REHEARSALS

Tyrone Guthrie Directs Hamlet

BY ALFRED ROSSI

UNIVERSITY OF CALIFORNIA PRESS
BERKELEY · LOS ANGELES · LONDON
1970

University of California Press
Berkeley and Los Angeles, California
University of California Press, Ltd.
London, England

Copyright © 1970, by
The Regents of the University of California

ISBN: 0–520–01719–6
Library of Congress Catalog Card Number: 70–115496
Printed in the United States of America

Designed by Dave Comstock

For the original Minnesota
Theatre Company, and especially
Pat Slingsby, my brother-in-law
and fellow-actor in *Hamlet*, who died
during the run of the production

FOREWORD by Alan Schneider

I don't remember exactly when I first met Tony Guthrie—my favorite director in the English-speaking world, and maybe in a few foreign languages as well—but I remember vividly when I first began chasing after him. Just after the war, the Theatre Guild brought before my youthful Washingtonian eyes a spectacular production of Andreyev's *He Who Gets Slapped*, replete with Stella Adler, Dennis King and directorial virtuosity and pyrotechnics such as I had only heard about and not seen. I dashed off my first (and last) fan letter to a director, one Tyrone Guthrie, in care of the Theatre Guild, detailing my enthusiasms and thanking him for having set me on fire. There was no answer to the letter. (I still wonder if Guthrie ever received it.) That was the first disappointment of a long line.

Not too many years afterward, when as resident director at Dartington Hall in England, I was being introduced to the special pastoral delights of Devonshire, as well as to the general richness of the current British theatre, I started hearing about a touring production of *Henry VIII*, directed by that same magical creature, Tyrone Guthrie (with settings by a Tanya Moiseiwitsch), as well as rumors of something called *An Satyre of the Three Estates* to be presented by him at the Edinburgh Festival in its second season (1948).

Immediately, I wrote a second letter to Mr. Guthrie explaining that I, too, was a director, young, gifted, and American, and terribly anxious to watch him at work. Could I come to a rehearsal somewhere in the Midlands, or wherever? Once more, no reply. Another letter; the same silence. Had I had enough shillings and a mastery of Button A and Button B of the British phone system, I might have telephoned; I didn't.

Instead, I journeyed all aglow to Edinburgh to watch, with practically mesmerized admiration, as on that bold tongue of a stage at the Assembly Hall there unrolled before me the rich tapestry of Guthrie's production of *The Three Estates*, a marvelously counter-

poised blend of *Henry V* and the Marx Brothers, which introduced me to the thrust stage, as well as determinedly and forever into
the ranks of the Guthrie worshippers. Of Guthrie himself, however,
hard at work with a flock of candelabras for another Festival production, I had only a glimpse and half a dozen fast words: Oh, dear,
yes he *had* gotten my letter. Who would want to watch *him* rehearse! In any case, he wasn't sure this would be possible because
he didn't know where or when, if ever, he'd be working again. (No
words about the current candlelight.) Yes, do keep after him if I
wanted to. Foiled again! I had, however, discovered something to
set my young blood roaring: Tyrone Guthrie did exist, albeit very
busy—and perhaps a bit vague.

Then, in 1953, something called the Stratford (Ont.) Festival began, and Zelda Fichandler and I (newly installed as Artistic
Director of the recently established Arena Stage) drove breathless-
ly through interminable wheat fields to Stratford's historic opening
night. Arriving there a night early, we scrambled down to the site to
catch our first glimpse of that glorious tent, and to hear a series of
frustratingly indistinct mutters from the rehearsal going on inside.
No amount of friendly persuasion or American guile could con-
vince a collection of Canadian watchdogs to let us sneak inside. We
had to be content with watching successions of off-duty actors attired
in glorious Moiseiwitsch costumes (the show was *Richard III*) pace
about, smoking or trying to make themselves comfortable. Eventually the rehearsal was over, and a little man emerged, got on a bicy-
cle stacked among many and peddled off past the trees. "My God,
that's Alec Guinness." He was followed by the "Master" himself, a
shirt-sleeved Guthrie, almost entirely bisected by a tremendous tu-
reen stacked full of props. He said hello without stopping forward
motion. Oh, yes, so glad we'd come all this way to see it—and him.
Yes, he remembered me indeed. Yes, he'd love to do a show for
Arena sometime: how about *Volpone*. As to seeing rehearsals? Oh
dear, we weren't really serious, were we?

And so on. Many times, many years. When Guthrie was
directing Thornton Wilder's *Matchmaker*, the predecessor to *Hello
Dolly!* in Philadelphia, I was getting ready to do that "celebrated"
second edition with Helen Hayes and Mary Martin of *Skin of Our
Teeth*. We had a drink in Thornton's hotel room. Could I watch
Tony's rehearsals? Oh, dear, he'd much rather watch mine. When
he was doing *The Tenth Man* on Broadway, I sent echelon after eche-

lon of my directing colleagues to the Booth Theatre to watch his in-
credibly skillful orchestration—à la New Yorkese—of that play's
inner movement and rhythms. Did I get to a rehearsal? No. When
his production of *Tamburlaine* came to the Winter Garden and laid
a big jeweled egg with the critics, I sat night after night in that practically empty theatre marveling at all of Guthrie's golden arrows,
literal and metaphorical. But I never even saw an understudy rehearsal. His failures were always more interesting than most people's
successes.

There were countless Guthrie productions, successes and
failures, which I somehow always managed to see: *Oedipus Rex,
All's Well That Ends Well, Gideon, Troilus and Cressida* at the Old
Vic, *Six Characters in Search of an Author* at the old Phoenix. But
did I see a rehearsal of his? Or watch him work? Or see how he dealt
with actors, or arranged those marvelously swirling crowd scenes,
or did a scene from scratch, or developed some lovely piece of business—like Lechery mocking Dame Chastity in the stocks by shaming
her with his finger and calling her "Chastititee"? Oh, dear, no!

Finally, Minneapolis gave birth to the Guthrie Theatre, and
I flew up after an afternoon's rehearsal of *Threepenny Opera* at the
Arena Stage to see the opening night of George Grizzard's *Hamlet*
—flying back the next morning in time to rehearse again. And one
bright day, shortly afterwards, I heard the persuasive voice of Tyrone
Guthrie, himself, on the phone, asking me if I'd come to the Guthrie
the following summer to direct *Skin of Our Teeth*. Would I! Yes,
I would—whatever the terms—but only if he'd let me watch him rehearse! Jolly laugh. Of course, my dear boy, if I were silly enough to
want to. Couldn't imagine why.

The next summer, for various subtle reasons, I directed *The
Glass Menagerie* instead of *Skin*, and I saw Guthrie all over the place,
including for tea and cocktails and we even had some political discussions. But rehearsals? Somebody in the scheduling department
was determined to keep us apart by always putting our rehearsals
together. I got to watch the voice coach and the movement coach all
right, and lots of Douglas Campbell; but Tony might as well have
been still at Edinburgh as far as I was concerned. Oh, yes, the night
Henry V went on, I watched for two hours while Tony was moving
some banner bearers hither and yon and George Grizzard, playing
Henry, and his Katherine stood around and got nervous. And Tony
did get to a *Menagerie* rehearsal to tell me he thought it was going to

be all right (it wasn't) and he didn't have many suggestions (he had a few).

All of which brings me to the subject of Mr. Rossi's labor of love—and observation. How startling it is, finally, to watch Tony Guthrie in rehearsal! How gratifying and how necessary. Because if one cannot get in in person—and you can see how hard I tried—at least in these all too few pages, one can get the flavor and sense of what was happening during this particular production and with this particular director in charge. I could wish that Mr. Rossi had now and then provided a bit more for us (or, sometimes a tiny bit less) of what actually went on or why. But for those of us who are directors, as well as for those of us who would like to be directors (and does that leave anyone out?) these pages are extremely enlightening—and often amusing, serious, understanding, and characteristic of the process and the man. And, forgive me, it is all much more "relevant" than something, say, by Alexander Dean—or some of his latter-day equivalents.

Thank you, Al, for finally getting me to Tony's rehearsals. They were worth the wait.

PREFACE

Less than a century ago an event took place which was to have an incalculable influence on the production of plays for the stage. On May 1, 1874, an unknown company of players under the aegis of George II, Duke of Saxe-Meiningen, opened an engagement in Berlin and the era of the modern stage director was born.

Since that auspicious day the importance of the stage director has grown astonishingly; not altogether a surprising fact, if one considers the astonishing individuals whose exceptional creative talents have graced this period. The names of Saxe-Meiningen, Antoine, Brahm, Stanislavsky, Nemirovich-Denchenko, Vakhtangov, Copeau, Jouvet, Poel, Granville-Barker, Meyerhold, Reinhardt, Belasco, Clurman, Kazan, Brook, and the subject of this work, Tyrone Guthrie, are as important to the history of world theatre in this period as those of any playwright, actor, or designer—perhaps more so. Their contributions to the image of the director as régisséur, the overseer of all aspects of a production, the one creative artist responsible for the unity of the *mise en scène*, are enormous.

Their work was, and is, however, as evanescent as it is prodigious, so that, except for film direction done by a few of these men, there is no way of re-experiencing their creative efforts. This is the inevitable fate of the theatre artist whose magic conjures a unique experience for his audience—it happens once and only once. Theatre experiences are unequivocally transient: they make their effect through ephemeral means and are almost impossible to analyze validly. Each observer at the two hours' traffic has a unique experience in the truest sense of the word, no two experiences are alike. They, unlike the phoenix, will never rise again, at least not in the same way.

Just as it is difficult for the artist to determine why a certain effect is made on an audience member, it is also difficult for the spectator to determine the techniques by which the effect is produced. Perhaps it should be. If when we view a work of art—in this case a play performed by living actors in the presence of an audience—it is easy to see all its pieces fitting into the aesthetic puzzle, it may be something less than a work of art. The total art experience does not lend itself to such scrutiny, at least not at the time of the experience. When techniques of construction are salient, be it on canvas, in a symphony, or on the stage of a theatre, the result is, generally, less satisfying than when the whole subsumes its parts. This is the chief reason for the difficulties which arise in analyzing a work of art, or, we may add, the workings of an artist. The stuff of which art is made is not always easily definable simply because the stuff of artistry is even less definable.

We can assume that in all creative artists there is a communality: inspiration, the essential without which no work of art can be created. But the nature of inspiration is inscrutable, its variances kaleidoscopic, the degrees of influence unknown, and its patterns unpredictable with as many specific instances as there are artists to experience them.

Since we cannot turn to the study of inspiration in determining the composition of artistry, what then is our course? What follows in this book is an attempt to present one method by which this elusive goal might be achieved: a record of the practical work of a creative artist of the theatre in the daily rehearsals of a play culminating in presentation before an audience.

The artist with whom we are concerned is Tyrone Guthrie; his artistry is directing plays. The play thus recorded is *Hamlet*, presented as the premiere production of The Minnesota Theatre Company at The Tyrone Guthrie Theatre in Minneapolis in 1963.[1]

The first day of rehearsals for this initial season was March 11; closing night was September 22. During this period The Minnesota Theatre Company rehearsed and performed four productions: *Hamlet* and *The Miser* opening on consecutive nights, May 7 and 8; *The Three Sisters* on June 18; and *Death of a Salesman* on July 16.

As a member of the playing company who appeared in all of the productions, and, as Assistant to the Director on *Hamlet*, I compiled a rehearsal log for the season's productions. The entries in the *Hamlet* log were originally written during rehearsals or shortly thereafter in an attempt to record the techniques of a master stage direc-

---

1. For a history of the founding of this theatre, the reader is referred to Tyrone Guthrie's own account: *A New Theatre* (New York: McGraw-Hill, 1964).

tor, with no attempt made to analyze or evaluate these notes at that time. The rehearsal log herein, however, does include editorial comments and observations not found in the original text. I found that I could not do this without bringing to bear upon the work a hindsight knowledge, so that the augmented log is, then, a combination of actual words, incidents, and observations during the *Hamlet* rehearsals and comments upon them made at a later time.

This book also includes the promptscript used for the *Hamlet* production. It is fortunate that Edward Payson Call, who compiled this script, executed his work with such perception, skill, and care, because it is an unusually clear record of the choreography of the production. It is unusual because the method employed consists mainly of verbalization of the action, instead of relying chiefly on staging diagrams, as is the common practice. As a result, his notations serve as a record of *stage directions* and not merely a record of *movement*, and the script is an invaluable document illustrating the results of Guthrie's rehearsal techniques. [In addition to the description of the action, Mr. Call included staging diagrams for all the group scenes—the first court scene, the Play scene, Ophelia's funeral, the finale, etc. Some of these diagrams are included here.]

The Minneapolis *Hamlet* was a modern-dress version with scenic and costume design by Guthrie's long-time collaborator and friend, Tanya Moiseiwitsch. A representative selection of Miss Moiseiwitsch's original designs are reproduced in this volume, as are production photographs.

It is my hope that the combination of the above—the *Hamlet* log, the promptscript, designs, and photographs—will present a meaningful record of the directorial techniques of a creative artist who has earned a place at the summit of his profession through a productive career as varied as it is international in scope and significance, an artist who has earned a rightful place in the line of succession which started with the Duke of Saxe-Meiningen.

ACKNOWLEDGMENTS

The author wishes to thank the following for help and co-operation in bringing this book to fruition: Tyrone Guthrie, first and foremost; The Cambridge University Press for permission to include its edition of *Hamlet*, Edited by J. Dover Wilson; *Drama Critique*, in which excerpts from the *Hamlet* log were printed; George Grizzard; Tanya Moiseiwitsch; Alan Schneider; Dan Sullivan of *The Los Angeles Times*; The Tyrone Guthrie Theatre Foundation; The University of Minnesota Library, and especially Mrs. Maxine B. Clapp, Archivist; WLOL-FM, Minneapolis; and Peter Zeisler.

HAMLET CAST LIST

Directed by Tyrone Guthrie   Designed by Tanya Moiseiwitsch
Music by Herbert Pilhofer

(Cast in order of appearance)

Francisco	William Pogue
Barnardo	Gordon Bryars
Horatio	Graham Brown
Marcellus	Paul Ballantyne
Ghost	Ken Ruta
Claudius	Lee Richardson
Gertrude	Jessica Tandy
Cornelius	Charles Cioffi
Voltimand	John Lewin
Laertes	Nicolas Coster
Polonius	Robert Pastene
Hamlet	George Grizzard
Ophelia	Ellen Geer
Reynaldo	Clayton Corzatte
Rosencrantz	Alfred Rossi
Guildenstern	Michael Levin
Player King	John Cromwell
Player Queen	Ruth Nelson
Lucianus	John Going
Prologue	James Lineberger
Musician	Katherine Emery
Musician	Carol Emshoff
Osric	Clayton Corzatte
Fortinbras	Claude Woolman
Captain	William Pogue
Sailor	Charles Cioffi
1st Grave Digger	Ed Preble
2nd Grave Digger	Ken Ruta
Priest	John Lewin

Court Ladies   Helen Backlin, Judith Doty,
Janet MacLachlan, Joan van Ark,
Selma Hopkins, Marion Miska

Officers and	Donald Forsberg, Thomas Nyman,
Councillors	Franklin Peters, Ronald Rogosheske,
	Kenneth Schuman, Pat Slingsby,
	Charles Stanley, Hans Von Mende
Sailors	Hans Von Mende, Ronald Rogosheske
Footmen	Edmond Poshek, Howard Moody

Production Stage Manager   Rex Partington
Stage Managers   Edward Payson Call, Gordon Smith
Assistant to the Director   Alfred Rossi

SCENE BREAKDOWN

Page	Script Scene No.				Our Scene No.	Description
1	Act 1,	scene	i		1	Battlements
9	”	”	”	ii	2	Court
19	”	”	”	iii	3	Laertes Departure
25	”	”	”	iv	4	Battlements
29	”	”	”	v	5	Hamlet-Ghost
37	Act 2,	scene	i		6	Reynaldo-Polonius
42	”	”	”	ii	7	Court-Arrival Players

FIRST INTERMISSION

63	Act 3,	scene	i		8	Court-Nunnery
70	”	”	”	ii	9	Advice to Players
74	”	”	”	ii (cont'd)	10	Play scene
85	”	”	”	iii	11	King's Bedroom
89	”	”	”	iv	12	Closet
98	Act 4,	scene	i		12A	
99	”	”	”	ii	13	Hide Fox
101	”	”	”	iii	14	Sending to England
103	”	”	”	iv	15	Fortinbras

SECOND INTERMISSION

106	Act 4,	scene	v		16	Court (Mad scene)
115	”	”	”	vi	17	Court (Letter to Horatio)
116	”	”	”	vii	18	Court (King-Laertes)
119	Act 5,	scene	i		19	Graveyard (Has plotting from 18 inserted at end)
132	”	”	”	ii	20	Court (Osric)
140	”	”	”	ii (cont'd)	21	Court (Finale)

CONTENTS

THE <u>HAMLET</u> LOG

March 11 – May 7, 1963

MARCH 11, 1963

In the zero degree cold of a Minneapolis morning I arrived
shortly before 10:00 A.M. at the still incomplete Tyrone Guthrie
Theatre. The Minnesota Theatre Company had been called together
for an official welcome by Tyrone Guthrie and Douglas Campbell,
the Assistant Artistic Director.

My initial impression of the theatre was that it was smaller
than I had imagined, but this was probably because of my previous ex-
posure to this theatre's model, the Stratford Ontario Festival Theatre, which seats 2258, while the capacity here is 1437. The theatre
has an intimacy which Stratford lacks, and a marvelously festive
feeling pervades the auditorium because of the seats of red, orange,
purple, gold, beige, blue, green, and yellow. Not all the seats have
been installed and workmen continued to do so, while members of
the press, radio, and television prepared to record for posterity this
first coming together of the company. The stage itself has a beautiful
warm, reddish glow, and appears to have been highly polished recently. The backstage area is entirely visible, since the moveable
back wall has not yet been installed.

There was a good deal of handshaking, milling around, and
coffee drinking, and then someone shouted, "Please remove your
overshoes before you come onstage." Guthrie then said, "Yes, take
off your boots," and those in the company thus outfitted did so, including the company's Hamlet, George Grizzard.

The company and other personnel of the theatre sat, stood,
and crouched on the stage and steps surrounding the polished oak
floor. When Guthrie began to speak, everyone quieted down:

> This will be a short address, highly spontaneous. Please do
> your best to look interested in my remarks.
>
> I bid you welcome to Minneapolis and to the theatre. I know
> all of you feel somewhat like a non-swimmer or non-diver
> who has got up on the high board. So do I.

3

As representatives of the various news media handled cameras, microphones, and notepads with professional aplomb, Guthrie gave the company its first direction: pose for the photographers. Campbell was given the choreographic assignment. The company walked to the rear of the stage, split into two groups right and left, and, as someone cried, "Esperance, Percy!" as inspiringly as the greatest Hotspur, the two flanks became a phalanx and thundered down center toward the grinding, exploding cameras.

Since neither the theatre itself nor the rehearsal room on the second floor is ready to accommodate rehearsals, the nearby Unitarian Church is to serve as a rehearsal hall for the next two weeks. After giving us this information, Guthrie told the company to assemble at the Center in "no more than ten minutes." With that gentle admonition the newborn cry of players struggled back into overshoes and coats, exited the theatre, and climbed the frozen hill in back of the building. On the way members of the company became more acquainted with each other, and spirits were high. Although I hardly think Guthrie planned it, the company's trudge through the snow, slipping on the icy slope, produced a salutary communal experience which unified the heterogeneous group in an unexpected way.

At the Center, in a large room on the floor of which the perimeter of the theatre's asymmetrical, pentagonal stage is outlined in masking tape, Guthrie's first piece of business was to read the entire cast list of *Hamlet* from the title role to the Fourth Undertaker. Since most of the McKnight Fellows[1] in the company and the extras did not know what their assignments were, this listing attracted a good deal of attention. The reading included every double or triple to be played by a member of the company, such as "Cornelius and Sailor: Cioffi," or "Lucianus, Soldier, and Undertaker: Going." The roster contained the names of 42 company members (including extras) and 52 roles (speaking and supernumerary, Shakespeare's and Guthrie's). There were some interesting listings: "Lifeguards," which we later learned were the King's personal bodyguards; "Undertakers," or pallbearers; and a "Ghost Double." The only characters cut from Shakespeare's text are the English Ambassadors in the last scene of the play.

---

1. There are twelve students from the University of Minnesota on McKnight Foundation Fellowships assigned to work at the Guthrie Theatre each in his own area of specialization. In the acting company there are six Fellows in acting, two in Directing, and the Playwriting Fellow.

When Guthrie read the name of the actor playing Hamlet, he pronounced it *Griz*-zard, at which George smiled, since he had introduced himself to members of the company as George Griz-*zard*. Guthrie's way does sound better with *Ham*-let.

During this time Tanya Moiseiwitsch, the theatre's designer, had been quietly arranging her costume designs in another part of the room. We were then invited by Guthrie to look at the costume sketches and at a cardboard and balsa wood model of the stage and furnishings which Miss Moiseiwitsch had constructed.

From previously published newspaper interviews, rumors, and now from the designer's sketches we learned that the play is to be done in modern dress, in this case modern meaning a period just before World War I. The court is to have a decidedly European look to it with men in full-dress, ceremonial uniforms and the women in long gowns and full-length gloves. A number of the men, including Hamlet, are to wear custom-tailored business suits, and Miss Moiseiwitsch apologized for not having designs for them: "I'm not very good at sketching suits."

I expected some comments from Guthrie or the designer about their conception of the play and the reasons for their visual choices, but they did not come—at least not to the company as a whole.

Douglas Campbell then read the cast list of *The Miser,* and informed the company that each rehearsal day there will be a half hour devoted to fencing and dancing lessons. These sessions are primarily for the actors involved in those specific stage actions in both plays, but all members of the company are welcome. The periods of special training are to be conducted by Campbell prior to each day's rehearsal.

Hamlet and *The Miser* are to alternate in the six-day work week (Monday off). Today was a *Hamlet* day, so, after scripts were distributed, Guthrie began rehearsing Scene 1 (Act I, Scene 1).

Guthrie handed me a Minneapolis Public Library copy of *Hamlet* in The New Shakespeare series published by Cambridge University Press, edited and with notes by John Dover Wilson. He said, "Keep this handy. Uncle Dover's notes are awfully good, don't you think?"

There were no general comments from Guthrie about the production, no discussion of the play with anyone, no reading of the play; in fact, no comments, discussion, or reading of the first scene of the play, which was put on its feet immediately. Guthrie is probably the world's most prolific director in writing about his philosophy of the theatre and his approach to directing.[2] In a number of places he has stated that he eschews discussion as a rehearsal technique, so obviously he was practicing what he preaches. I personally wanted a bit more to go on, as we embarked on this Shakespearean adventure, and my feeling was that others in the cast felt the same way, but the excitement of the opening rehearsal atmosphere assuaged these qualms and off we confidently went with only Guthrie, at this point, knowing where or how.

Guthrie told Bill Pogue (Francisco), "There is implicit drama in the house lights going out, so let that mood carry over into Francisco's attitude."

Directions were given to stress the cold and the apprehensiveness of the situation. "A lower tone of voice suggests darkness."

An actor should be able "to build the scenery around him." Francisco was blocked to follow the perimeter of the stage when he walks guard. "This indicates the shape of the battlements. Look down; that tells a story too."

As the scene progressed Guthrie kept reminding the actors not to play front, that it wasn't a proscenium theatre, that people were going to be seated all around them, and that "even the backs of heads can act."

In this first blocking (and reading) of the scene, Guthrie gave some of the actors line readings with particular emphasis on phrasing, pauses for breath, and cushioning the "r" sound in the middle of a word following a vowel as in "buried." This specific instruction on the technique of reading the verse, even going as far as word stress, was a surprise to me since Guthrie had stated, especially in *A Life in the Theatre,* that this kind of coaching was to be reserved for certain kinds of actors:

> In theory, a director should not instruct his actors in the detailed playing of their parts. General aspects of a scene or a speech must be directed . . .
>
> But frequently, with the less gifted or intelligent or experienced actors, the director must coach the performer, show

2. He has published over sixty periodical articles, eight books, and a score of commentaries on individual plays.

him where to breathe in a speech, which words to stress, when to move, when to keep still.[3]

The four actors with whom Guthrie was working at the time were, I suppose, to varying degrees gifted, intelligent, and experienced, but he gave them little opportunity to exhibit these qualities because he was doing it for them. He seemed to be unwilling to let the actors discover things for themselves. Whether this manifests a lack of trust in the actors he has cast I don't know, but it can't be very encouraging for them, particularly at this earliest stage of rehearsal.

Guthrie told Graham Brown (Horatio) that "Fortinbras is an impudent bastard." Later in the scene, Graham started to deliver the famous line, " . . . the morn in russet mantle clad Walks o'er the dew of yon high eastward hill." He stopped and asked Guthrie where the light will be coming from. Guthrie answered, "Why do you want a pink light when you have a line like that?" Graham's reaction: laughter.

Although he did not elaborate, this implies that Guthrie has decided again not to use colored gelatin in the lighting instruments, a practice he initiated when he was using the open stage at Stratford Ontario.[4]

In building the atmosphere of the scene Guthrie suggested to the men on watch that they are reluctant to say "ghost," so that they all substitute other names for it—"thing," "illusion," "image," "apparition," "spirit," "object." This direction has immediate, discernible results, since it created a very slight pause before each of these substitute references, thereby projecting the characters' fear.

There is to be a Ghost Double, a second ghost figure, in the first scene. Guthrie asked me to walk this added role until he selects one of the extras to play it. The second ghost appears just before the cock crows, so that when the "real" ghost, upon hearing the cock, moves from center stage out the left tunnel (downstage left), the ghost double, appearing up right, will exit the right tunnel (downstage right). This physical action is timed to the lines:

3. Tyrone Guthrie, *A Life in the Theatre* (New York: McGraw-Hill, 1959), pp. 150–151.
4. For Guthrie's articulation of his feelings about this kind of lighting, the reader is referred to *Thrice the Brinded Cat Hath Mew'd* (Toronto: Clarke, Irwin, and Co., 1955), pp. 166–167.

HORATIO:	Speak of it; stay and speak.
	Stop it Marcellus.
MARCELLUS:	Shall I strike at it with my partisan?
HORATIO:	Do, if it will not stand.
BARNARDO:	'Tis here.
HORATIO:	'Tis here.
MARCELLUS:	'Tis gone.

Although he did not tell the actors the reason for the added figure, one can surmise that it lies in the repeated " 'Tis here."

The scene was done three times with fewer directions (and stops) each time.

The first court scene, Scene 2 (Act I, Scene 2), was next on the rehearsal agenda. It was done without the extras, who are not scheduled to join the company again until three weeks before the opening. Guthrie told the actors, "Take these positions. We'll worry about how you get there later."

It was obvious that Guthrie had not planned any specific positions for most of the actors in the scene, although as the scene progressed it was equally apparent that he wants certain things to happen which *had been* premeditated. He did not refer to the text nor to notes of any kind during the rehearsal.

Guthrie sees the assemblage as a reception for a newly-wedded pair (Claudius and Gertrude). "You may have champagne glasses for toasts." The scene will open with a sound cue, joyous bells.

The court is obsequious throughout the King's first speech, "Though yet of Hamlet our dear brother's death the memory be green. . . ." Claudius plays to the court for their open approval. Guthrie set a couple of applause cues. Polonius is to act like a stage manager throughout the proceedings, literally cuing the court for applause, reactions, movements, etc. He is also the first one to laugh at the things the King implies are funny; the court follows.

Just prior to the mention of Cornelius and Voltemand, Polonius motions them to step forward, then stops them just in front of the King. At the point where Claudius speaks the line, "and we here dispatch you good Cornelius, and you Voltemand . . . ," Guthrie broke in saying to Lee Richardson (Claudius), "You forget his name," pointing at John Lewin (Voltemand).

Hamlet's first line, "A little more than kin and less than kind," is not going to be treated as an aside, as is sometimes done. Guthrie wants it said after a pause. He said to George Grizzard (Hamlet), "It's a riddle, like his character."

When Claudius turns to Hamlet after giving Laertes permission to return to France, Guthrie told Bob Pastene (Polonius) to move the court away from the Prince. A few speeches later Guthrie demonstrated to Lee how he wants him to put his arm around Hamlet, "like a naughty child," and walk in a half-circle in front of the court "to pose for the photographers." No, cameramen have not been added to the scene.

Gertrude is very concerned about Hamlet's behavior, and is affectionate near the end of the scene. Guthrie told Jessica Tandy (Gertrude) to kiss Hamlet on both cheeks. At the end of the scene the royal couple sweep out followed by the court. Hamlet has been directed to follow, but the double doors which are to be up center will close in his face.

Guthrie told George that Hamlet will have a small photo of his father to which he can refer in the first soliloquy.

This scene, of course, is the first in the play for both Claudius and Hamlet, as well as for other major characters, like Gertrude, Polonius, and Laertes. Guthrie, at this rehearsal, did not discuss the scene with any of them.

It should be noted that George Grizzard arrived ten days earlier than most of the company, and that he and Guthrie worked alone during this period. Prior to their working together, George had written to Guthrie about the play, production, and his role, to which Guthrie responded:

> January 16, 1963
> Annaghmakerrig, Doohat, Monaghan, Ireland
> Dear George—
> Your multi-purpose letter of Dec. 28 only reached me yesterday. Perhaps instead of sending it by air (did you know they have FLYING machines now?) you specified sailing ship.
> Anyway, I hope the lateness of my reply won't stand between you and the Caribbean beach. *Plans*: I expect to reach Minn. by Feb. 14 and am ready to begin work as soon after that as

suits yourself. I think we should start our "private" work not later than Feb. 25 or so.

I've read a lot of books too and I agree there comes (really rather soon) a moment when one says to hell with all this scholarly poking about, let's just take a bash and see what it *sounds* and *feels* like.

You can stop right now depending on me for 98% of the performance. I know you don't mean it and only put it into your letter partly because you thought it was appropriate to neophyte Hamlet writing to elderly director. In fact the performance will be, *must* be almost entirely yours. You'll have to depend on me for the "set-up" of the scenes (largely dependent on casting) as well as tempo and positions (sorry, "Blocking"), but the interpretation must be YOU. I shall try and help you by advice and criticism, and, of course, we'll discuss each scene, each speech, each sentence together, but what we arrive at will be determined by your personality —appearance, tones of voice, rhythm, and so on. To put it another way: I shan't try (or anyway not consciously) to change YOU; only to help you to express what is already in you to express.

All the same, mind you, I don't think one can undergo the marvelous experience of seriously pretending to be Hamlet without it changing one quite a bit.

Sorry I shan't get a chance to see you in *V. Woolf*, because tho' we reach N.Y. on Jan. 28, I have to go right to Minn., then back to New York after a day or two. So I'll miss you. Have a good rest and a fine time—And you can't be looking forward to our grapple more than I am.

I'm sure there'll be HELL because of its being a new building. We shall rehearse with hammers banging and painters whistling, and there'll be acoustic problems in the hugest way.

Tanya's designs are (I think) splendid—highly expressive and where required "sumptious." The set couldn't be simpler—a minimum of scene-changing and no "realism," but I think it can always be clear where we're pretending to be. Hope you can read my handwriting. I ought to have typed, but somehow typing doesn't seem to flow quite naturally. I use it for "business" letters.

Ever,

T.G.

George later said about the work of this prerehearsal period:

> He answered my six months' worth of questions in one morning session. Then we just read thru the play together a little at a time—making decisions on anything that I felt was not clear in my interpretation. After that day we spent several other mornings talking and reading the play. Tony was swell as Gertrude! That's about all the *hard* work we did. It didn't take long. Doug (Campbell) and I worked every day on the dueling scene, since I had never fenced before. He choreographed the whole thing. We (Tony and I) would chat and read in the a.m. and Doug and I would fence in the afternoons.[5]

Possibly, Guthrie spoke with other cast members individually prior to rehearsal. I know that last night at a welcoming party for the company, Guthrie told Lee Richardson some of his thoughts about Claudius:

> Claudius is not a villain. He's not ashamed of what he's done; maybe he had to do it for the good of the state, or so he thought. Try to get as much out of the political implications as possible.

MARCH 13

The first scene was worked again. Guthrie told his actors, "You must act with your bodies and reactions to make up for the things we don't do with gauze and eerie lighting."

The position of the Ghost might change. As it is now, the soldiers imagine it first, then it appears in the tunnel left as though "searching for something."

5. Letter from George Grizzard to Alfred Rossi, February 24, 1968.

Scene 4 (Act 1, Scene 4) was done for the first time today. This is Hamlet's first meeting with the Ghost. Guthrie told George to "suggest you are high up over the country."

Hamlet has been directed to have a sense of the Ghost's impending presence twice before the spirit appears: after ". . . the pith and marrow of our attribute," and after ". . . that too much o'er leavens the form of plausive manners."

When the Ghost does appear, Guthrie told Paul Ballantyne (Marcellus), "Marcellus is a Christian; he crosses himself." Guthrie also directed George to keep a very low, intense tone in speaking to the Ghost. Hamlet is physically drawn to the Ghost, and "he is shaking with cold."

Working on this scene, Guthrie stressed proper phrasing and breathing again. He has done this in all of the scenes to a degree, and particularly in long passages, in which the line of thought (and action) will be harmed by faulty word grouping through too many pauses. In this scene he worked especially hard with Horatio and Hamlet. Here are two examples of the kind of demands Guthrie is making on his actors; two speeches in which Guthrie specifically told the actors when and how to breathe:

HORATIO: What if it tempt you toward the flood my lord,
          (Breath)
Or to the dreadful summit of the cliff
That beetles o'er his base into the sea,
And there assume some other horrible form
Which might deprive your sovereignty of reason,
And draw you into madness? Think of it.
          (Breath)
The very place puts toys of desperation,
Without more motive, into every brain
That looks so many fathoms to the sea,
An hears it roar beneath.

Horatio's speech is to be delivered rapidly, loudly, and urgently. Guthrie made Graham Brown do the speech three or four times, each time instructing him to take deeper breaths at the two places indicated.

George Grizzard's problem is slightly different. It is a much shorter line, but Hamlet is, at this time, being forcibly prevented from following the Ghost by Marcellus and Horatio:

> My fate cries out,
> And makes each petty artery in this body
> As hardy as the Nemean lion's nerve.

George is expending a great deal of energy, both physical and vocal, during the line, and is allowing most of his breath to be released on a big "My fate cries out," literally crying out. He then breathes *after* the line. He has no choice. Guthrie is trying to get him to take a much deeper breath *before* the line and then follow through without another breath to the end of the third line.

As a general rule to his actors, Guthrie said:

> All energy should come from the diaphragm. Don't lose energy in gestures. Communication must be from the diaphragm to the audience.

Both Graham and George seem willing to abide by Guthrie's demands, but at the moment, their flesh is weak.

Near the end of the scene, Hamlet says, "Go on, I'll follow thee." Guthrie stopped George and told him he was making an "ugly sound." The vocal quality was too harsh for the line and moment.

Because the well-known line, "Something is rotten in the state of Denmark," usually gets a laugh in America, Guthrie, in order to bury it, is having Horatio come in quickly after Marcellus delivers the line.

Guthrie moved right into Scene 5 (Act I, Scene 5). The Ghost has been staged to give him physical domination over Hamlet, that is, Hamlet is always a step or more below the Ghost: crouching, kneeling, or sitting. Hamlet is physically as well as emotionally overwhelmed by the ghost of King Hamlet.

Guthrie's approach to the Ghost seems to lean toward making the Ghost sympathetic, with human qualities and *feelings*. Thus far there is no indication of the supernatural. Some of Guthrie's directions to Ken Ruta (Ghost) reveal his feelings about the character:

> Be near Hamlet, don't touch him.
>
> Once you say, "Brief let me be," get on with it. Pearl White's tied to the tracks; train's coming.
>
> Feel your body being fried in Hell.
>
> The Ghost can't stand the light.

Guthrie has given Ken some definite readings and movements in the scenes, demonstrating for him both vocally and physically; for example, on "burnt and purged away," Guthrie told Ken to really put a bite into the terminal consonants. Also, he showed Ken some of the full body gestures he'd like on the passage describing the effects of the poisoning: the Ghost is re-experiencing the physical pain of his death. The death is not a pretty one, but then the images conjured by the language are not very pretty: "And a most instant tetter barked about, Most lazar-like with vile and loathsome crust all my smooth body."

Guthrie demonstrated a spectacular oratorical effect on the following lines of the Ghost:

> Thus was I sleeping by a brother's hand
> Of life, of crown, of Queen, at once dispatched;
> Cut off even in the blossoms of my sin,
> Unhouseled, disappointed, unaneled,
> No reckoning made, but sent to my account
> With all my imperfections on my head—

Guthrie told Ken to do it "like they do at Habimah." He then illustrated what he meant, which was to increase volume and raise pitch in building to an emotional peak on "head." Guthrie didn't do it particularly well, but the idea must have been clear to Ken because he took the direction and, even this early in the game, started to make it work. Guthrie added a few more directorial notes: elongating the vowel sounds in "unhouseled, disappointed, unaneled," and also doing the last three lines on a single breath. Since Ken has one of the best voices in the company he was able to incorporate these directions quite readily.

It is apparent that an actor with great technical expertise, especially with the voice, makes Guthrie look very good indeed. In this case, at least, Guthrie's direction could not be more effective.

The Ghost and Hamlet want to touch each other at the end of the scene, but can't quite make it, the Ghost backing away down the left tunnel, and Hamlet collapsing on the stage.

George told me later in the season (September 11) that this scene had been the subject of much discussion in the prerehearsal work with Guthrie. They decided together that the Ghost Hamlet sees is really in his head, and that there is a change in the playing style after the Ghost leaves: "It's more realistic—like Odets." He didn't comment on the fact that others see the Ghost also.

According to George, Guthrie's approach to this scene when it was actually done in rehearsal was surprising:

> He also played a tiny trick on me concerning the relationship between Hamlet and The Ghost. I wanted a strong relationship between them and he agreed, so I played a real love and reverence for Ken, and he had him treat me like dirt—like a sniveling weakling—(*"Pity me not!"*) which put a whole different slant on the relationship. Also I disagreed with the staging: Ghost in center stage—Hamlet in the pit—and his big speech done as an aria—but you know how voice-worshipping Tony is and Ken does have a great voice. I felt the scene was mostly important because of its effect on Hamlet, and this staging didn't seem to achieve it. But we did it this way and finally, I think, after playing for awhile managed to get across what Hamlet was suffering.[6]

In reworking the first court scene today, Guthrie said that he would write out ad-libs for the opening, so that no anachronisms would appear.

He told the court to "do a Wimbledon." The court accents the amorous glances between Claudius and Gertrude by moving their heads back and forth, as at a tennis match: "Helps tip off the audience."

We moved to Scene 7 (Act 1, Scene 7) today, the first appearance of Rosencrantz and Guildenstern. Guthrie told us that he originally had thought of having Gertrude in riding clothes mounted on a dummy horse having her portrait painted, but he and Tanya decided it was too costly.

The scene opens with a footman pushing on a serving cart laden with various decanters of liquor. Rosencrantz and Guildenstern enter, look around, and Rosencrantz starts to help himself to a drink, but is interrupted by the entrance of Claudius and Gertrude.

Guthrie told Claudius that "you don't really remember their names, so you bluff it through with hearty handshakes." The first time Lee did this everyone, including Guthrie, really broke up. Lee mumbled something or other unintelligibly as he shook our hands, and his timing was perfect.

Guthrie is taking his cue from the script, because shortly thereafter these lines appear in the scene:

6. *Idem.*

CLAUDIUS:	Thanks Rosencrantz and gentle Guildenstern.
GERTRUDE:	Thanks Guildenstern and gentle Rosencrantz.

He has obviously interpreted these lines as confusion of identity on the King's part. Jessica Tandy applied Guthrie's earlier direction in the scene to give meaning to her line, so she read it as a correction of her husband.

It is possible that Guthrie has decided once and for all to make the definitive statement about Rosencrantz and Guildenstern.[7] They have been confused for centuries, probably because they always appear together, and, in dramaturgical terms, serve the same function. Also, the roles are often cut to shreds giving the actors (and the audience) even less with which to differentiate them. Guthrie has chosen, as he has with the whole play, to cut very little of these characters.

After the scene Michael Levin (Guildenstern) and I initiated a discussion with Guthrie about the characters. He gave us some of his thoughts about Hamlet's school chums:

> Rosencrantz and Guildenstern are not villains. There is no intrigue; they are just opportunistic climbers. They never knew that their packets contained orders for Hamlet's death. It must be a crime for Hamlet to have tampered with the letters.
>
> They really don't know what the King's designs are. They figure that doing him a favor will get them ahead. They're Royalists—loyal to the King and The Establishment.
>
> Besides, they probably weren't that close to Hamlet at Wittenberg.

MARCH 15

Several scenes were worked today, and a pattern seems to be emerging in Guthrie's work. He begins each rehearsal day with a

7. Remember, this was several years before Tom Stoppard's brilliant *Rosencrantz and Guildenstern Are Dead.*

run-through of the last scene done the day before; this is done with or without stops.

When approaching a new scene he works it very hard— three, four, five times in succession, depending on the length and difficulty of the scene. Usually the last time through he lets the actors go on without stopping.

In the Ghost-Hamlet scene today Guthrie gave a couple of directions to George and Ken: "George, don't shout at the Ghost."; "The Ghost should be simple in motioning."

The entrance of the Players was done today for the first time. Guthrie's concept of the troupe is not the one he has used in several previous productions of *Hamlet*, the strolling, down-at-the-heels variety. He has indicated that he sees the players as professionals, but not necessarily of top caliber. They're not a first-rate in-demand company, but are well-established in the European courts, and, like most actors, think just a bit too highly of their talents. The First Player (John Cromwell) and his leading lady wife (Ruth Nelson) are like E. H. Sothern and Julia Marlowe (and family) coming to the White House for a command performance.[8]

Guthrie established immediately that Hamlet is very glad to see the group, and particularly The First Player. He recognizes friends at a time when he desperately needs them. Remember, he has just been disappointed by his "good friends" from Wittenberg; at least, as George is now playing the scene, he suspects the motives of Rosencrantz and Guildenstern in coming to Elsinore.

Guthrie told George, "Royalty is always lonely. Hamlet should extend his hand first when receiving people like Horatio, Rosencrantz, Guildenstern, and The First Player."

The first intermission will come after Hamlet's soliloquy, "O, what a rogue and peasant slave am I."

We did the scene following the first intermission, Scene 8 (Act III, Scene 1), for the first time today. It begins offstage with Claudius ad-libbing angry, critical shouts at Rosencrantz and Guildenstern. Guthrie's directions to the actors in the scene were specific; he obviously knows what he wants, and there seems to be little freedom on the actors' parts—at least they don't seem to have the courage to ask for any.

8. Guthrie did not discuss this concept with the players as a group at this time or at any subsequent rehearsal, but did mention it in a published interview two weeks later: John K. Sherman, "Guthrie Takes Pains with Bits and Pieces of *Hamlet*," *The Minneapolis Tribune*, March 31, 1963.

Although Guthrie often says, "Feel free to argue, if you wish," he appears to be *so right* in his direction, or, perhaps more correctly, *so confident*, that the actors hesitate to suggest anything very different from what he has in mind. It is certainly true in my case, and, as I found in conversations with other members of the company, I am not alone in this feeling. I think if Guthrie said to the company, "On these lines all of you go to the roof of the building and jump off—it would be a great effect," we'd do it with nary a query.

Thus far, there is no denying that Guthrie's charisma is a strong factor in his relationship with the company. The power and charm of his personality often dissuade actors of talent and experience from the constructive questioning which usually occurs between actors and their directors in creating roles. Although not always separable, Guthrie's impact as a director seems as much a result of what he *is*, as of what he *does* or *says*.

Jessica Tandy's comment on the subject seems appropriate: "I often disagree with him, but I never think twice about it."[9] The company apparently doesn't either.

This question of the amount of freedom Guthrie gives actors is an interesting one. His point of view might be illustrated best by excerpts from three interviews which I conducted. The first was with William Hutt, an actor who worked with Guthrie at the Stratford Shakespeare Festival in Ontario. Hutt told me that Guthrie contributes "freedom, but not license, to an actor's performance."[10] Michael Langham, Artistic Director of the Canadian festival, when asked about the same point, said that Guthrie "gives the actor the *illusion* of freedom."[11] When told of these two comments, Guthrie paused, a glint coming to his eyes, and said, "Freedom *is* an illusion."[12]

This first scene of our Act II (Scene 8) is typical of Guthrie's directorial approach. It starts at a very high pitch offstage, then Rosencrantz and Guildenstern are backed onstage by a furious King and perturbed Queen, expressing their impatience with the failure of the two young men to find out the cause of Hamlet's "confusion."

9. Interview with Jessica Tandy, Minneapolis, September 9, 1963.
10. Interview with William Hutt, Stratford, August 29, 1962.
11. Interview with Michael Langham, Stratford, August 29, 1962.
12. Interview with Tyrone Guthrie, Minneapolis, September 6, 1963.

All cues are picked up briskly, and the scene is paced rapidly until the exit of Rosencrantz and Guildenstern.

Guthrie did not take time out before doing the scene to explain how he thought the scene should be played, or how the scene relates to what has gone before in the play. He seems to imply in his direction that by doing the scene three or four times we'll understand what he thinks of it. I must say it works, because he is *clear* about what he wants. It is, however, sometimes a shock, particularly if an actor has thought of the scene in another way.

After doing the scene a few very hectic times, Guthrie said that Rosencrantz and Guildenstern were distraught at the King's censure, but that "they weren't plumbers who wandered into the court." The direction: maintain a sense of dignity; don't fall apart completely.

When we finished working on the scene Guthrie said, "This will wake 'em up after the break." Obviously, he wants to start the second act with the proverbial bang.

Guthrie to Claudius: "England is a synonym for assassination."

MARCH 18

Guthrie distributed some shamrock he received from Ireland for St. Paddy's Day.

So far, during rehearsals, there has been very little discussion of play, scene, or character.

The more we see of Hamlet's scenes, the more we see that Guthrie and Grizzard's prerehearsal work was tentative and incomplete; it appears that they only made a sketch—now comes the painting. George is, for example, still searching for the key to the nunnery scene, which is not unusual, of course, at this stage of rehearsals. Guthrie, tonight, suggested that Hamlet is close to tears in the scene, and it seemed to be a surprise to George. The scene began to play better.

Another example. George, after doing the "Words, words, words," scene with Polonius a couple of times, stopped and asked Guthrie directly about his relationship to Polonius: he said he wasn't sure what Guthrie wanted. Guthrie did not articulate the relationship, but in physical terms, by altering blocking and indicating some line readings, made the scene clearer to George.

This type of direction, at this point in rehearsals anyway, is characteristic of Guthrie's way of working. Direction is concerned with gesture, both verbal and physical, that is, language, movement, and technical facility. He rarely speaks in analytical terms or enters into discussions of character development or relationships.

Again tonight Guthrie's work showed a pattern: when working a scene, work it hard. This repetition of scenes has a method in it, since he is shaping and polishing the scene as he goes along. However, it seems unusual to be doing this so early in the rehearsal schedule. It could be that he has enough time—"Thank God," as he once said at the start of rehearsals. At this point we have blocked and run nine scenes in four days.

Overheard as I was leaving: Guthrie and Grizzard planning the next rehearsal:

> Let's get on with the Closet scene. It's the key scene for you, so we should do it, and see how we stand.

George, also, must have felt that this scene was extremely important, because later in the season in a radio interview he said that this scene was the climax of the play. It's Hamlet's first overt action (the killing of Polonius), and the scene which frightened him most. He also felt that it's the best written scene in the play.[13]

MARCH 20

The Ghost-Hamlet scene is very powerful. Ken Ruta is the most human Ghost I've ever seen; he writhes in purgatorial torment.

Guthrie has put in an illuminating bit of staging. The Ghost, by speaking directly into Hamlet's ear, poisons him with words of revenge, just as his own ear and "the whole ear of Denmark" were physically poisoned by Claudius. Grizzard, after the scene, was prompted to subtitle the play, "Lend an Ear."

13. Interview of George Grizzard by Sheldon Goldstein, WLOL–FM, Minneapolis, June 3, 1963.

The entrance of the Players was worked hard tonight, and Guthrie enjoyed the session immensely. In shaping this scene Guthrie added bit upon bit to establish Hamlet's rapport with the visiting troupe. One thing is clear: Hamlet is an amateur talking to professionals. During the course of doing the scene three or four times, Guthrie has planted some positive clues that tell a great deal about the relationship of the Prince and the Players, and about the Players as a company.

When Hamlet asks The First Player if he remembers "Aeneas' Tale to Dido," the old man doesn't. When his wife whispers in his ear, his face lights up. Hamlet, meanwhile, has continued recalling the speech, "The rugged Pyrrhus, like th' Hyrcanian beast." The actor shakes his head and finger negatively, and Hamlet says following this cue: "tis not so, it begins with Pyrrhus—" The First Player and the rest of the company nod "Yes." Hamlet then goes into the speech again, this time several members of the group mouth the words along with him. He dries up; they mouth "he whose sable arms." He remembers. He then falters after "dread and black . . . ," and a young player puts a hand to his own cheek. Hamlet happily cries, "complexion," at which point all laugh.

Hamlet, heady with getting through a couple more lines without error, really starts to get involved in his acting out of the famous speech. He saws the air too much with his hands (where have we heard that before?). Guthrie has George getting caught in an awkward position, off-balance, feet seemingly nailed to the floor, arms close to his sides, with gestures going out from the elbows. At the end of the speech, ". . . old grandsire Priam seeks . . . ," Hamlet is out of breath literally. He gulps some air and says, "So proceed you." From this performance there is no doubt in anyone's mind that Hamlet is an amateur actor having a fling at histrionics, or as Guthrie might say, "tearing a cat."

After The First Player launches into the speech, he is interrupted by Polonius, and is deeply offended. In a huff he goes to the side of the stage where his whole company-family surround him in consolation. Hamlet goes to him and begs him to continue. He reluctantly goes back to center stage, gives the chancellor a devastating look, sets himself, and *then* continues. At the end of the speech Hamlet moves to the player, who has "turned his color and has tears in his eyes," and fondly puts a hand on the old man's shoulder in a touching gesture.

Hamlet and Guthrie seem to be best in the comic touches, but the occasional juxtaposition of serious moments, like the one mentioned, gives dimension to both.

In sessions like the one tonight, one can sense a great rapport building between Guthrie and the company. Guthrie exudes an unabashed delight in working on a scene, and it's infectious. The company is enthused, and each rehearsal is a vibrant, exciting adventure, never dull for an instant. Guthrie's use of humor is a rehearsal technique in itself; it certainly relaxes actors. He never seems to let anything become too serious. As a result the rehearsal atmosphere is most congenial. Joy of actively working in the theatre pervades the entire environment, and rehearsals are anxiously anticipated.[14]

MARCH 22

The Closet scene is proving to be very exciting. Guthrie really gets involved in directing George and Jessica Tandy; often he physically demonstrates actions for them. Guthrie has directed Hamlet to come close to physically assaulting his mother. In the heat of the scene Guthrie cried, "Go on, beat her!" Gertrude moves off a bench onto the floor and crawls away from Hamlet's tirade against her. Guthrie told her, "Carry on, Jessie, like a madwoman rolling about."

The scene after the Play, Scene 11 (Act III, Scene 3), was worked today for the first time. The first part of the scene is very often cut, so it opens with Polonius telling the King that Hamlet is going to his mother's chamber. Guthrie has chosen to do the whole scene, including the opening portion with Rosencrantz and Guildenstern. His approach to the scene, at least from today's rehearsal, makes an interesting point about the insecurity of rulers and their dependence on functionaries like Rosencrantz and Guildenstern.

The scene's physical action involves these two men helping Claudius into his dressing gown, which Rosencrantz will carry on. Guthrie, in a rare instance, took time to explain what his idea for

---

14. Guthrie is especially articulate about what he tries to accomplish in rehearsals in his recording, "Directing a Play," Folkways Records, Album No. Fl 9840. Album transcript included. In this instance, his theory and practice are coincident.

the scene was by telling us an anecdote about the coronation ceremony of Elizabeth II of England. He described the young Elizabeth
being undressed to a shift by various bishops. Then she was invested
with all the clothes of royalty, the traditional vestments of kingship.
She progressed from the look of an infant to the power-figure sym-
bolized by her accoutrements. "And it was all laid on by the same
bishop who's been handling the robes since 1301."

Guildenstern undressing the King (taking off his formal
dress coat and vest) symbolizes the divestiture of kingship that will
come.

The King at the beginning of this scene is terribly shaken by
the events of the Play scene. Guthrie told Lee to push Guildenstern
before him onto the balcony, where the scene will be played, to make
sure it is safe for the King to enter.

Before we started rehearsing today Guthrie told us, in answer to a question, that the speeches concerning the nature of kingship were "sincere." But as the scene was repeated again and again,
other things seemed to happen. Rosencrantz became a little sadistic
in his attempt to capitalize on the King's distraught state. On the
lines, "The cease of majesty dies not alone," Guthrie had me slowly
advance behind the seated King and speak from behind his right
ear, reaching a soft, insinuating climax on "falls," at which point
Claudius winced and made a half-gesture to his ear. I surmised
Guthrie's reason for this ironic bit of action is to link Claudius' poisoned ear in this scene with his poisoning of the senior Hamlet's ear
in the precurtain murder. It also ties in with the Ghost-Hamlet scene.

I have the distinct impression that Guthrie has vivid individual scenes in mind, and, undoubtedly a general "plan" for the
whole play. What is lacking now is a continuity between scenes and
characterizations. Individual scenes are brilliantly conceived and
directed, but, as yet, nothing links them together. The same can be
said of many of the characterizations; consistency of behavior is
lacking. What seems of prime importance to Guthrie is the effect
of each *scene*. Despite these reservations, I have the feeling that the
company is being brought along like a fine racehorse for our Derby
Day, May 7.

Guthrie has abandoned the idea of Claudius forgetting the
names of Rosencrantz and Guildenstern completely; now he hesi-
tates, and then remembers.

The scene in which Hamlet gives the advice to the Players is starting to shape nicely. Guthrie is following through with the idea set in the first meeting between the Prince and the troupe: he is an amateur, and they are professionals.

The small company is seen preparing for the performance of *The Murder of Gonzago*, every member of the group doing something: vocalizing, combing out a wig, sewing a costume, practicing a recorder, polishing a sword, and the actor who is going to play Lucianus, the Murderer, rehearsing "The croaking raven doth bellow for revenge." There is a great deal of physical activity in the scene, but Hamlet still gets the focus, for several reasons. The Player King and Queen, seated on an artificial mossy bank, never turn their backs to royalty, and since Hamlet is moving about a great deal, they, every few lines, have to shift their positions to face him. There is some nice by-play between Hamlet and a nearsighted recorder player; also with the clown of the troupe who laughs on the line, "And let those that play your clowns speak no more than is set down for them." The lines, "Speak the speech I pray you . . . ," and "Nor do not saw the air too much with your hand thus . . . ," are given directly to the player doing Lucianus. The professional actor shows indignation at being coached by an amateur, be he royal or not.

The other notable aspect of the scene is that Hamlet is very excited over the prospect of catching the King's conscience. He personally arranges the pillows and chairs brought on by servants during the scene, making sure that everything is just right. Guthrie also indicated that lighted candelabra will be brought on during this scene.

I think that Guthrie has chosen to do the scene this way for two reasons. First, it builds the excitement for the Play scene, and, second, Guthrie wants to make the audience forget that this is one of the most famous speeches in all of Shakespeare. Guthrie mentioned the other day that in England where this play is even more familiar to audiences than it is here, the audiences say the famous speeches in the play along with the actors—they mouth the words. It's my guess that Guthrie is giving the audience so much to look at in this "Advice to the Players," that the speech will be over before they notice it. It also happens to have a basis in truth, being a perceptive statement about an excited young man giving unwanted advice.

After doing the dumb show in the Play scene, Guthrie said that it might not be done. "We'll keep it a week."

MARCH 25

"Hide fox, and all after."

Hamlet says this line at the end of Scene 13 (Act IV, Scene 2), after he has been questioned by Rosencrantz and Guildenstern about the whereabouts of Polonius' body. Hamlet is on the main stage, Rosencrantz is on the balcony above, and Guildenstern comes in from a tunnel behind Hamlet.

Guthrie said that we will come in with revolvers drawn, "meaning business." Hamlet and Rosencrantz exchange insults. Guthrie wants me to be rude and brash with the Prince, and use a "steely" voice. Hamlet steps back slowly and bumps into Guildenstern, and after the "fox" line, Hamlet runs off. Guthrie told George to move first toward one tunnel, where Guildenstern blocks him, then up center, where Guthrie told me to block his path. Since I was to be on the balcony about ten feet in the air, I asked him how I was to do it. He replied very simply, "Jump down." I said, "Oh," and simulated the leap by jumping about four inches off the rehearsal room floor and landing with a menacing thud. Apparently this will be enough to stop Hamlet and, prompted by Guthrie's direction, he will turn and run down another tunnel. Guthrie said that the two men chase after him, and "there'll be a wild shot."[15] I hope that Rosencrantz doesn't appear in the next scene with a broken ankle.

At this stage of rehearsal it seems difficult to justify this rough handling of Hamlet, especially drawing guns on him.

The next scene we did, Scene 14 (Act IV, Scene 3), proved even more difficult to motivate. The scene deals with the interrogation of Hamlet by Claudius followed by his being sent to England. Guthrie told me that Hamlet has led Rosencrantz and Guildenstern a merry chase through the castle, but that he has been caught and

15. Guthrie used shots in the pursuit of Hamlet in another production at the Gate Theatre in Dublin (1950). A review of the production was written by J. J. Hayes, "Ronald Ibbs as The Dane," *Christian Science Monitor,* July 22, 1950, p. 6. In addition to this production, Guthrie has directed the play onstage three other times, all at the Old Vic: in 1937 with Laurence Olivier (a production which later played at Elsinore Castle in Denmark); in 1938 with Alec Guinness; and in 1944 with Robert Helpmann.

"roughed up," so that when I appear near the beginning of the scene, I'm out of breath from the physical exertions belowstairs. Guthrie has directed Mike Levin to be twisting Hamlet's arm as the Prince is brought out from a tunnel; Mike then throws him to a position downstage center on the stairs.

The first time we did the scene today, Guthrie, after an exchange of dialogue between Hamlet and Claudius, pointed at me and snapped, "Rosencrantz faints." An actor's job is not to wonder why, etc., so Rosencrantz fainted. A couple of others in the scene (the King comes in well-attended) pick me up and cart me off to the side of the stage to revive. Of course, I have to revive in about four speeches to be handed a letter from the King for Hamlet's "safety" in going to England. Guthrie didn't tell me why Rosencrantz faints; I'm sure he feels I can figure out something that I can play. I do know that this is an action that Guthrie planned prior to rehearsals, because I now recall that he said something about "Rosencrantz being the weak one who faints when the going gets tough," at the welcoming party on March 10. It's possible he did the same thing with another Rosencrantz in another production.

I don't remember whose idea it was, but Hamlet kisses Claudius on the cheek when he says the line, "Farewell, dear mother."

Guthrie moved on to the Mad scene. He gave Ellen Geer (Ophelia) some specific images to work with in the scene. He told her to think of a wild animal scratching and clawing at the ground. This seems to fit very well, since Guthrie is playing the center section of the stage as Polonius' imagined grave. Ophelia scratches the floor, and, in her madness, goes on hands and knees to outline her father's resting place, as though making a ridge of earth around it. Later, Guthrie had Ophelia persuade Laertes to kneel with her at the grave and clasp his hands in prayer, as though they were young children. The various flowers she names are picked from around the grave. Ellen and Guthrie have established that the rosemary is for Laertes, pansies for Hamlet (which she crushes), fennel and columbines for the King, and rue for both her and Gertrude.

Guthrie had me refer to John Dover Wilson's notes on this scene several times during the rehearsal.

Other specific images Guthrie gave Ellen were of a women's insane asylum, and maternity ward screaming. The latter relates to what Guthrie wants Ellen to emphasize in this scene: Ophelia's pregnancy. This is the first time we've gotten a suggestion of it, because there has been no implication of that condition in Ophelia's earlier scenes.[16] Her singing in the first part of the scene accents the bawdiness in the song, and Guthrie has her hugging Marcellus and making a half-grab at his groin. She has been directed to be very harsh and loud on, "Young men will do it when they come to't, *by cock they are to blame* . . ." At one point Guthrie demonstrated how she should hit her abdomen, all the while making the sounds of a woman in labor.[17] Obviously, Hamlet's treatment of *this* Ophelia contributed greatly to her aberration, and, as a result, her actions to the men in the scene are particularly disdainful.[18]

Guthrie has put in a theatrical bit of staging. Ophelia, after the line, "Indeed without an oath I'll make an end on't," runs diagonally across the stage and leaps off the stage toward the left tunnel, but Horatio, standing on one of the stair levels surrounding the stage, moves over quickly and catches her in one arm and forces her back. As she leaves for the first time in the scene, she signals to Horatio for her coach and directs the "good night, sweet ladies" lines to the men in the scene.

Guthrie's enjoyment of his work shows itself at every rehearsal, as well as his warmth, whether it be in making light of an acting criticism, giving a compliment to an actor (not often, but sincerely), or laughing at his own invention or his actors'. His criticism is always couched in humor; the actor laughs at his own failings, so that a directorial reprimand becomes more palatable and effective. It struck me today that his use of humor while directing is very much akin to a technique that Moliere uses in *The Miser* (as do many

16. In a radio interview with Sheldon Goldstein (WLOL–FM, Minneapolis, July 22, 1963), Ellen said that on the first day she was called for rehearsal Guthrie came over to her and said, "Hamlet and Ophelia have had a relationship, don't you think?" although she added, "We never discussed it."
17. Later in the run of the play Ellen began hitting herself on the hipbones instead of the abdomen, because she actually *was* pregnant. In fact, she left the company in midseason to join her husband, Ed Flanders, in San Diego, and she was replaced as Ophelia by Zoe Caldwell, who was already appearing in *The Miser* and *The Three Sisters*.
18. This interpretation of Ophelia is very much in keeping with what Guthrie had written about the character shortly before this time. In fact, a number of things in this production closely align to his theories expressed in this same source: *Shakespeare's Ten Great Plays* (New York: Golden Press, 1962), pp. 6–11, 288–289, *passim*.

other playwrights in many other plays)—making men laugh at
their own foibles, so that criticism implied is easier to swallow. It
seems to work for Monsieur Poquelin and Sir Tony.

Another noticeable thing about Guthrie's direction is his
flawless timing when suggesting a line reading. In dealing with the
text he always communicates the *idea* of the speech, if not always
the technical process to achieve it. This clarity of communication
contributes greatly to the feeling of creative joy at rehearsals which
I mentioned earlier.

MARCH 27

The Play scene tonight was an exemplar in the art of direction. Guthrie built the scene beautifully. There were quite a few
things he did that can be singled out as veritable Rules-to-Follow
in directing a crowd scene. He demonstrated how to get maximum
visual variety and emphasis in a scene with a large number of people
but more than one focal point—in this case, Hamlet, Claudius, and
Gertrude, and the enactment of the murder of Gonzago. Guthrie
told the court audience to focus on the action in several stages, not
to face the action directly. He then showed how an actor can contribute to the focus of the scene by first looking over a shoulder at
the action, then, on a reaction, making a quarter turn, then, perhaps
a little later, facing the action directly, or turning to a partner nearby
and exchanging glances, or even leaning across the partner to whisper something to someone two persons away. He didn't give every
person in the court a specific move to make at a certain time, but
his demonstration and explanation left no doubt about the effect
that could be achieved by each individual in the group finding a
variety of positions in giving focus. He said that there is "nothing
duller than seeing a small part person moving back to the same
position after a reaction."

Tonight he also made a good point about the use of silence.
Just as The Poisoner pours the distillment in The Player King's ear,
Claudius, as directed by Guthrie, gives an uncontrolled gasp, a loud
one. This, plus Hamlet's quick move to center stage confronting his
seated uncle, abruptly cuts off the very evident whispering by which

the court has been expressing shock at the subject matter of this playlet being acted in front of them. In other words, the court is way ahead of Claudius.

When this silence occurs Hamlet can then take his rather telling line, "He poisons him i' the garden for his estate," very softly. And Guthrie makes the most of it by having Claudius break up the line by phonated fearful reactions: "He poisons him" (reaction) "i' the garden" (another reaction) "for his estate" (reaction again). Then a few seconds later the King rises as though to hit Hamlet, who dashes downstage center past him. Guthrie said that at this point Hamlet will take a portable spotlight away from a servant who has been focusing it on the playlet, and shine it in the King's face. Claudius then cries, rather ironically, "Give me some light. Away!"

The confrontation between Hamlet and Rosencrantz and Guildenstern after the Play scene was done today. Cut in most productions, Guthrie has chosen to play it as written. In one exchange of dialogue about playing a recorder, Shakespeare succinctly illustrates the entire relationship among the three men. Guthrie's sense of the whole must have prevented him from deleting this valuable, beautifully written scene. Indeed, the playing of *Hamlet* "in his eternity," as Old Vic actors were wont to call full-length productions of the play,[19] gives the fullest possible dimension to the title role, and will, I believe, be illuminating to our audiences, even those who thought they *knew* the play.

We rehearsed the scene for an hour or so—about four times —each time adding a bit of blocking or business. Guthrie has Hamlet causing a great commotion among the players, finally grabbing a snare drum from one of them and beating it in elation because of the effect the Play scene had on Claudius. Guthrie told George to ignore Guildenstern and me as we try to give him the message from Gertrude for him to come to her chamber. The more Hamlet beats the drum, the louder, shriller, and more frightened Guildenstern becomes. Guthrie specifically told Mike Levin to use a high-pitched voice in trying to get through to the Prince. As we did the scene, Guthrie told Hamlet to throw the drum to Guildenstern, who is shocked. He is at a loss to get rid of it and becomes more upset. At this point Guthrie told Mike to "throw it to Horatio." The whole

---

19. Audrey Williamson, *Old Vic Drama: A Twelve Years' Study of Plays and Players,* Vol. I (London: Macmillan, 1948), p. 26.

bit of action developed into a game of Musical Snare Drums. I don't know why Rosencrantz was left out, but then, this is the first time we've worked the scene.

Guthrie wants Rosencrantz to be very tough in this scene, impatient with Hamlet's antics. He is rude and sharp with the Prince, and Guthrie, with characteristic limpidity, told me to "use a ballsy voice." This particular vocal approach obviously is meant to contrast with Guildenstern's stridency, thereby giving the characters more differentiation. Guthrie does a great deal of this type of directing, almost as though he is saying, "Do this now. Figure out why you do it later."

Because of the nature of the friction Guthrie has set up between Hamlet and Rosencrantz in the scene, he is able to accent it in a physical way. Hamlet motions Rosencrantz to come closer to him (he is on a 6″ platform). Rosencrantz does, but warily, because Hamlet's look is threatening. Also, the hand with which Hamlet motioned is poised above his head as though to deliver a karate chop. Then, in a quick move, Hamlet places both his hands on Rosencrantz's collarbone and presses firmly during the next few lines of dialogue—a suggestion of strangling. Guthrie illustrated this bit of action for George, but without telling us what he was going to do. In two very quick moves he (as Hamlet) slammed one hand and then the other around the lower portion of my throat. It was shocking, menacing, and smarted a bit. It also helped me get a truthful reaction, which I later used when George did it—gently at first, then more firmly, when he was sure he wasn't hurting me.

The way Guthrie is doing the scene it is clear that Hamlet has totally rejected his former classmates, and they him, to a large extent. Hamlet is disgusted with their hypocrisy. He comes close to hitting Rosencrantz, and then, taking a recorder from one of the musicians, brilliantly illustrates the hurt he feels in being betrayed:

> HAMLET: O, the recorders! Let me see one. To withdraw with you, why do you go about to recover the wind of me, as if you would drive me into a toil?
>
> GUILDENSTERN: O, my lord, if my duty be too bold, my love is too unmannerly.
>
> HAMLET: I do not well understand that. Will you play upon this pipe?

GUILDENSTERN: My lord, I cannot.

HAMLET: I pray you.

GUILDENSTERN: Believe me, I cannot.

HAMLET: I do beseech you.

GUILDENSTERN: I know no touch of it, my lord.

HAMLET: It is as easy as lying; govern these ventages with your fingers and thumb, give it breath with your mouth, and it will discourse most eloquent music. Look you, here are the stops.

GUILDENSTERN: But these I cannot command to any utterance of harmony; I have not the skill.

HAMLET: Why, look you now, how unworthy a thing you make of me! You would play upon me; you would seem to know my stops; you would pluck out the heart of my mystery; you would sound me from my lowest note to the top of my compass: and there is much music, excellent voice, in this little organ; yet cannot you make it speak. 'Sblood, do you think I am easier to be played on than a pipe? Call me what instrument you will, though you can fret me, yet you cannot play upon me.

MARCH 28

No *Hamlet* rehearsal today, but Tanya asked if I would go down to Juster's, "a nifty men's store," and try on the suit that had been custom-made to my measurements in New York and sent to Minneapolis. I am to be used as a test case; if mine fits, the others ordered for the production should be all right. Peter Zeisler (Production Director of the theatre), Tanya, and Guthrie accompanied me.

Guthrie, who has been known to wear white tie and tails with not-so-white sneakers, must have had some concern for his appearance that day, because just outside the entrance to the store he adjusted his tie, turned to me, and in his usual clipped, brisk British manner said, "Al, do I look all right?" He was wearing a tan gabardine suit, blue shirt, yellow tie of some mysterious material—

perhaps hopsack or burlap—and forest green socks peeping over his favorite red and black Scotch plaid felt house slippers. Although Ophelia would hardly call him "the glass of fashion, and the mold of form," I thought he was just beautiful.

> In the store great care was given to my fitting:
> . . . a half inch higher on the coat . . . a quarter inch lower on this jacket button . . . only a slight break at the shoe top.

The material and cut of the suit look expensive, and should be effective for the performance. And with such distinguished supervisors, the fit has to be first-rate.

MARCH 29

The company has started rehearsing Psalm 118 to be spoken as part of the dedication ceremony on May 5. Guthrie is acting as choral director and seems to relish this kind of work as much as he does staging the play. His enthusiasm is contagious. We are going to spend 15 or 20 minutes a day on the psalm prior to each day's rehearsal. The company has been divided into groups according to voices. The arrangement is antiphonal with men and women alternating stanzas or lines, and finishing strong with all 30 voices (plus Douglas Campbell, who must count for at least two more).

Guthrie is death on midwestern speech habits, particularly the flat "a." In working on the piece Guthrie told us to think of the consonants as percussion, and vowels as strings.

The famous "precepts" speech given by Polonius to the departing Laertes in Scene 3 (Act I, Scene 3) is being done in a delightful and different manner. Guthrie suggested this approach to the speech at the first rehearsal of the scene, but Bob Pastene was not able to make it work, so Guthrie has left him alone to work it out. Today Bob's timing of line and gesture started to jell, and Guthrie exclaimed happily, "That's it, that's what I mean."

Guthrie has added Reynaldo to the scene, and his function is to hold a portfolio upon which rest various state documents that are being read and signed by Polonius while he delivers his well-known maxims. The speech is done with economy of voice and gesture, with bits of physical action accenting words such as "vulgar," "beware," and "gaudy." I believe that Guthrie's reason for doing the scene this way could be the same as his handling of the advice to the players—it's a very well-known speech, so it is important to get the audience's mind off the words by doing something visually fresh. This approach also happens to be very funny, and makes a telling comment about the statesman: his business affairs come first, *then* he'll show his love for his children—when it is convenient. Every time Guthrie seems to be doing something for novelty's sake, I find, after some thought, valid reasons for his approach.

There is a funny bit of business on the line, "Farewell, my blessing season this in thee." As Polonius says "this" he reaches into his pocket and hands Laertes a bill. Guthrie said magnanimously, "Give him a $100."

This is one scene in which Guthrie has given Bob a good deal of freedom, and it seems to be paying off, because he has contributed some fine things, both vocally and physically. Guthrie seems to enjoy Bob's casual, underplayed, throw-away delivery; he laughs loudly and often.

And that is another thing I have noticed in watching Guthrie direct. You always know that he is interested; nothing seems to slip by him. As he sits, stands, or paces watching a scene he makes enough different sounds to fill a zoo, expressing approval or disapproval through a myriad of phonations.

When he decides to stop the action for a comment, Guthrie brings everything in the rehearsal room to a stop with a resounding clap of his hands, followed by a brisk snapping of fingers. He sometimes shouts the direction from the far side of the room; sometimes he rushes onstage with words cascading in a sharp, precise delivery.

APRIL 4

Guthrie functioned very well in the running of the second act tonight (Scenes 8–15), generating particular excitement in the Play scene. It is really starting to shape; small bits of business planted a couple of weeks ago have developed into beautiful accents of dramatic action.

The dumb show and the play that follows are being played *very* grandly—not a burlesque of nineteenth century romantic acting, but definitely suggesting the oratorical delivery of that era. (Coincidentally, Tanya Moiseiwitsch told me later in the season that The Player Queen's reddish-orange pig-tailed wig was patterned after one worn by Ellen Terry as Lady Macbeth.)[20]

Guthrie has done an interesting thing with Lucianus, the Poisoner (Jack Going). He is the same fellow who is being coached by Hamlet in the Advice to the Players, rehearsing, no doubt, part of that "speech of some dozen or sixteen lines," which Hamlet has given to the players to interject into the regular script of *The Murder of Gonzago*. The audience has heard him rehearsing the line, "The croaking raven doth bellow for revenge," when Hamlet tells him to pronounce it "trippingly on the tongue." Now in the Play scene the audience hears the line once more, not from Lucianus, but from Hamlet. Guthrie has decided that the actor playing Lucianus "dries up," and he cannot remember the first line of his new dialogue. Hamlet, as would any callow playwright on opening night, gives him the line in an intense whisper. He is, however, prompted to it by the actor's obvious embarrassment in trying to remember the line. The "damnable faces" that Hamlet tells the actor to "leave" are manifestations of a very uncomfortable thespian. Finally, Lucianus, still nervous, leaps into the middle of his speech, "Thoughts black, hands apt, drugs fit, and time agreeing." Hamlet's review of his performance is a perturbed look and a gesture of disapproval. Once into the speech the player overacts outrageously to compensate for his poor beginning. Here again, Guthrie has based a novel approach on a common human trait—opening night jitters.

The small part of the player who speaks the prologue to the playlet is played by James Lineberger, and Guthrie has made him the clown of the touring group. When he speaks his three brief lines before the dumb show he is so nervous that he can hardly wait to get off the stage; in fact, he runs off to the laughter of the court.

During the dumb show everyone onstage is watching intently as the Poisoner begins to pour the "mixture rank" into the ear of the sleeping Player King. At this point Guthrie said to me, "Rosencrantz starts to laugh." "The court hushes him," he then told the

20. Interview with Tanya Moiseiwitsch, Minneapolis, July 24, 1963.

actors near me. He probably wanted this as a conscious use of contrast; he does this often, setting up a mood, then deliberately breaking it, so that when it is again established, interest is heightened.

Guthrie worked the end of the scene a few times, and already a sense of hysteria has been established as the court, shocked by the proceedings, scatters in near panic. Guthrie told Helen Marie Backlin, a lady-in-waiting, to go off "screaming hysterically." Helen Marie does so magnificently.

Obviously, this kind of melodramatically spectacular finish to the scene will work only if it is justified by what has gone before— if the tension has built to such a point that nothing short of this effect *can* happen. From what I have seen so far, I certainly wouldn't bet against Guthrie pulling it off. And the extras haven't even been added!

During the scene he worked with the court to get the right kind of whispering effect after their discovery that the playlet being performed for them makes indiscreet implications about the present monarch. Guthrie told an anecdote to illustrate the sound he wants:

> At an opening night in London a young actress making her debut was quite disturbed after she made her first entrance. The audience, it seemed to her, was being very inattentive and whispering to each other. Later, she went to the stage manager to find out the trouble. She discovered that the audience, *en masse,* were saying to each other, "She's Gladys Cooper's sister, Doris."

You can be sure that none of us said anything but that line in the Play scene all evening, and broke up every time we did it. Guthrie, by the way, delivers punch lines beautifully.

Guthrie never lets things get too serious, even though we are working on what is considered to be one of the world's greatest "serious" plays. He makes the company conscious of the fact that it *is a play,* and not an earthshaking event that will alter the lives of millions by its success or failure. Jessica Tandy expresses Guthrie's attitude this way: "It's a play, not the end of the world, so enjoy it, have fun with it. If it fails, well, it's a *play.*"[21]

His general attitude prompts one to say, with qualifications (as an escape clause), that the process might be an end unto itself. The audience participation later, at performances, is almost a fringe

21. Tandy interview.

benefit. The kind of creative joy with which Guthrie imbues his re-hearsals, and thereby his actors, is as much a part of his rehearsal techniques as more tangible features, like the handling of a crowd scene. No little of this effect is created by Guthrie's incisive, witty criticisms and directions; also, his penchant for storytelling—non-time-wasting, pertinent, and effective.

Another feature of Guthrie's building of a creative atmos-phere is his attention to minor details. The result is that every actor believes that nothing he is doing onstage is going unnoticed by the director. This, of course, helps develop the actor's feeling that he *is* contributing to each scene, whether or not he has the main focus or even a few lines. In short, Guthrie makes all the actors feel im-portant, indeed *essential*, to the action. Admittedly, he only gives each actor his due amount of attention, but each actor does get *that much*. This technique reads like an equation: the amount of atten-tion (read direction) given is directly proportionate to the im-portance of the character to the action of the moment.

Guthrie budgets the actors' time extremely well. When they are called for a scene, they work, and usually very hard. There is little time wasted, Guthrie's or anyone else's. This contributes a great deal to a happy rehearsal situation.

Guthrie truly acts as "an audience of one" at rehearsals, sticking to his own advice.[22] He reacts as a sounding board for his actors, many times in an audible way—a plethora of sounds emanate from his huge frame. These physical reactions are only the external manifestations of the role Guthrie plays for his actors. His excellent powers of observation enable him to make comments about the most subtle of gestures, both vocal and physical. Through this acute per-ception he is able to suggest things to his actors in specific terms. This, of course, is also the result of his especially effective use of language, judiciously chosen and vividly delivered.

It is this combination—perception and communication—which enables him to supply for his actors the ingredient so necessary in this creative period of rehearsal, and which can be expressed in the question every actor asks his director in one way or another, im-plicitly or explicitly, "How am I doing?" Invariably, Guthrie will answer—one way or another—as he did tonight, "It's coming along nicely."

22. Tyrone Guthrie, "An Audience of One," *Directors on Directing,* Toby Cole and Helen Krich Chinoy, eds. (New York: Bobbs-Merrill Co., 1963), pp. 245–256.

APRIL 6

Today we did the Graveyard scene in the theatre. Although parts of the rehearsal room floor are removable for a pit effect, Guthrie wanted to work on the stage as long as it was available. Our work in the theatre has been limited to evening rehearsals, because there are many workmen laboring there during the day. For some reason it was free today.

Guthrie sees the Graveyard scene as a comment on mortality. He feels this is coincident with Hamlet's preoccupation with death, so that an "autumnal feeling" should pervade the scene.

The trap will open in the blackout, then The First Grave-digger (Ed Preble) will start singing. At this point, Guthrie started experimenting with the comic possibilities of the pit. A hand is seen throwing things out of the grave on one side. Then another hand throws something out on the other side. Then two hands throw things out at the front and rear of the grave respectively. Then *four* hands are seen at once, while, all the time, *one* voice sings. Guthrie played with variations on this theme for a time, and then moved on. He seemed to enjoy this game, like a kid with a new toy. So did the actors.

Guthrie doesn't want the gravediggers done with any sort of regional accent. (Cockney is used often.) A word about characterization: "These workmen are not absolute nitwits, simply because they're members of the lower orders." To Ed Preble:

> The gravedigger is a man going about his daily work, and the action intrudes upon his job. He carries on with it, although he reacts to the interruptions of this fellow he doesn't know to be Hamlet. Don't play him as a funny man; let the laughs come incidentally.

"The scene must be full of singing, like Ophelia's mad scene." Hamlet will enter dressed as a sailor. "He's occupied with death images; Horatio is wary and watchful." Guthrie wants George Grizzard to sing the four lines starting with "Imperious Caesar, dead and turned to clay," to a simple melody, but George seems reluctant. He said he doesn't sing, but he'll learn it.

After the gravedigger's line, "Why here in Denmark," Guthrie wants the actors to suggest that it is beginning to rain. There will be two planks over the grave upon which Ophelia's casket will rest for the brief ceremony. Also two spades, a couple of burlap bags, some bones and skulls, but *no* dirt. The Second Gravedigger (Ken Ruta in an interesting double) goes out to "fetch a stoop of liquor," and returns singing a bawdy song just as the priest is about to begin final rites. Embarrassed, the workman sidles off to the edge of the stage.

Guthrie is concerned about the pacing of the Closet scene, particularly about getting enough vocal variety in Hamlet's tirades against his mother. Guthrie to Grizzard: "George, screw every ounce of dirt out of the charges against your mother."

Guthrie has blocked the scene so that Gertrude is practically in the Ghost's arms after he appears to Hamlet. They are very close, but do not touch. When Gertrude tells Hamlet that she sees, "Nothing at all . . . ," she looks directly into the eyes of her dead husband.

At the evening rehearsal we had a run-through of our first act (Scenes 1–7: through Act II, Scene 2). Guthrie and I sat in the center section of the house. Some comments during the course of the evening:

> On Barnardo (Gordon Bryars): He's better—more relaxed and confident.
>
> On Horatio: He's worked out his long speeches quite well. (Guthrie, after one of Graham Brown's scenes, got up and went to far house left where Graham was sitting, said a few words, and came all the way back. Graham was smiling.)
>
> On Laertes (Nicolas Coster): He's got a nervous tick. Good voice.
>
> On Marcellus: He adds so much to the battlement scenes; he looks like a grizzled Sergeant Major.
>
> On Hamlet: He's developing into a good speaker.
>
> On The Ghost: Wonderful voice. (On the Ghost's line, "If thou hast nature in thee, bear it not," which Ken delivers very powerfully, Guthrie hunched into his seat and said, "Jesus!")

I include these comments to illustrate what a barometer Guthrie is for his actors. As mentioned before, he reacts vocally to much of what is happening. The actors, to be sure, don't hear comments like those described above, but they do get the various laughs, giggles, gasps, etc., which permeate the rehearsal.

As in the case of Graham Brown, Guthrie has the knack of dropping just enough of a compliment to an actor to bolster his confidence, to encourage him. Guthrie certainly isn't prodigal in his praise, but it always seems honest. He also seems to imply to the actor who is being directed: "Don't take any of this personally. If I shout at you, it's only my way of making you more objective about your character. Don't let me frighten you."

Guthrie tends to dispense with the chaff of a performance, both vocally and physically. The company is constantly being directed to eliminate needless gestures, and to read lines with less stress. In one instance with the soldiers on the battlements, he justified cutting down on the physical aspects of the scene by saying, "You'll all have heavy clothes on." I believe he feels that a "fussiness" of words or actions will cloud the ideas of the verse. This seems particularly true of those very few actors in the company who are Method-oriented.

At this rehearsal Guthrie expressed concern over the fact that a number of the actors were not intelligible in certain speeches, and several of them were difficult to understand on most of their lines. A notable exception was Jessica Tandy, who is crystal clear in her delivery. I don't know whether or not he was rationalizing these deficiencies in some of the actors when he said, "Well, I don't think we should be too worried about audibility until the carpets and back wall are in, do you?" I said that I thought that it would make some difference.

He then asked me to think of some kind of standard opening for the beginning of the play:

> At Stratford Ontario we had cannon fired, then the house lights went dark, but we really can't do that here. Think of something.[23]

23. Opening night found the audience directed into the theatre by an impressive flourish of herald trumpets composed by Herbert Pilhofer, and similar in effect to that used at the Stratford Ontario Festival Theatre. An undeniable sense of excitement and *occasion* is the intent and the result.

APRIL 9

Tonight was the first time I have seen Guthrie initiate a discussion of a scene with his actors, while the rest of the company waited. It was in the Closet scene; more specifically, Hamlet's panic in lugging off Polonius' body. Guthrie started with this point, but then went on to a discussion of the whole scene, particularly of Hamlet's motivations. Guthrie kept the discussion intimate with George, Jessie, and Bob and few things were heard by the company. One thing that was heard was a statement about the reappearance of The Ghost in the scene. Guthrie said that the Ghost is a projection of Hamlet and has come to intervene, because Hamlet has gone too far with Gertrude. At the end of the talk, Guthrie, aware of using rehearsal time in a way he had not planned, checked the time with the stage manager.

The scene itself starts out very high; it is paced quickly with Hamlet giving a great deal of steam and punch to his opening exchange with his mother. After the murder of Polonius he becomes more intense, but in a lower key. Then in the charges against Gertrude, he bacomes almost sadistic in his verbal, and, as has been noted, nearly physical attack on her.

Guthrie has done an interesting thing on an exchange of lines late in the scene. The speeches are:

> HAMLET: Not this by no means that I bid you do:
> Let the bloat King tempt you again to bed,
> Pinch wanton on your cheek, call you his mouse
> And let him for a pair of reechy kisses,
> Or paddling in your neck with his
> damned fingers,
> Make you ravel all this matter out
> That I essentially am not in madness,
> But mad in craft. 'Twere good you let
> him know,
> For who that's but a queen, fair, sober, wise,
> Would from a paddock, from a bat, a gib,
> Such dear concernings hide, who would do so?

> No, in despite of sense and secrecy,
> Unpeg the basket on the house's top,
> Let the birds fly, and like the famous ape,
> To try conclusions in the basket creep
> And break your own neck down.
>
> GERTRUDE: Be thou assured, if words be made of breath
> And breath of life, I have no life to breathe
> What thou hast said to me.

In the middle of Hamlet's speech, after the line about his being mad in craft, he laughs. He then delivers the rest of his speech jokingly, and the Queen begins to laugh in a strange way. She continues the laughter during her speech. Guthrie wants it played as though both Hamlet and Gertrude are on the verge of hysteria after the great emotional turmoil of the scene, and the laughter takes on a frightening quality. Actually, the panic in Hamlet about the removal of the corpse and about the murder in general has been building throughout the scene, and Guthrie's discussion with George and Jessie was concerned with its first salient appearance, which could be at this point.

Scene 15 (Act IV, Scene 4) is being staged in a way which Guthrie used in his production of the play at The Old Vic in 1944, with Robert Helpmann in the title role.[24] There is a dramatic contrast between Hamlet and Fortinbras, between the man of thought and the man of action.

Guthrie has put Fortinbras (Claude Woolman) on the balcony upstage center, so that he has dominant focus, while Hamlet is below him on the main stage, at times looking up at the figure whose commands will send 20,000 men to their deaths for ". . . a fantasy and a trick of fame . . ." Fortinbras has binoculars, and his two men a field telephone.

APRIL 15

Tonight the extras appeared for the first time since the opening day of rehearsals, March 11. Guthrie's opener to them was, "Have

24. Williamson, *op. cit.,* pp. 166–167. Also mentioned in E. Harcourt Williams, *Old Vic Saga* (London: Winchester Publications, Ltd., 1949), pp. 174–175.

you all read the play?" A lot of the assemblage laughed, but it's a logical beginning. Guthrie then introduced each of them (nine men, two women) by name, first and last, to the regular company. And he got them all right—without notes!

In the three hours of rehearsal (with one 15-minute break) we did the first Court scene and the Play scene three times each.

In Scene 2 Guthrie gave the extras general directions, like "All of you will enter through the double doors upstage center. Pair yourselves off, a lady with a gentleman." This pairing, of course, included many of the women in the regular company, who, up until this time had been working without male escorts in all the court festivities. Because the company had been in rehearsal for over a month and were familiar with the action of the scene, they were able to guide and coach the extras. Guthrie encouraged this, in fact, he asked the company earlier to be prepared to do so. He feels that this gives the new members of the cast confidence in what they're doing, and also makes them feel they're contributing to the ensemble that much sooner.

The first time through the scene Guthrie did not stop very often. He did interject things like, "Everyone applauds here—politely." Or "The court laughs." The various moves which had been set with the company were, in the main, retained. The extras, guided throughout the scene, moved when and where told. Polonius' stage managerial duties took on a practical, as well as a dramatic, function.

The second time through Guthrie refined some of the choreography, switching a couple from one part of the stage to another, or taking an earlier cue to move away from Hamlet when Claudius comes down to speak with him, etc. After the third time through the scene had a definite shape, with the extras already being bold enough to do bits and pieces on their own.

Guthrie didn't give directions to all of the individuals in the scene. He gave general directions, with specific things to just a couple of people. What seemed to happen, however, is that all of the people in the scene could get something from the directions given severally. There is a certain extension which can be made with most of his direction, so that the *essence* of the directorial note can apply to many people.

We were given a short break, and one of the extras, who had been assigned as a footman to open and close the double doors up center, was overheard saying, "You know, when you're out of this for five or six years, you get stale."

During this break, all the members of the court were given four sheets of "Additional Dialogue—Scene 10." Guthrie had written some lines for the actors to say at the opening of the scene. He did this, I believe, for several reasons: to make the extras feel a part of the ensemble; to give more reality to the scene by having specific lines being delivered to specific people (rather than relying on the inspired ad lib); and to lessen the possibility of inappropriate dialogue being heard by the audience, the closest members of which, in this theatre, are only a few feet away from the playing area.

As proven in the rehearsal of the first court scene, having the regular company well-versed in their assignments has paid a dividend with the choreography of the extras. Again the extras were coached by their more experienced colleagues, although, with this scene, there was some adjustment of positions. This was the result chiefly of the fact that Guthrie's new dialogue designated specific exchanges— Marcellus with an elderly court lady, Barnardo with a young girl, the Queen's lady-in-waiting with a court guard. This required some rearrangement, although not as much as one would have imagined. The dialogue was never rehearsed; Guthrie never went over it or gave comments about it. Actually, it is not meant to be heard, but simply to aid in creating the excitement which the court experiences in the anticipation of watching a play. It also helps to animate the entrance of the court, and the company seems to enjoy delivering the lines, many of which are quite funny:

CORNELIUS (to SLINGSBY):	I love a play. The prince, I hear, has penned a speech in this.
FORSBERG:	Prince Hamlet?
CORNELIUS:	Who else?
FORSBERG:	And will they speak his speech?
CORNELIUS:	Can you doubt it? They have no choice. Besides they get well paid.

MARCELLUS:	This way, Madam, they give the play in here.
HOPKINS:	I hope it's warm. I hate a chilly room.

MARCELLUS (to HAMLET): Good even, sir. (To HOPKINS)
Sit here. It won't be long.
The play I hear is short.

HOPKINS: I'm glad of that.
I hate your long, long plays
    of death and doom.
Enough, I say, of sorrow in
    real life.

MARCELLUS How true. Excuse me, madam,
one calls. I'll take my leave.

DOTY: You've been abroad?

CIOFFI: I've just returned.

DOTY: Alas!
I'd love to travel. Don't you love to
    travel?

CIOFFI: My duties keep me traveling night and
    day,
By land and sea.

DOTY: I envy you.

CIOFFI: Indeed?
Then let us change our places; you shall
    be
Assistant to that fool Cornelius. I
Will stay at court, feast nightly and
    sleep sound.

DOTY: Nothing but feast and sleep? Let's place
    us here.
The players make their entrance from
    this side.

BARNARDO: Let's watch the play together.

MACHLACHLAN: Mother says,
These actors are the finest in the world.

BARNARDO: Lord Hamlet thinks so too.

MACHLACHLAN: He does?

BARNARDO: Indeed,
One told me he had writ this play for
them.

MACHLACHLAN: No, there you're wrong. For Rosencrantz declares
The play's an old one, rarely staged of
late.

BARNARDO: Rosencrantz, standing by the King?

MACHLACHLAN: The same.

BARNARDO: He and his friend are close friends of
Lord Hamlet.

VAN ARK:
(joining them): Speak you of Hamlet? Shall I tell you
something?
I had it of a friend, who heard it—
wait—
It is so secret that I cannot say it.

MACHLACHLAN: Tell.

BARNARDO: You must tell now.

VAN ARK: Later. The play begins.

BACKLIN: Give me a merry play with songs and
dances.

SLINGSBY: Agreed. I hate your melancholy plays.

BACKLIN: And poetry—don't you *hate* it?

SLINGSBY: Yes, I do.

BACKLIN: Your Aeschylus, your Sophocles and
stuff
Let them all burn, say I, they're garbage
all.

SLINGSBY: I hear that murder is the theme tonight.

BACKLIN: Murder? Now murder I can relish well.
Stabbing or how?

SLINGSBY: Indeed, I know not how.

BACKLIN: Stabbing, I hope, or strangling. No loud
bangs.
I hate loud bangs. The player folk, I
hear,
Get paid more money if they're knocked
about;
They call it danger money. . . . Peace,
break off,
The play begins. God spare us from
loud bangs!

MISKA: In here? I'm dizzy. All that wine . . . .

FIRST HUZZAR: This way.
We'll find a chair.

MISKA: The King—so hospitable.
Such a kind King. Such lovely, lovely
wine.

SECOND HUZZAR: Fetch her some coffee—black.

FIRST HUZZAR: It is too late.
The play begins.

SECOND HUZZAR: Not yet.

MISKA: *Such* a kind King.

FIRST HUZZAR: Ay Madam. Sit and watch the play.

MISKA: I will.

SECOND HUZZAR: Pray God she do not fall asleep and
snore.

PETERS: A seat, my dear young lady?

OPHELIA: Thank you, sir.

PETERS: It's quite a treat to see a play at court.
They visit us too seldom. Ah, young sir,
I can recall when Yorick played at
court.

THIRD HUZZAR: Yorick?

PETERS: The old King's jester.

THIRD HUZZAR: Why, he's dead.
I think I heard my grandad speak of him.

PETERS: No doubt. *He* was an artist; but, alas
Such talents are no longer valued here.

VAN ARK: You've been among the actors.

ROSENCRANTZ: Yes, I have.

VAN ARK: How *wonderful*! Are they like us? I mean
Do they eat supper?

ROSENCRANTZ: Yes, I think they eat.

VAN ARK: How *wonderful*! Tell me, who wrote the play?

ROSENCRANTZ: It's secret. (whispers)

VAN ARK: (runs to BARNARDO and MACHLACHLAN)

The play itself is done center stage, on or near the green mossy bank which butts against the balcony upstage center. The area below the balcony is curtained off, and the players use it for their entrances and exits. It works throughout this production of *Hamlet* like the inner below of the Elizabethan stage—sometimes open, sometimes closed.

The court enters in a state of excitement, and Guthrie has arranged them on all five sides of the stage focusing on the action of the play stage center. Claudius and Gertrude are seated on thrones aligned in front of the left tunnel on the stage level. No one is allowed to get close to the royal couple. Both Polonius and a man who is later identified as Osric keep the members of the court at a respectful distance. Hamlet starts out near Ophelia at stage right, but during the course of the action moves to various places among the court.

Everyone seems to be enjoying the performance until The Player Queen has some lines which, to say the least, are indiscreet:

In second husband let me be accursed;
None wed the second but who killed the first.

The court, at Guthrie's direction, begins to react to this apparent breach of decorum on the part of the players. They start to whisper among themselves, and Hamlet, eyeing his uncle, says, "Wormwood, wormwood." But the leading lady continues her speech:

> The instances that second marriage move
> Are base respects of thrift, but none of love.
> A second time I kill my husband dead
> When second husband kisses me in bed.

Of course this adds oil to the fire of suspicion racing through the court; they increase their whispering. Guthrie, at this point, told several people on far stage left to begin moving toward down center stage on the lowest level of the playing area, the space between the first row of the audience and the first step going onstage. During this action the leader of the players, who is performing The Player King, takes in the situation, and, in his next speech, pointedly tries to silence the disrespectful audience with increased volume and sharpness of delivery, all to no avail.

The tension builds with The Player Queen's line, "If once a widow, ever I be wife." At this point, Guthrie has Hamlet springing from the steps behind Gertrude's chair and delivering very sharply and intensely the line, "If she should break it now!"[25] Gertrude is startled, not only because of her tenseness, but because Hamlet delivers the line from behind her ear. Jessie's gasp cuts the air like the proverbial knife.

The tension thus broken, it builds again. By the time Hamlet confronts Claudius with the line, "He poisons him i' the garden for his estate," the court has moved to a position opposite the King and Queen. They are in a huddled mass on the right side of the stage. Guthrie indicated certain lines on which three or four people at a time would make a move. The only motivation Guthrie implied was that these people wanted to tell other people their thoughts on this

---

25. Robert Helpmann also used cat-like movements in this scene in Guthrie's 1944 Old Vic production. Williamson, *Idem.*

> In Grizzard's letter to me he commented on this particular line and action: The only disagreement we had (and he won!) was my interpretation of the line in the play scene, "If she should break it now." I wanted to say it to Horatio in reference to Gertrude—meaning if she should stop the play before Claudius realized what it was about. Tony insisted that it be said to Jessica about the Player Queen breaking her word to the P. King. Of course his way makes more sense, and I had originally conceived of it that way—but found the other reading more interesting and tension-making.

embarrassing situation. He did this at various points during the last part of the scene, so that by the time Claudius rises to hit Hamlet, he is almost isolated. Gertrude moves away when the King rises, and the only one near him is Osric, who, we infer, is a bodyguard. The visual impression is, I'm sure, telling: the lone figure of the King versus the court massed in back of Hamlet.

At the end of the scene, when everything seems to explode into hysteria, Guthrie simply said to the new members of the company, "Everyone go out by the nearest exit, as quickly as possible." He then gave some directions like, "You four out this way. You two out there. You grab this chair, and take it off here." He said that there will be a lot of things to strike in this scene, and a few of us would help. He also told the servants who are going to be operating the two portable spotlight stands that "the lights would shine about wildly" at the end of the scene.

APRIL 16

A number of copies of *Drama Survey* were delivered to the theatre today. Virtually the entire issue is devoted to The Tyrone Guthrie Theatre—its architecture, directors, designer, plays, and productions. It was eagerly perused and read by members of the company, particularly the articles on the two plays currently being rehearsed. Of special interest was Guthrie's article on the reasons for choosing to do *Hamlet* in modern dress. Since he had never discussed these reasons with the company, it filled a gap in our work which had been felt by a number of us. Included below are the most significant parts of that article.

> . . . the term "modern dress" is rather misleading. We shall not try to make the play look as though its action were happening in 1963. The Court Scenes will suggest European, rather than specifically Danish, Royal Occasions, with the men in full-dress, ceremonial uniform and the women in long skirts and long gloves. Such occasions even now do not suggest any specific date. The uniforms are traditional and the women's dress is completely formal and only faintly related to contemporary trends of fashion.

I do not pretend that there will be no anachronisms . . . there will be some incongruity between modern, or even semi-modern, dress and certain archaisms in the play's language.

But, while here and there the language differs from that of our own day, most of it is surprisingly and utterly modern; and we wish to stress the modernity of the play, not to exhibit it as an antique.

Granted certain incongruities, what are the positive advantages of modern dress?

First: the characters look more real; it is easier to accept them as human creatures like ourselves, rather than as animated illustrations, or worse, stereotypes of Hero, Villain, Ingenue, Nobleman . . . The Gloomy Dane . . . we shall aim at showing a young man dressed as any young man of means and good family might be dressed for a formal occasion shortly after his father's death. The actor and the text will then reveal gradually what sort of a young man he is . . .

Second: in my opinion the characters and the play will look handsomer. It simply is not true to say that "period" dress is interesting or picturesque whereas "modern" dress is dull. Dowdy modern dress is dull; dowdy period dress is even duller. I do not think that our dresses will be dowdy.

Third: we can, and habitually do, at a glance deduce all sorts of information from people's clothes . . . we can place them as high or low, rich or poor, soldier or civilian . . . relevant *facts* can be conveyed with force and economy. Modern dress does just that.

Fourth: the clothes help the actors to convey both where the action is to be supposed to be taking place and also to establish the time and atmosphere of particular scenes.

Guthrie cites the middle section of the play: no time lapse between Hamlet's advice to the Players and the first Fortinbras scene.

. . . As the sun is rising, Hamlet, with an overcoat covering the wreckage of his evening clothes, will meet a Fortinbras whose practical service dress will contrast significantly with the elaborate, impractical finery in which we have seen the Danish officers. All this will convey, I believe, something which is not apparent in period costume: that this whole sequence of the play occurs pell-mell, without interruption; it represents the events of a single, terrible night.

But I do not wish to leave the impression that modern dress is primarily useful in conveying facts . . . More importantly it brings the tragedy back from the remoteness of a long-by-gone era . . . and compels us to regard the characters as men and women subject to the same passions, the same confusions and perplexities, as ourselves.[26]

I'm not sure that this explanation will appease those critics who accuse Guthrie of being the dean of the Wouldn't-It-Be-Fun (Just for a Change) School of Production, but it certainly helped us.

Guthrie has added some of the extras in Scene 7, the arrival of the players. Several of the servants in the palace will carry on some of the company's luggage and stage properties. The whole scene has begun to shape very well. Guthrie has added bits and pieces at each rehearsal, and they are beginning to jell.

At the beginning of The First Player's long speech (which John Cromwell is doing excellently), the actor takes a sword out of his cane. At the same time the leading lady of the company pulls an old, well-used script out of her handbag, and "holds book" for him. (This particular bit of business developed, I'm sure, from the fact that Ruth Nelson is John Cromwell's wife, and she simply held a copy of *Hamlet* from which he could get prompts, if necessary, during the speech—a prompt for *John*, not The First Player.)

Guthrie has a group of soldiers entering from the left tunnel just as The First Player is about to start his reading. This bit of action is typical of the way Guthrie works. At first they simply entered noisily, then he added a dirty story and laughter, then a whistle, and now, while the actor taps his foot impatiently as the soldiers file in, one of them stumbles and falls against another. *Then*, all action having come to a stop, the actor begins.

There are several things which George Grizzard is doing during the Priam's slaughter speech that mark Hamlet as one of those "guilty creatures sitting at a play . . ." which the Prince mentions later in the scene.[27] George reacts physically at the mention of "Pyr-

26. Tyrone Guthrie, "Hamlet in Modern Dress," *Drama Survey*, III (Spring-Summer), 1963, pp. 73–77, *passim*.
27. Later in the season (September 11) George told me that this is one of the things which he and Guthrie decided upon prior to rehearsals.

rhus' ear" and also after the Player's lines, "So as a painted tyrant Pyrrhus stood, and like a neutral to his will and matter, did nothing." As you can imagine, the line "Aroused vengeance sets him new a-work" also stirs him up no little. Hamlet really becomes involved in the speech, since it relates strikingly to his own situation. In this way the "O what a rogue," soliloquy has a solid preparation.

It becomes, in essence and execution, an immediate com-ment upon a *fact* in the play. This is the general approach to all the soliloquies, with "To be or not to be" the only exception. All the rest are discernibly the result of a direct response to a stimulus just pre-sented, as in the Player's Hecuba speech. Guthrie (and Shakespeare) have provided this Hamlet with a positive action to prompt the re-action of the soliloquies, so that what is going on in Hamlet's psyche is extremely limpid. In fact, Guthrie's approach to the play is taking a simple narrative line: to make absolutely clear what is going on, chiefly by vocal and physical means, and, in so doing, to *show* the play to the audience.

Our rehearsal schedule does not seem to be very favorable to George. Scenes may not be touched for a week, then worked hard, then not touched for a week, etc. I think he needs continuity to bring his performance into a "line," if I may borrow from Mr. Gielgud.

APRIL 18

Guthrie was really rolling in the Graveyard scene tonight, as the extras were added for the first time.

The funeral procession enters from the left tunnel. It is led by the priest, then the casket carried by four "undertakers," then Laertes, then Claudius and Gertrude, then the rest of the court. Ham-let and Horatio hide under the balcony upstage center.

Most of the members of the cortege hold black umbrellas. (You remember that it started to rain during the Hamlet-Gravedigger scene?) Guthrie had used this approach to the scene before in his modern-dress production of the play in 1938 at The Old Vic with Alec Guinness as Prince Hamlet. Audrey Williamson describes Ophe-lia's funeral in that production as a "dreary vista of wet umbrellas and dripping mackintoshes . . ."[28] A few members of the cast were heard to remark, "Shades of *Our Town*." (Coincidentally, that play was written in 1938, and Thornton Wilder is one of Guthrie's favorite playwrights. I'll make no further inference.)

Guthrie has the umbrella-holding members of the court ringing the grave (trap) center stage. It's quite an effect. Again the extras fitted in smoothly; so did the umbrellas. Guthrie made a comment about them:

> Let those brollies act for you. They can express much. If they are used right, it will seem as though we have hired fourteen more actors.

Most of the choreography involving the brollies comes after Hamlet leaps into the grave to wrestle with Laertes. Guthrie seems to have a pattern for this scene. He'll give a direction, then run it, stop and refine the first direction and add a new one, run it, stop and refine the second direction and add a third. He doesn't give directions to all the actors onstage, but he will show some few specifically what he wants done. For example, he took an umbrella from an extra and illustrated the kind of movements which can be done with a brolly.

When Hamlet leaps into the grave there is a great deal of movement by the court: the women get out of the way, some of the men move immediately to the graveside and attempt to pull the combatants apart, Claudius moves toward Osric for protection. Those who lay hands on Hamlet and Laertes must get rid of their umbrellas, thereby creating sweeping movements with them. Some of the courtiers now have two umbrellas. When these people move later in the scene, as the two principals struggle to get at each other after being pulled from the grave, they create doubly strong visual effects.

Guthrie told one extra he was "to run across the stage with the brollies waving about" when Hamlet and Laertes are pulled from the grave. Then, a few lines later, as they lean across the pit, one on each side of the opening, arms held by courtiers, Guthrie told the same extra, "Hans, now run back, and wave those brollies."

Because Guthrie is so specific to a few people, the others take on a certain boldness of their own, and the scene comes alive.

28. Williamson, *op. cit.*, pp. 106–107.

Guthrie once again made a point of telling people not to return to the same place after a reaction, to find a slightly different position in the same area.

The emotional tension of the scene is released by Gertrude's speech beginning with "This is mere madness . . ."

As Guthrie creates the dynamics of this and the other crowd scenes, it is readily apparent why he has been called by more than one critic the greatest director in the world with more than six people onstage.

Near the end of the scene there are some lines by Claudius:

> Good Gertrude set some watch over your son.
> This grave shall have a living monument:
> An hour of quiet shortly shall we see;
> Till then, in patience our proceedings be.
>
> (Exeunt.)

Between the first and second of these lines Guthrie has interpolated a major portion of Act IV, Scene 7, the scene in which Claudius first reveals his plan to murder his nephew in the fencing match. The section begins with Claudius' line to Laertes, "Will you be ruled by me?" It continues until the line, "Our purpose may hold there," which is just before Gertrude's recounting of Ophelia's demise. Then the "living monument" line is picked up, and the scene comes to a close.[29] Guthrie told Lee Richardson to kick a nearby wreath into the grave on "living monument."

Nick Coster, as Laertes, is having a good deal of trouble in playing this scene. It has been in rehearsal for quite a while, and Nick hasn't been comfortable in it. The chief problem is that Guthrie wants it played rather quickly, and Nick seems to need more time to say his lines. Guthrie finally told Nick:

> There is no realistic way of playing this scene. It is too late in the evening for pauses and psychologizing. You must be sacrificed to the shape of the evening.

I don't think Nick was very pleased with Guthrie's abruptness, and Guthrie's tone made it clear that there was nothing further to consider.

---

29. Guthrie did the same interpolation in the 1944 Old Vic production. Williams, *op. cit.*, p. 175.

This is not the only scene in which Nick and Guthrie are in disagreement. Nick seems to have trouble accepting the action of the scene earlier in the play in which Laertes returns to avenge Polonius' death. Guthrie has Nick entering the King's chamber and threatening Claudius with a revolver. In the course of the action, the King succeeds in getting Laertes to give up the weapon, from which, unseen by the young man, he removes the bullets.

At a recent rehearsal Nick told Guthrie that he couldn't understand why "a guy who breaks into the palace looking for vengeance for his father's death would give up his gun so easily." Guthrie replied, "Because it says so in the script." Nick didn't seem impressed by the answer. A bit later Guthrie took Nick over to a corner of the stage to speak with him privately about the scene.

Guthrie's control over his actors and the production gets stronger with each passing rehearsal. The occasional dissenting voice, in this case Nick Coster's, is being silenced for the good of the performance as a whole. Guthrie has listened reasonably to the few actors who have questioned his directorial choices, but I sometimes get the feeling that the game is being played with marked cards, and Guthrie, as dealer, is the only one who knows how it will come out.[30]

APRIL 19

There is a grotesque comic effect at the end of Hamlet's first scene with the Ghost, triggered by Hamlet's lack of certainty about having seen the Ghost. It starts with the exaggeration of the falconer's cry, "Hillo, ho, ho, boy! come, bird, come." It continues in Hamlet's strange behavior during his attempts to get Horatio and Marcellus to swear to secrecy about the night's events. Marcellus, in particular, seems very doubtful, and places his hand on the sword hilt in a comically reluctant manner, almost as though saying, "Oh, this is all too silly."

Hamlet now faints after the line, ". . . o cursed spite, that ever I was born to set it right." He is caught by the two other men,

---

30. In speaking about the production later in the season (September 6) Guthrie told me: "I hope that the actors were able to see what I was about one way or another, perhaps implicitly, if not always in an explicit fashion."

and revives to give the tag line of the scene, "Nay come, let's go together." Guthrie said this emphasizes Hamlet's "need for help and friendship."

Guthrie has Lee Richardson back to mixing up Rosencrantz and Guildenstern on their first entrance. The King remembers the *names* but not the *faces*; Claudius says, "Welcome dear Rosencrantz . . . ," but then looks from one to the other for an acknowledgment before extending his hand. He also pours glasses of sherry for the two students as he explains why they were brought to the castle.

Guthrie's review of the first Hamlet–Rosencrantz–Guildenstern scene today: "Sounds like the fourth act of Strindberg."

Today the balcony was in place for the first time, and several bits of action had to be adjusted. One of them was Rosencrantz's leap off the balcony to stop Hamlet in the "Hide Fox" scene. Before we did the scene, I asked Guthrie if I should try the jump; he said to go ahead; I did; and it was cut. He said, "The scene will be dark anyway." He might have been prompted by the look of shock on my face as I landed; it was a real jolt—more than I had expected. (My soles stung for an hour after.) I think that Guthrie would like to keep the leap in for its spectacular effect, but his concern for my safety militates against it. Since I would have to do the leap in patent leather dress shoes (part of my Play scene costume), I'm glad it's been cut.

Guthrie added the extras in this scene, and the visual concept is an encirclement of Hamlet by the King's guards. They will enter from the tunnels and also from the aisles through the audience. The scene will be very dark, and all of us surrounding Hamlet will have flashlights trained on his face. At the end of the scene, he will bump into one of the guards and bolt down the left tunnel with all in pursuit. Guthrie has cut the revolvers which we were to be carrying in the scene.

The decision to cut the jump from the balcony made necessary a complex plan for me to be able to appear at the beginning of the next scene from the right tunnel, out of breath from the chase of Hamlet and his subsequent rough handling below stairs. When Hamlet bolts away in the "Hide Fox" scene, I exit left from the balcony, down a flight of stairs to the waiting elevator which takes me down to the basement; then run at the fullest and safest speed possible. through the basement (under the stage), up a ramp, through a corridor, up another ramp and onto the stage through the tunnel.

Obviously, there'll be no acting required to give the impression that Hamlet has led me a merry chase through the bowels of Elsinore.

Hamlet is anxious to relate to Horatio the story of the pirates and the fates of Rosencrantz and Guildenstern, and does so with fervor. Horatio is shocked, but Hamlet argues in defense of his actions. Later in the scene, Osric enters, and Hamlet proceeds to make a fool of Claudius' pawn, much to Horatio's pleasure. Osric (Clayton Corzatte) pronounces Laertes as "Lay-ur-tease," elongating the second vowel.

In this scene one senses an hostility (racial prejudice?) in Osric's attitude toward Horatio. This is the only scene in the play in which Horatio's color is played upon for any specific emphasis, and it is done with subtlety. Guthrie's casting of a black actor in the role was deliberate, to give a more contemporary look to the play, but he is not creating undue focus on Graham Brown. Of course, Graham is not simply a black actor, but a talented black actor, who is doing very well in the role.

APRIL 21

Today was not a *Hamlet* rehearsal day, but Guthrie used the morning to set lights. Douglas Campbell was there to help, as were all of the stage managers and the technical director. Jack Going and I were asked to walk through some of the actors' positions.

Guthrie seems no different from most other directors in his approach to this aspect of staging a production. He was concerned with the same problems, had the same considerations—although always allowing for his concept of the theatre making it effect not by means of illusion, but by ritual; that is, the enjoyment of a play is not dependent on illusion, and that includes technical illusion.[31]

The lighting instruments in this theatre are, in the main, ungelled. White light is more consistent with the function of this kind of stage, according to Guthrie.[32] It was interesting that Guthrie has decided to have two exceptions to this rule: blue light is used in both the Ghost-Hamlet scene in the first act and the Graveyard scene in Act Three.

31. Guthrie is eloquent on the subject in *A Life in the Theatre,* pp. 349–350.
32. Cf. Footnote 4.

APRIL 23

Shakespeare's Birthday! The company spent it appropriately, rehearsing one of the most blatantly melodramatic and theatrically effective scenes in all of dramatic literature: *Hamlet*, Finale—All Hands.

The scene had never been done by the full company, so it was a new experience for all of us except George Grizzard and Nick Coster. They had been working on the fencing match under Douglas Campbell's expert tutelage since the beginning of rehearsals, so that action was far along. In keeping with the modern dress approach to the play, the duelists use foils, and don masks and jackets.[33]

Guthrie's opening direction to the company was to tell them to think of the action as "a jolly fencing bout after dinner." He wants a great deal of gay chatter at the beginning of the scene (this time there are no especially written lines), and it continues until the match begins. He said this "will pay a dividend" for the silence later. It subsides during the exchange between Hamlet and Laertes, but starts to build again as the two young men get into their fencing costumes. Each man has two seconds, one of Hamlet's being Horatio. Osric is the official judge, and as he parts their foils with his the match begins, and the court—taking his cue—is silenced abruptly. After the first hit, Guthrie told the court to applaud. They also applaud when Claudius first offers the cup to Hamlet. Guthrie told George Grizzard:

> Ham it up. Take the cup. Remember, there are people in the audience who won't know the play. They think Hamlet is going to drink the poison.

Guthrie encouraged the court to cheer on their favorite in the match, to make comments about the style of the fencers, to gasp at a particularly exciting exchange, and, as indicated previously, to applaud the hits.

In working on the scene Guthrie came on the stage and moved about as though a court member, shouting various comments to the

33. The same approach was used in the 1938 modern-dress version with Guinness. Williamson, *op. cit.*, p. 107.

combatants and to other court members. While the bouts were being played, you could see him, for instance, say something to a court lady and then give her a firm push in the direction of a guard six feet away—and she'd run to the fellow and point at the action excitedly; or he might pound a nobleman on the back as a hit was made. His physical and vocal presence *among* the cast seemed to generate even more excitement in an inherently exciting scene. This, coupled with the fact that the whole scene was fresh—that the company had never seen the well-practiced bouts—made the rehearsal vitally spontaneous.

Guthrie stopped at various points in the scene to give a general choreographic direction. For example, on the third bout the court gets so excited that they crowd in on the contestants, and they have to be restrained by the seconds. They move back and forth with Hamlet and Laertes, as the two men move diagonally across the stage, from up right to down left and return. Even the servants get involved in the action and contribute to the visual dynamics.

There is another choreographic pattern which lays the basis for what Guthrie is doing with Gertrude's drinking of the poison. After each bout, the duelists and their seconds switch positions, so that six men, three on one side, three on another, cross each other at midstage. Guthrie has timed one of these mass moves to happen right after Claudius' line, "Gertrude do not drink." He then makes a move to stop her, but finds a traffic jam in front of him.

Hamlet will get hit in the palm with the poisoned tip. He then disarms Laertes, and, after switching the foils, attacks him viciously. Laertes will die very grandly, with Hamlet stabbing him in the side downstage center. Guthrie spent time arranging some courtiers on the stairs just below Laertes' moment of truth. He then told Nick to turn slowly—"in shock and pleasure; pleased that it's over"—take a couple of steps forward, let the foil clang to the floor, then fall stiffly forward into the arms of the waiting noblemen. The men don't reach out to grab Nick; he falls to them—they just wait. It's a very theatrical effect.[34] In fact, Guthrie has mentioned "the showy theatricality of the scene" several times already.

Guthrie is interpreting Hamlet's line, "Ho, let the door be

34. It is interesting to note that Guthrie used a similar effect in the 1937 *Hamlet* with Olivier, but then it was Gertrude who fainted from a high rostrum into the arms of terrified courtiers. Both Williamson, p. 84, and Williams, p. 144, mention the death plunge.

locked," in a literal way, and he creates an impressive moment. As Hamlet cries, "O Villainy!" Osric, who is in on the treachery, bolts for the double doors up center. On Hamlet's command about locking the doors, the portal is closed with a loud slam by a servant Guthrie has placed in readiness. Osric then moves to his left toward another door at the far right of the back wall; this, too, closes forcefully. He then makes a move toward the left tunnel, and the noise of a door underneath the audience (another part of the castle) stops him. Thereupon, yet another slam is heard from the right tunnel. Trapped! Claudius has *not* been unmindful of these prophetic sounds. Ignoring the underling, Osric, Hamlet concentrates on bigger game.

During this sequence Guthrie handled the court like a chorus and has arranged some excellent effects. He made the court a multiple shadow of Claudius. As the King moved upstage away from Hamlet, Guthrie had the court move upstage also on the far sides of the stage. His fear was their fear; his fearful phonations were theirs also. Guthrie asked one extra if he was a Catholic. The reply was in the affirmative, to which Guthrie replied, "Think you're following Jesus to Golgotha." He also spoke of the intake of breath before a great effect, which he called "the single most thrilling thing in the theatre." This comment came as he directed the sequence of the King's death. The best way to illustrate this whole action is list the steps in order:

> Hamlet stalks the King, the court following.
>
> Hamlet stabs him as the court has a great shocked intake of breath.
>
> The King groans.
>
> The court echoes the expression of pain by making a keening sound starting high and loudly and finally going through a long diminuendo.
>
> At the same time each member of the court acts as though Hamlet's sword has penetrated his body, as well as the King's. (Guthrie mentioned "the death of the corporate state.")
>
> The King tops this sound with "Oh yet defend me friends, I am but hurt," as he slumps against the wine table.
>
> Hamlet grabs the poisoned cup, pours the liquor down Claudius' throat, and then releases him.
>
> Claudius rises slowly, and in one final summation of energy raises his arm as though to strike Hamlet.

A moment of frozen tension by all.

Claudius falls backward, upsetting the table with a great clamor.

As Guthrie directed this sequence it was obvious that he had done some homework. There was never any hestitation about any of it; every direction was given quickly, clearly, and confidently. Through all of this the company reacted very well: they seemed to be having as much fun as their director.

Although the scene is choreographically complex, Guthrie did not refer to the text or a staging diagram during the entire session. This is not unusual, I might add, since it has been his practice for every scene in the play.

APRIL 25

The Ghost Double has been cut. Guthrie had told me to instruct an extra in the moves of the double, which I had been walking all this time, but the extra never got a chance to do it. It was cut after I learned—and reminded Guthrie—no costume has been designed for this added character. It is probably a case of the designer holding off on a costume until the director was sure whether he really wanted it or not, and Guthrie eventually decided against it.

The opening of the first court scene was done with sound effects today; and it seems very good. The peal of joyful sounding bells are heard (wedding bells?), the double doors open upstage, and Hamlet comes through them sideways looking back over his shoulder; he then puts his hands to his ears and moves all the way downstage center. The court enters after a beat or two, and, at the same time, four musicians (three trumpeters and one drummer) enter on the balcony, take positions and begin to play a specially composed entrance march. It heralds the arrival of the King and Queen, who enter, make a circle around the stage acknowledging the court, and come to a stop at a V-shaped bench at stage right.

The end of the scene reverses the choreography, with Hamlet following the royal couple and the court toward the double doors, but finding them shut in his face. He then touches his cheek which Gertrude has kissed, and begins his first soliloquy, "O that this too

too solid flesh would melt . . ." Guthrie's interpretation of the scene as a wedding reception provides an immediacy for this soliloquy which allows the audience to share more fully Hamlet's anguish and depression of the moment. The choice has been an extremely valuable one for George, and he is effective in his reactions throughout and after the scene.

Gertrude kissing Hamlet in the scene allows a nice bit of character development: Claudius had been turned away from them during the kiss, but sees them as he says, "Be as ourself in Denmark." He then sharply says, "Madam . . ." and pauses as he restrains his jealous anger, then says, ". . . come." Gertrude is pleased with her new husband's concern.

In working on the finale tonight Guthrie deleted a few details he set previously. The courtiers no longer block the King's path to Gertrude as she is drinking the poison. Gertrude drinks more quickly, and Claudius doesn't reach her in time. Guthrie also cut the second door slam after Hamlet's command to lock the door, so that there is the double door slam, then one from each tunnel. This bit of action really takes advantage of one of the special features of this theatre—those marvelous tunnels under the audience.

Guthrie told Osric "to find something showy" as Hamlet stalks the King.

Guthrie gave Nick Coster a few words of advice about what he (Guthrie) called "interior acting." He wanted Laertes to die more simply with less emoting:

> Your job is to let Shakespeare's lines be heard clearly and distinctly. They will do the rest. You don't have to find the psychological basis for saying the lines; Shakespeare has done it for you.

I get the impression that Nick knows he can't win, but has too much integrity not to question those directions with which he is in disagreement. Although the question is academic and no value judgment is implied, I wonder what this production would now look like had more of us done the same thing.

At the end of the scene Fortinbras comes in on the balcony with two soldiers, each bearing a furled flag. As the four captains with the body of Hamlet on their shoulders move upstage, the flags will unfurl.

APRIL 28

A memorable day! For the first time I felt that the company was really that—a vibrant acting ensemble working for a common goal. This happy event can be attributed to one thing: the first run-through of the entire play with minimal stops. Up to this time we have run through only individual acts.

The experience revealed more clearly the enormity and imagination of Guthrie's "plan." This rehearsal came at a particularly important time (by design, no doubt)—nine days before our first and only preview. It came at a time when the company badly needed the continuity, particularly the actors in the major roles, and, above all, George Grizzard. Working for this long time (seven weeks) on the play without a run-through has made it impossible to achieve continuity in any production element. Obviously, Guthrie must know this. He must also know, from his vast experience, that this type of rehearsal schedule *can* work. In fact, he was confident enough to give the cast a few extra days off earlier this month (for the "Easter hol").

Seeing George Grizzard's performance today showed us a very well-deliberated characterization, the keynotes of which are honesty and simplicity. This Hamlet will never win him an award for dynamic acting, but is thoroughly human, the most believable Hamlet I've seen. In George Grizzard, Guthrie cast an actor who could exist believably as Hamlet in the reality Guthrie has been creating from Shakespeare's text. This is a Hamlet who could be a college student; have a Black for his best friend; have gotten his girl friend pregnant; be deeply hurt by the duplicity of his old school chums; be an amateur actor, playwright, and fencer; in addition to grappling with the most fascinating psychological problem in dramatic literature.

This run-through did wonders for George, as it did for all of us. As I watched as much of the run-through as I could, I came to the conclusion that Guthrie's margin for acting errors was a wide one, and the direction of the play has been so securely structured that only embarrassingly poor performances—God and Thespis forbid!—could alter the impact of the production. In *Return Engagement*, his sequel to *Moscow Rehearsals*, Norris Houghton makes some comments about Guthrie which seem to have been written precisely for our Minneapolis *Hamlet*:

> My admiration for Guthrie's directorial genius is immense, but the impression I usually take from his presentations is of his staging rather than of any single actor's unique contribution. I used to have the same reaction years ago to productions directed by Orson Welles. It is an impression that presumably cannot be avoided when an intensely creative director is at work.[35]

The show ran well over four hours today, including the two intermissions. I'm sure that it will eventually be shorter than this, (since there were a few stops) but the production has been advertised as a full-length, uncut version of the play, and while this is not literally true, we are using what is very close to being a complete text.

In an introduction to a published version of *Hamlet* Guthrie had expressed his qualms about cutting a script drastically:

> The result is that Hamlet, who, in a full-length version is still the dominant figure, but who dominates a pretty considerable and interesting group of characters, is in a heavily cut version, left the single interesting figure against a background of cardboard dummies; while the play, deprived of its intended rhythm, jerks phrenetically from one unprepared and therefore incredible and melodramatic climax to another.[36]

Obviously, Guthrie doesn't intend this to happen in our production, since no scenes have been deleted and only two *very* minor characters have been cut: the Lord and the First Ambassador in the final scene of the play.

The major emendations made by Guthrie are as follows:

1. Shifting part of the Claudius-Laertes plot to the graveyard scene. Also, cutting eleven lines in it.

2. Cutting the exchange between Hamlet and Rosencrantz

35. Norris Houghton, *Return Engagement* (New York: Holt, Rinehart, and Winston, (1962), p. 100.
36. *Shakespeare's Ten Great Plays*, p. 289.

about the children's theatre, just prior to the entrance of the players.

3. Cutting four lines in the first Laertes-Reynaldo scene.

4. Cutting seven lines in the Polonius-Reynaldo scene.

5. Cutting eight lines in Hamlet's welcome to the players.

6. Cutting twelve lines in the speeches of the Player King and Queen.

7. Cutting three lines in the Closet scene.

8. Cutting fourteen lines from a speech of Hamlet's in the Gravedigger scene.

9. Cutting fifteen lines from Hamlet's story of the pirates.

Because of the relatively few textual deletions in this production, all of the characters around Hamlet have been given full opportunity to develop. As a result, Hamlet is seen in the fullest dimension possible, not only through the soliloquies but through the relationships with the characters left intact by Guthrie.

After the rehearsal Guthrie for the first time gave written notes taken by him in the house. We were amazed that there were so few of them, five sheets of yellow legal paper. Many of them were about the lack of clarity in speaking the verse. Indeed, some actors are less intelligible than others. Everyone, except Jessica Tandy, is having some degree of trouble. The theatre itself is partly—but *only partly*—to blame, as it is in any nonproscenium arrangement. The house has some bad spots, particularly in the audience right section, called affectionately by the company "The Alpine Climb" because of its steep, unbroken line from first row to last.

APRIL 30

Tonight's rehearsal didn't seem to have the spark and vitality of the first run-through, but it was still profitable.

Guthrie asked me to sit in various sections of the house whenever I had the chance (the first and third acts) and take down any words I missed from the actors. I took about three pages of notes.

Guthrie's notes were mostly on lost words and phrases, with a few about a couple of bits of business. Nothing major. Listening to Guthrie give notes is much fun; it seems that every note he gives ends in a punch line. He convulsed the company with this one:

> When Ophelia exits in the Mad scene, don't all of you officers follow her off the same way. It looks as though the five of you are going to rape her.

That's rather typical of Guthrie's humor. Again, it is evident that Guthrie's criticisms are purposely couched in humor, but it is never merely to get a laugh. There is always some truth in the gag, and he gets his point across in the most pleasurable way possible, for us as well as for him.

Remarkable about these notes is that they have yet to generate substantial changes. Obviously, what he has worked for all this time is there; the notes are polish.

MAY 2

Today we had another run-through, but with stops. Typically humorous things happened to contribute even further to the relaxed atmosphere which has characterized the whole rehearsal period.

Guthrie worked the play scene to sharpen it, and—onstage at least—it is quite exciting. The last time through, the scene had an exceptional tension to it, and Guthrie shouted form the house (just before Hamlet confronts the King), "Wonderful. That's the best all of you have ever done it. It's fine. On." George Grizzard, his concentration broken: "Thanks." A company laugh.

Later Guthrie took a little time to refine the finale, and a couple of interesting things were said:

> About an offstage cry: "Gordon, Duse couldn't have done it better, but it was a silly idea of mine. Forget it."

> To George Grizzard asking for a piece of "crimson" for his cut in the duel: "Oh no, George. It would be a great mistake. It all goes in with the nonrealistic idea."

On Claudius' death: "That dumping of the table, which I planned to be a big moment, doesn't come off at all, because the table is under the balcony." (He restaged this to his satisfaction.)

The costumes were worn today for the first time. The production is stunning. There was a dress parade before the rehearsal, and each actor had to wear each of his costumes. Guthrie, Tanya, and two costumers from New York, Ray Diffen and Jane Greenwood, all passed judgment on the finery. Guthrie has a keen eye for costume details.

Life magazine is going to do a spread on the opening of the theatre, and their photographer, under Tom Prideaux's direction, took what seemed like a couple of hundred photos. Someone wanted to pose Jessica Tandy in her first costume (an off-white gown) against the multicolored seats of the theatre. Guthrie objected:

> The gown was made to look regal, and Jessie to be regal in it. Sitting like that would make her look dumpy.

The notes after the run-through took about 25 minutes— they filled four sheets of yellow paper.

MAY 3

At this last rehearsal before our preview performance, things went very smoothly. The note session was over in 15 minutes with Guthrie giving only a page and a half. I've mentioned the amount of notes taken because we all assume it is an indication of how confident Guthrie is about the production.

One interesting note was given to Graham Brown about Horatio's speeches after Hamlet's death. Graham has been doing the lines more and more emotionally as the rehearsals progressed. Guthrie told him today:

> It's a disembodied voice. Don't go for the easy tear and pathos. The play is above that emotion by this time. It has risen above it. Far greater.

In thinking about this later I remembered Guthrie's comments about his production of *Oedipus Rex* at Stratford Ontario in 1954, and they struck me as particularly apropos of his intention for the end of *Hamlet*:

> The performance of a tragedy must aim higher than at an audience's susceptibility to pathos. An audience will cry readily; the death of little Willie or a pretty girl singing the sorriest rubbish will melt to tender tears the hardest-bitten men and the hardest-biting women. The emotion aroused by even a half-decent performance of great tragedy cannot be measured in terms of chewed hankies and misted specs. The full impact of great tragedy is not immediate; it takes effect slowly. It lies in wait on the fringe of dreams. It wakes one with a start in the small hours. It can shake the confident and strengthen the weak, stop the clock, roll back the seas. It can give a new meaning to life, and an old meaning to death.[37]

The dominant mood of the production is relaxed with confidence among the company and emanating in abundance from the director. I have never been in a production which exuded more assurance. It is particularly interesting that, with so much at stake for so many people, there is still a relaxed atmosphere. There is a feeling of faith in what Guthrie has asked us to do, a feeling that whatever reservations one might have about certain things—not the least of which concern our own performances—all will fit perfectly and successfully on opening night. The magnitude of Guthrie's talent evokes a great trust in his actors, not unlike a childlike awe for the prodigious feats of a father. There is a loyalty in the company to an extent rarely seen, except, perhaps, in productions directed by Tyrone Guthrie.

MAY 5

The dedication service was a singularly inspiring event. The Minnesota Theatre Company gave a choral reading of Psalm 118. As the company took the stage, there was a great feeling of pride and *esprit de corps*, which began to form for the first time last Sun-

37. *Thrice the Brinded Cat Hath Mew'd*, p. 113.

day at the first run-through. It has built all during the week, and a unified spirit moved the company at the ceremony.

MAY 6

A couple of hours before our first performance before an audience (an invited audience composed mainly of the workers who constructed the theatre, cab drivers, and hospital personnel), Guthrie was asked in a radio interview what he wanted an audience to get from their experience with this production of *Hamlet*:

> I'd be satisfied if the audience said, "Well, I really don't know what it all adds up to, but we've certainly been through a variety of very interesting experiences, and I don't know why, but I find Hamlet an oddly sympathetic and endearing person."
>
> If Shakespeare had intended to make the meaning clear, he was a good enough craftsman to do so. No great art completely reveals itself. There is always an element of mystery. The main thing is for you to find enough in it to make it interesting and to make you speculate and ponder upon the mystery. Ponder *Hamlet* and you'll find much which is applicable to your own lives, if you take time after the performance to do so.[38]

The preview performance before an excited, packed house was, to my way of thinking, not a fully satisfactory evening. The first act seemed terribly slow, the second and third better, but uneven. The performance lacked that extra spark, vitality, inspiration—whatever.

George Grizzard was very nervous, and consequently off form. He read some lines as he had never done in rehearsal. In addition, he blew lines in various places—he went momentarily blank in the "What a piece of work is man" speech, for instance. Off stage during the second act Mike Levin and I asked George how his voice was (it's hoarse from "smoking too much"), and he said his voice was all right, but he felt "empty inside."

The audience applause at the end of the performance was

38. Interview of Tyrone Guthrie by Sheldon Goldstein, WLOL–FM, Minneapolis, May 6, 1963.

good, but not as strong as for last night's preview performance of *The Miser*. The Play scene and Ophelia's Mad scene both stopped the show with applause.

Guthrie, in spite of what many of us considered a disappointing performance, gave no notes.

I think maybe this let-down was good for the company. Perhaps we had gotten a little too cocksure about our work. This question mark should spur the cast on to a fine performance for the opening (I hope).

MAY 7 (G DAY)

The long-awaited opening night of The Tyrone Guthrie Theatre has come and gone. And it was a *great* night.[39]

The excitement seemed to hang in the air, both outside and inside the building. Press, radio, and television coverage was exceptional. The call board was inundated with telegrams from theatre companies and personnel from all over the world, a veritable "Who's Who in the Theatre." The Green Room was filled with flowers for the company and for individual cast members.

My objectivity about the performance is understandably clouded by my personal excitement, but most of the cast felt that the performance was considerably better than the night before. The audience—for whatever combination of reasons—seemed to enjoy the show immensely. Applause after scenes and exits seemed the rule rather than the exception; particularly well-received were the Ghost-Hamlet, Play, and Mad scenes. There was a standing ovation at the finish—more for the entire venture, I think, than for the production or any one actor's performance. I don't really see how it could have been otherwise, considering the civic pride of the audience. It was an emotional audience that wanted to applaud as appreciatively as possible for this realization of a magnificent dream.

I saw our director only once all evening. After the performance Dr. Guthrie, a picture of uncomfortable elegance in tails, poked his head into Dressing Room 14 and said with characteristic briskness, "Well done, boys. Good job."

39. For Guthrie's version of opening night the reader is referred to *A New Theatre*, pp. 108–111.

AFTERWORD

The evaluation of the results of any creative process (in this instance, rehearsals) is best left to those for whom the artists involved in that process practice their art and craft: the audience. The production of *Hamlet* at the Guthrie Theatre in 1963 played 46 performances to 50,000 people (75.6% capacity in the 1437-seat house). Statistics, of course, are far from the whole story, and most actors and directors are more interested in audience reaction to their work after the tickets have been taken.

The general audience reaction to the production was, in my opinion, favorable. In fact, most audience members who anticipated seeing *Hamlet* that season in Minneapolis were genuinely excited and enthused about the prospect. Early in the run this excitement was as attributable to the new theatre *per se* and partaking in the *event* of the Guthrie's first season as it was for attending the performance of *Hamlet*. This feeling contributed greatly to the audience reaction at early performances. Later performances of the play, attended by patrons who might have seen other productions in the season (*The Miser, The Three Sisters, Death of a Salesman*), did not have this welcome dividend of civic pride and curiosity influencing the enjoyment of the experience. Nevertheless, audiences throughout the last two months of the twenty-week season seemed attentive, responsive, and appreciative, if understandably less excited than their counterparts in the months of May, June, and July.

No audiences for the entire run of the play were more enthusiastic than the special matinees for junior high and high school students. Lee Richardson echoed the general feeling of the cast about going back to adult audiences after the exhilaration of performing before these exceptionally responsive audiences: "Bring back the kids."

Critical reaction in newspaper and periodical reviews was, as

71

they say, mixed. It is typified by the heading of a newspaper article containing excerpts of the major reviews:

"Critics Don't Agree on Guthrie:
Pay Your Money and Take Your Choice"[1]

Reading these notices it is difficult to believe that the critics all saw the same production. Obviously they didn't, if the thoughts expressed in the preface to this work are valid. The main areas of disparity, excepting contrary opinions about certain supporting performances, seem to be centered on two things: Guthrie's modern-dress approach, and the performance of George Grizzard in the title role.

That this should be the case is not surprising, and was least surprising to Guthrie and Grizzard. There will always be those to whom "tradition" in producing Shakespeare is sacrosanct, and the attempt to present a classic in anything resembling modern dress will be looked upon by some as The Wrong Idea. Similarly, an actor who plays the most famous character in dramatic literature invariably invites comparsion, however unconscious, with other actors who have performed the role, particularly in the recent past. This is inevitable, and will occur every time an actor accepts the challenge of the great roles which stand as a measure of an actor's right to be called "great." Guthrie and Grizzard, you can be certain, were well acquainted with these facts, but being potential targets for the slings and arrows of drama critics did not dissuade them from taking a crack at the Melancholy Dane together.

It is not my purpose to evaluate evaluations. I have appended a representative selection of reviews so the reader may have an opportunity to do this for himself.

1. Dan Sullivan, "Critics Don't Agree on Guthrie: Pay Your Money and Take Your Choice," *The Minneapolis Tribune,* June 2, 1963.

THE HAMLET PROMPTSCRIPT

Key to Promptscript Abbreviations

Characters

BAR:	Barnardo	OPH:	Ophelia
CAPT:	Captain	P. KING:	Player King
CORN:	Cornelius	P. QUEEN:	Player Queen
FORT:	Fortinbras	PLAY K.	Player King
FRAN:	Francisco	PLAY Q.	Player Queen
GDS:	Guards	POL:	Polonius
GUI:	Guildenstern	PRO:	Prologue
HOR:	Horatio	REY:	Reynaldo
LAE:	Laertes	ROS:	Rosencrantz
LUC:	Lucianus	RPS:	Rest of Players
MAR:	Marcellus	VOLT:	Voltemand

Names of Company Members

BACK:	Backlin	SLING:	Slingsby
FORS:	Forsberg	STAN:	Stanley
MACL:	MacLachlan	VAN:	Van Ark
NYM:	Nyman	VON MEN:	Von Mende
ROGO:	Rogosheske	VON M:	Von Mende

Levels (five levels are indicated in the stage diagram)

4: highest level
3: highest step level
2: next step

1: next step
0: pit level (lowest)

Movement

CW: clockwise
CC: counter-clockwise

Xing: crossing
Xes: crosses

Stage Areas
C: center
DC: down center
UC: up center
L: left
DL: down left
UL: up left
R: right
DR: down right
UR: up right
R TUN: right tunnel under audience
L TUN: left tunnel under audience
C BEL: area under center of balcony upstage
L BEL: area under left section of balcony upstage
R BEL: area under right section of balcony upstage
SKENE: upstage center balcony, supported by four pillars, with playing
  above and below (this section capable of being enclosed by
  curtains)
PLAT: platform at perimeter of stage between 8:00 and 10:00
BENCH: V-shaped seat on platform
POLE: Pillar supporting skene or balcony
Clock numerals (see diagram) are used to indicate positions on the
  perimeter of the stage.
Relative positions are expressed in fractions to indicate placement be-
  tween stage center and the perimeter of the stage, e.g., ½ 9:00
  means halfway between stage center and 9:00.

Miscellaneous
PANTO: pantomime in Play Scene
TROL: drink trolley used in Scene 8
Sound and Light cues are noted in the right-hand margin of the prompt-
  script.

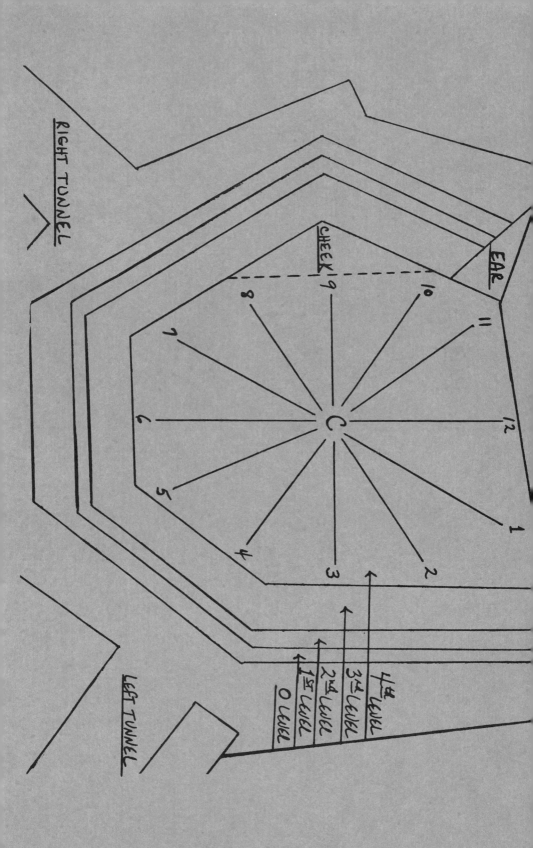

Scene 7(Act II, scene ii)

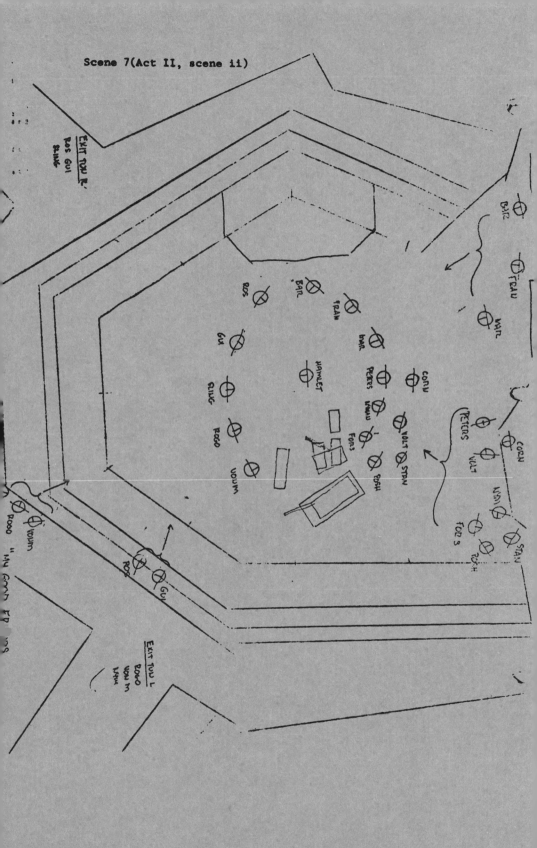

Scene 10(Act III, scene ii)

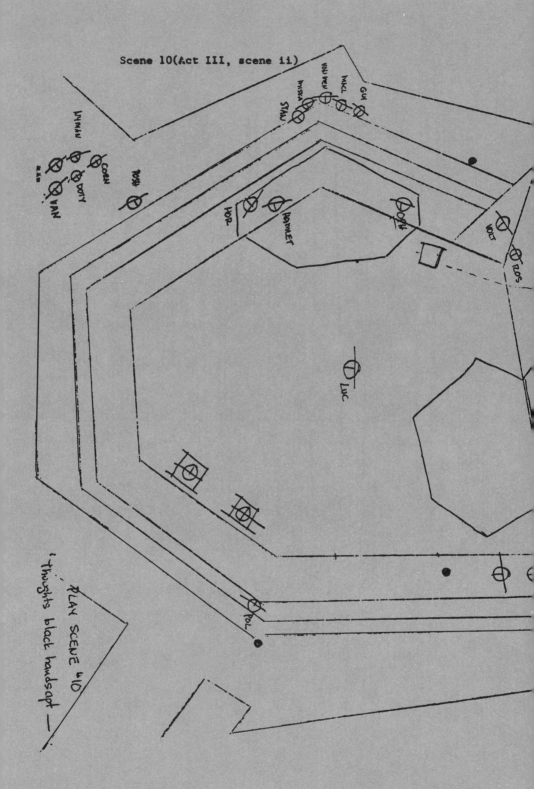

LYMAN

B.B.

CORN

DOTY

VAN

ROS

STAU

MISEA

VOU MEU

MACL

GU

HOR

HAWLEY

ODU

VOLT

FLOS

LUC

POL.

PLAY SCENE #10
'Thoughts black handsapt —

Scene 21(Act V, scene ii)

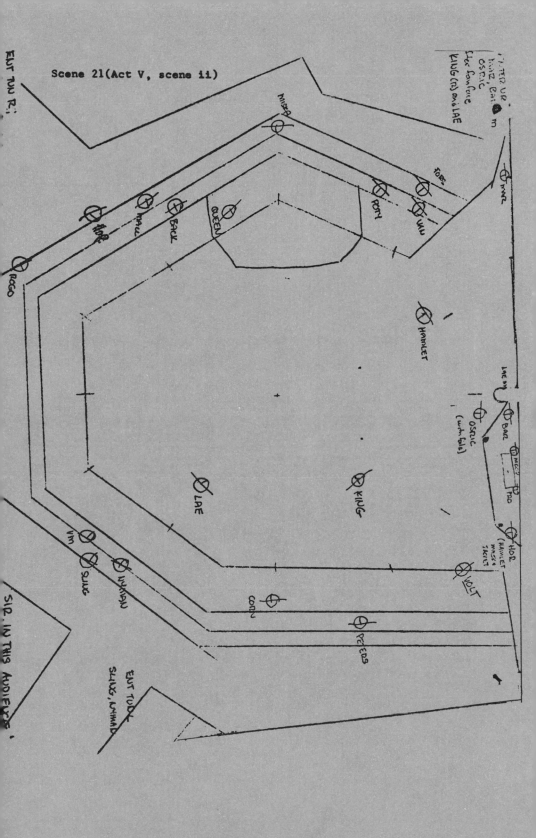

CHECK LIST

Before House Opens:

CHECK CUE LIGHTS: Below
Orch
UR
Prompt
Trap   L Ramp

CHECK INTERCOM: Backstage
Ramps
Basement
Orchestra

CHECK MONITOR

CHECK TIME

CHECK FLASHLIGHT

SOUND CHECKED AND READY

LIGHTS CHECKED AND READY : House at full and controlled
Works out
Pre-set in
Catwalk lights off
Catwalk doors closed
Aisle Lights
Exit Lights
STAGE CHECKED AND READY: Aud. door open plug struck < Sister
                                                                              plat.
Doors open above
— UR and Below doors closed
Drapes across R Below door
Bench set
balustrade set

NITE LITE STRUCK -
SUIT-UP
BOOTH WORKS ON
VOL II.

Half Hour Call

Fifteen Minute Call

Five Minute Call

Places   Ready in Ramps: Marcellus
Horatio
Barnardo
Ghost

Starters Ready Backstage

Orchestra Ready Backstage

Light and Sound Operators Ready in Booth

Go From PSM _____

O Monitor on   O   VOL II
O Goose neck off
O Suit up
O Xmas lites out
O Backstage works out

STARTERS ?

WARN
HOUSE (30)

L#1 (8), L#2, 2A

m#1, 1A, (1B)

C-LITE BEL

CHECK COMPLETE ▪═══════════════════════ m#1, HOUSE

RED LITES ON

END m#1, COUNT 2 ▪═══════════════════ m#1A, L#1

COUNT 8 ▪━━━━━━━━━━━━━━━━━━━ C-LITE BEL

START m#1B ▪━━━━━━━━━━━━━━━━━ L#2

AT RISE: FRAN at ½ 8:00 SWORD DRAWN IN R HAND, LOOKING OUT, TURNS STARTS SLOW X CC
TO 3:00. BAR STARTS IN FROM TUN R. FRAN STOP AT 3:30, THEN X → 3:

STOPPING ON 1 AND 0

TURNS, XES IN TO C

XES IN TO FRAN BRISKLY. THEY MEET C   ⊗   FR

SALUTES WITH SABRE, THEN RETURNS IT TO SCABBARD

TAKING OUT SABRE SALUTING FRAN

XES LOF   BAR. ON WAY OUT R TUNNEL. BAR XES UL A FEW

TURNING BACK TO FRAN

STOPPING AT EDGE OF 4, TURNS. BACK TO BAR.

FRAN XES ON, STOPS OU 3 WHEN BAR SPEAKS AGAIN

BAR X TO 1:00 IN SENTRY WALK

PEERING INTO TUN L

HOR AND MAR START IN TUN R. MAR LOF HOR AND FOLLOWING.
HOR XES RIGHT UP TO 2 AT 8:30 STOPS, MAR STOPS OU O TO
TALK TO FRAN WHEN HE XES DU STEPS ● BAR XES TO ¾ 2:00

X DU STEPS
KING IN TO O.

1

Act 1 Scene one (1)

    Elsinore. A platform on the battlements of the

    Castle. Enter Francisco on guard. Then enter

    Barnardo.

BARNARDB Who's there?

FRANCISCO Nay, answer me. Stand and unfold yourself.

BARNADO   Long live the king.

FRANCISCO Barnardo?

BARNARDO   He?

FRANCISCO You come most carefully upon your hour. *salute*

BARNARDO   'Tis now struck twelve, get thee to bed Francisco.

FRANCISCO For this relief much thanks, 'tis bitter cold,

    And I am sick at heart.

BARNARDO Have you had quiet guard?

FRANCISCO Not a mouse stirring.

BARNARDO   Well, goodnight

    If you do meet Horatio and Marcellus,

    The rivals of my watch, bid them make haste.

FRANCISCO   I think I hear them.

                            replace salone

         ENTER HORATIO AND MARCELLUS.

    Stand ho, who is there?

HORATIO   Friends to this ground.

MARCELLUS And liegemen to the Dane.

FRANCISCO   Give you good night.

MARCELLUS O, farewell honest soldier.

    Who hath relieved you?

XING OUT TUNNEL R VIA L OF MAR

XING ONTO I AND O

TURNING, HAVING XED TO 2:00

MAR & HOR X IN   TO MEET BAR WHO XES IN. TO 1/4 8:00

HO & MAR SHAKE HANDS   • HOR X ↷ ABOVE BAR TO   3:00 . BAR XES DS A FE
●CLICKING HEELS SMARTLY FOR MAR WHO DOES SAME AT 3/4 8:00

TURNING. XING TO 11:00 THEN DS TO DS BENCH _

_XING TO 12:15

BAR XES DS TO BENCH PLAT

LOOKS OFF UR XES R A FEW STEPS THEN BACK .

AT 1/2 3:00

IN FRONT OF DS BENCH

SITS DC ON BENCH, HOR STARTS TO X TO BENCH PLAT.

XES IN. SITS US ON BENCH, MAR X TO STAND UR OF BENCH ON 3 AND 2

MAR

HOR

BAR   POINTING DL

2

FRANCISCO　♠Barnardo hath my place;

Give you good night.　　　(Exit

MARCELLUS　♠Holla, Barnardo!

BARNARDO　　　　　　　　　　♠ SAY _____

What, is Horatio there?　　　　　　　　　　　　　　　　　L*2A

HORATIO　　♠A piece of him.

BARNARDO　　♠Welcome Horatio, ♠welcome good Marcellus♠

HORATIO　　What, has this thing appeared again to-night?

BARNARDO　　I have seen nothing. ♠

MARCELLUS　♠Horatio says 'tis but our fantasy,

And will not let belief take hold of him

Touching this dreaded sight (turn to Hor. twice seen of us)

Therefore I have entreated him along

♠With us to watch the minutes of this night,

That if again this apparition come,

He may approve our eyes and speack to it.

HORATIO　　♠Tush, tush, 'twill not appear.

BARNARDO　　　　　　　　　♠Sit down awhile,

And let us once again assail your ears,

That are so fortified against our story♠

What we have two nights seen.

HORATIO　　　　　　　　　♠Well, sit we down,

And let us hear Barnardo speak of this.

BARNARDO　　Last night of all,

When♠yond same star that's westward from the pole

Had made his course t' illume that part of heaven

Where now it burns, Marcellus and myself

GHOST STARTS IN TUN L

MAR STARTS AS IF SEEING GHOST UC ☐ ALL FOLLOW GHOST AS IF IT WERE MOVING FROM
UL TO DL ● MAR XES SLOWLY TO 3 ABOVE BENCH
BAR RISES .   .   .   HOR RISES SLOWLY

GHOST STOPS ON O DL,

GHOST XES UP TO 3
    PAUSE - HOR X IN TO CENTER THEN BACK UP 2   .   THEN SPEAKS
    WHEN HOR X IN MAR X OUT TO 11:00

GHOST TURNS XES OUT L TUNNEL

    MAR AND BAR. X IN MAR TO ½ 2:00 BAR TO ¾ 6:00
    X TO ¾ 3:30
    THEY LOOK ABOUT AND ABOVE AS IF GHOST HAS DEMATERIALIZED.

        X ↙ → ½ 8:00

    X TOWARD HOR   STOP AT ½ 3:00

3

BARNARDO   The bell then beating one------

ENTER GHOST

MARCELLUS   Peace, break thee off.‖ [Look] where it comes again.

BARNARDO   In the same figure like the King that's dead.

MARCELLUS   Thou art a scholar, speak to it Horatio.

BARNARDO   Looks 'a not like the King? Mark it Horatio.

HORATIO   Most like. It harrows me with fear and wonder.

BARNARDO   It would be spoke to.

MARCELLUS   Question it Horatio.

HORATIO   What art thou that usurp'st this time of night,

            Together with that fair and warlike form

            In which the Majesty of buried Denmark

            Did sometimes march? By heaven I charge thee speak.

MARCELLUS   It is offended.

BARNARDO   See it stalks away.

HORATIO   Stay, speak, speak, I charge thee speak.

                        (EXIT GHOST.

MARCELLUS   'Tis gone and will not answer.

BARNARDO   How now Horatio, you tremble and look pale.

            Is not this something more than fantasy?

            What think you on't?

HORATIO   Before my God I might not this believe,

            Without the sensible and true avouch

            Of mine own eyes.

MARCELLUS   Is it not like the King?

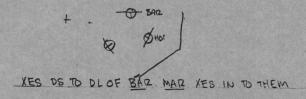

XES DS TO DL OF BAR. MAR XES IN TO THEM

XING TO LOOK OUT R TUN AT 7:00 on 3. HOR FOLLOWS SLOWLY XING
TO CROTCH DURING SPEECH, STARTS OVER ON 'CANON' MAR XES TO 3 AND 2

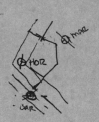

XING TO UL OF HOR, PACE FROM BENCH (3/4 10:00) TURN BACK
HOR XES ACROSS HIS PATH

SITTING IN CROTCH. BAR FINISHES REST OF X TO 1 AND 2 D R OF BENCH
LEANING ON SEAT

4

HORATIO   As thou art to thyself

Such was the very armour he had on,

When he the ambitious Norway combated;

So frowned he once, when in an angry parle

He smote the sledded Polacks on the ice.

'Tis strange.

Marcellus   Thus twice before, and jump at this dead hour,

With martial stalk hath he gone by our watch.

HORATIO   In what particular thought to work I know not,

But in the gross and scope of mine opinion,

This bodes some strange eruption to our state.

MARCELLUS   Good now sit down, and tell me that knows,

Why this same strict and most observant watch

So nightly toils the subject of the land,

And why such daily cast of brazen cannon,

And foreign mart for implements of war,

Why such impress of shipwrights, whose sore task

Does not divide the Sunday from the week,

What might be toward that this sweaty haste

Doth make the night joint labourer with the day.

Who is't that can inform me?

HORATIO   That can I.

AT least the whisper goes so; our last King,

Whose image even but now appeared to us,

5

HORATIO   Was as you know by Fortinbras of Norway,

Thereto pricked on by a most emulate pride,

Dared to the combat; in which our valiant Hamlet--

For so this side of our known world esteemed him----

Did slay this Fortinbras, who by a sealed compact,

Well ratified by law and heraldry,

Did forfeit, with his life, all those his lands

Which he stodd seized of to the conqueror.

Against the which a moiety competent

Was gagèd by our King, which had returned

To the inheritance of Fortinbras,

Had he been vanquisher; ~~as by the same Covenant~~

~~And carriage of the article design~~ed,

~~His fell to Hamlet~~, Now sir, young Fortinbras,

Of unimprovèd mettle hot and full,

Hath in the skirts of Norway here and there

Sharked up a list of lawless resolutes

For food and diet to some enterprise

That hath a stomach in't; which is no other,

As it doth well appear unto our state,

But to recover of us, by strong hand

And terms compulsatory, those foresaid lands

So by his father lost; and this I take it

Is the main motive of our prerarations,

The source of this our watch, and the chief head

Of this post-haste and romage in the land.

USE OF EUPHEMISMS FOR GHOST - 'ILLUSION' 'PORTENTOUS FIGURE' EC.

_____

HOR RISES X OUT 1 STEP FACE 5:00, MAR COUNTER OUT 2 _____

LOOK OFF AT 6:00 HIGH _____

GHOST STARTS IN AD   SLOWLY, STOPS AT 10:30. _____
    ● ALL FEEL PRESENCE, MAR FACE DS. HOR TURNS SLOWLY VIA RIGHT

HOR X QUICKLY TO ½ 4:00 FACES GHOST, IN PLACE BY "STAY"
BAR BACKS TO 7:30 ON 1 AND 2. MAR TO AGAINST DS BENCH, GHOST LOOKS
1st AT MAR WHO CROSSES SELF THEN AT BAR WHO BACKS DOWN A STEP
_____

6

WARN

L#2B
S#1

BARNARDO   I think it be no other but e'en so.

Well may it sort that this| portentous figure

Comes armed through our watch so like the King

That was and is the question of these wars.

HORATIO   A mote it is to trouble the minds eye.

In the most high and palmy state of Rome,

A little ere the mightiest Julius fell,

The graves stood tenantless, and the sheeted dead

Did squeak and gibber in the Roman streets;

As stars with trains of fire, and dews of blood,

Disasters in the sun; and the moist star,

Upon whose influende Neptune's empire stands,

Was sick almost to doomsday with eclipse.

And even the like precurse of ~~feared~~ fierce events,

As harbingers preceding still the fates,

And prologue to the omen coming on, Gh k in

Have heaven and earth together demonstrated

Upon our climatures and countrymen

Re-enter Ghost

But soft, behold, lo where it comes again. L#2B

HORATIO XES TO C ▨

(Ghost spreads its arms.

I'll cross it, though 'it blast me. Stay illusion ||

If thou hast any sound or use of voice,

Speak to me

If there be any good thing to be done

That may to thee do ease, and grace to me,

GHOST MOVES TOWARD HOR   THEN SLOWLY RAISES RIGHT ARM

GHOST AT 11:00

GHOST HOLDS HANDS UP DEFENSIVELY   THEN XES QUICKLY VIA R
OF HOR OUT LEFT TUNNEL.
                    . HOR XES TO 3/4 8:30 FOLLOWING. BAR FOLLOWS TO
6:00
  X TO C

AS IF SEEING GHOST DR ON 4 AND 3 AT 6:00

AT C OF TRAP . HOR XES UP THEN BACK TO PLACE

XES IN TODR OF MAR

X → 3:30

  X IN SLOWLY TODR OF MAR

7

LATE SEATING ?

CALL HOUSE MGR.; TELL RAMPS

HORATIO   Speak to me.

If thou art privy to thy country's fate

Which happily foreknowing may avoid,

O speak.

Or if thou hast uphoarded in thy life

Extorted treasure in the womb of earth,

For which they say you spirits oft walk in death   S#1

(Cock crows.)

Speak of it; stay and speak. Stop it Marcellus.

MARCELLUS   Shall I strike at it with my partisan?

HORATIO   Do, if it will not stand.

BARNARDO   'Tis here.

HORATIO   'Tis here ||

(Exit ghost.

MARCELLUS   'Tis gone.

We do it wrong, being so majestical,

To offer it the show of violence;

For it is as the air invulnerable,

And our vain blows malicious mockery.

BARNARDO   It was about to speak when the cock crew.

HORATIO   And then it started like a guilty thing

Upon a fearful summons I have heard,

The cock, that is trumpet to the morn,

+MAR
—————⊕—————————————————————————————————————

⊕ HO

⊗ BAR

LOOK OUT L TUNNEL ———————————————————————————

HOR TURN IN TO FACE MAR ————————————————————

LOOKING AT 1000. THEN DO MAR + BAR ————————————

                    all
TRIO STRETCHES - START X DR A PACE THEN ————————
STOPS TURNS TO THEM   ⊗ MAR
              BAR ⊕   ⊗ HOR

LOOKING OVER RIGHT SHOULDER TO TUNNEL L ————————————

LOOK TO CHECK BAR THEN
MAR X BETWEEN THEM ON "AND" XES TO EXIT TUNNEL R FOLLOWED
B4 HOR THEN BAR

        ⊗ BAR

      ⊗   ⊗ HOR

     MAR

L#3
IN#2A (Flash)
S#2,3,2A

HORATIO Doth with his lofty and shrill-sounding throat

Awake the god of day, and at his warning,

Whether in sea of fire, in earth or air,

Th' extravagant and erring spirit hies

To his confine; and of the truth herein

This present object made probation.

MARCELLUS It faded on the crowing of the cock.

Some say that ever 'gainst that season comes

Wherein our Saviour's birth is celebrated,

This bird of dawning singeth all night long,

And then they say no spirit dare stir abroad;

The nights are wholesome, then no planets strike,

No fairy takes, nor witch hath power to charm,

So hallowed and so gracious is that time.

HORATIO So have I heard and do in part believe it.

But look the morn in russet mantle clad

Walks o'er the dew of yon high eastward hill.

Break we our watch up, and by my advice

Let us impart what we have seen to-night

Unto young Hamlet, for upon my life

This spirit dumb to us will speak to him.

Do you consent we shall acquaint him with it,

As needful in our loves, fitting our duty?

MARCELLUS Let's do't I pray, and I this morning know

Where we shall find him most convenient. L#3 S#2

(Exeunt.

CHIMES ◼_____ S#3

POLONIUS ENTERS ◼_____ M#2A(Flash) S#2A

HAMLET SOLUS THEN BELLS HEARD AND COURT ASSEMBLES

QUEEN ENTERS R OF KING. THEY CIRCLE STAGE (J) KING ALMOST
PIVOTING AT C. QUEEN CIRCLES HIM. INCLINING HEAD TO COURTIERS
WHO BOW, CURTSEY OR CLICK HEELS, GUARDSMEN HAVE HELMETS UNDER
ARMS

POL AT 11:00 HAS DIS. CASE   KING WITH QUEEN ON PLAT
AND AGENDA SHEET

                                    KING X TO ABOVE C

A PUBLIC SPEECH

    TURNING IN FULL CIRCLE AS HE SPEAKS

APPLAUSE, X ABOVE QUEEN ON PLAT   THEN TURNING ON STAGE

    POLITE LAUGHTER, POL XES TO SHOW MEMO TO KING, HE SCANS IT THEN WAVES
    HIM OFF, POL RETURNS TO PLACE

Scene Two (2)

The Castle. Enter Claudius and Gertrude to Council,
with Polonius, Laertes, Voltemand, Cornelius, Lords,
and Hamlet.

CLAUDIUS   Though yet of Hamlet our dear brother's death

The memory be green, and that is us befitted

To bear our hearts in grief, and our whole kingdom

To be contracted in one brow of woe,

Yet so far hath discretion fought with nature,

That we with wisest sorrow think on him,

Together with remembrance of ourselves,

Therefore our sometime sister, now our Queen,

Th' imperial jointress to this warlike state,

Have we as 'twere with a defeated joy,

With one auspicious, and one dropping eye,

With mirth in funeral, and with dirge in marriage,

In equal scale weighing delight and dole,

Taken to wife, nor have we herein barred

Your better wisdoms, which have freely gone

With this affair along—for all, our thanks.

Now follows that you know young Fortinbras,

Holding a weak supposal of our worth,

Or thinking by our late dear brother's death

Our state to be disjoint, and out of frame,

Colleagued with this dream of his advantage,

He hath not failed to pester us with message

Importing the surrender of those lands

Lost by his father, with all bands of law,

POL X TO KING AGAIN

   SCANNING NOTICE , THEN TAKING DISPATCH FROM POL, POL RETURN TO PLACE

   WAVE IN CORN AND VOLT, THEN SIGNALS THEM TO STOP ON EDGE OF 4

KG

⌀CORN

⌀VOLT   (2ND HIGH SIGN FROM POL . CORN AND VOLT TO BEFORE KING
           POL COUNTERS TO ½ 12:00 WHEN COR AND VOLT MOVE IN
           CORN SLIGHTLY PRECEDES VOLT TO PLACE. ON COUNTER POL PUTS AGENDA
           INSIDE COAT
              .GIVES DISPATCH TO CORN

VOLT STARTS TO SPEAK BUT THE KING CUTS HIM OFF

   KING SQUELCHES ANOTHER TRY, POL MOVES IN TO ASSIST THEIR DEPARTURE

     BOW BACKING   US TURN AND EXIT UR ● KING GIVES HELMET TO COURTIER

SLIGHT PAUSE AS KING LOOKS TO POL WHO GESTURES TOWARD LAE   THEN KING XES
OVER TO L   LAE XES IN   WHEN NAME IS MENTIONED, BOWS
POL BACKS TO ABOVE AND BETWEEN THEM.

   GIVES LAE A BACK HANDED CLAP ON THE CHEST AND MOVES AWAY A BIT
   QUEEN GIVES BOUQUET TO BACK XES SLOWLY TO KING'S SIDE.

   MEET AT TRAP TOP

   KING ⌀   ⌀ LAE

GX ⌀

CLAUDIUS To our most valiant brother. So much for him.

Now for ourself, and for this time of meeting,

Thus much the business is--we have here writ

To Norway, uncle of young Fortinbras,

Who, impotent and bed-rid, scarcely hears

Of this his nephew'w purpose, to suppress

His further gait herein, in that the levies,

The lists, and full proportions, are all made

Out of his subject: and we here dispatch

You good Cornelius, and you Voltemand,

For bearers of this greeting to old Norway;

Giving to you no further personal power

To business with the King, more than the scope

Of these delated articles allow.

Farewell, and let haste commend your duty.

CORNELIUS and
VOLTEMAND In that, and all things, will we show our duty.

CLAUDIUS We doubt it nothing. Heartily farewell.

CORNELIUS We shall my lord (Exeunt Voltemand and Cornelius.

CLAUDIUS And now Laertes what's the news with you?

You told us of some suit; what is't Laertes?

You cannot speak of reason to the Dane,

And lose your voice. What would'st thou beg, Laertes,

That shall not be my offer, not thy asking?

The head is not more native to the heart,

The hand more instrumental to the mouth,

Than is the throne of Denmark to thy father.

①. POL

① LAE ½ 3

KG.

X IN 2

QUEEN X INTO R OF KING

X IN TO LAE. CLAP SHOULDERS, POL X ↓ TO DL OF LAE ON "BEST GRACES"

LAE BOWS RETURNS TO PLACE. KING FOLLOWS QUEEN'S GLANCE TO HAMLET. SPEAKS WITH
FORCED JOVIALITY.   POL DISCREETLY SIGNALS COURTIERS DL TO MOVE US. XES SELF TO 4:00 ON
KING AND QUEEN X TO ABOVE HAMLET ON 4. KING 3/4 5:00, QUEEN DR OF HIM.

X ONTO 3

KING LOOKS TO QUEEN WHO THEN SPEAKS TO HAMLET

11

CLAUDIUS   What wouldst thou have, Laertes?

LAERTES   My dread lord,

Your leave and favour to return to France;

From whence though willingly I came to Denmark

To show my duty in your coronation,

Yet now I must confess, that duty done,

My thoughts and wishes bend again toward France,

And bow them to your gracious leave and pardon.

CLAUDIUS   Have you your father's leave? What says Polonius?

POLONIUS   He hath my lord, wrung from me my slow leave

By laboursome petition, and at last,

Upon his will I sealed my hard consent.

I do beseech you give him leave to go.

CLAUDIUS   Take thy fair hour Laertes, time be thine,

And thy best graces spend it at thy will.

But now my cousin Hamlet, and my son.

HAMLET(aside) A little more than kin, and less than kind,

CLAUDIUS   How is it that the clouds still hang on you?

HAMLET   Not so my lord, I am too muhh in the sun.

GERTRUDE   Good Hamlet, cast thy nighted colour off,

And let thine eye look like a friend on Denmark.

Do not for ever with thy vailéd lids

Seek for thy noble father in the dust.

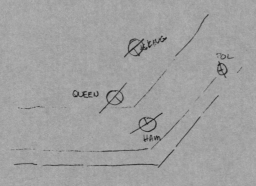

KING IS TURNED L SOMEWHAT EXCHANGING GLANCES WITH POL

KING LOOKS AT POL

HAMLET   START X UR AND ONTO STAGE STOPPED ¼ 8:00 BY KING'S NEXT LINE
                         HAMLET STAYS FACING US
TURN C THEN XES TO UL OF HAMLET, WIDE

X IN 2 TO UL OF HAMLET

X TO HAMLET TOUCH ARM - HAMLET XES UR ¼

(KG STARTS SLOW X AROUND HAMLET CC, STOPS FIRST UL OF HIM

12

GERTRUDE   Thou know'st 'tis common, all that lives must die.

                Passing thru nature to eternity.

HAMLET   Ay madam, ti is common.

GERTRUDE   If it be,

                Why seems it so particular with thee?

HAMLET   Seems madam? Nay it is; I know not, seems.

                'tis not alone my inky cloak, good mother,

                Nor customary suits of solemn black,

                Nor windy suspiration of forced breadth,

                No, nor the fruitful river in the eye,

                Nor the dejected haviour of the visage,

                Together with all forms, moods, shapes of grief,

                That can denote me truly. These indeed seem,

                For they are actions that a man might play,

                But I have that within which passes show---

                These but the trappings and the suits of woe.

CLAUDIUS   Tis sweet and commendable in your nature,Hamlet,

                To give these mourning duties to your father.

                But you must know, your father lost a father;

                That father lost, lost his, and the survivor bound

                In filial obligation for some term

                To do obsequious sorrow; but to persever

                In obstinate condolement. 'tis unmanly grief.

                It shows a will most incorrect to heaven,

                A heart unfortified, a mind impatient,

                An understanding simple and unschooled.

AT UL OF HAMLET   (POL AT 4:00 ON 1)

CONTINUING X G HAMLET

_FINISHING EMPHATICALLY, QUEEN XES TO HIM, MEET ½ 6:00. HE SOFTENS ATTACK, XING US 2

HAMLET TURNS QUICKLY CW TO LOOK AT KING WHO CLAPS SHOULDERS. THEN
KING PUTS LEFT ARM ABOUT HAMLETS SHOULDERS THEN X UP AND SWING
AROUND TO FACE DS AT C, QUEEN FOLLOWS XING STRAIGHT UP TO JOIN THEM
AT ½ 12:00   KG   HT   BOTH HAVE ARMS AROUND HAMLET
            ⊕ ⊕ ⊕ QN
                  F

APPLAUSE THEY POSE FOR A FEW BEATS THEN THE KING TAKES
HAMLET QUICKLY DS TOWARD 5:00, ARM ABOUT SHOULDER. QUEEN FOLLOWS
XING ACROSS THEIR PATH TO R OF KING

TOUCHES KING FORBEARINGLY ON R ARM. KING STOPS AT ½ 5:00 LETING
HAMLET GO. HAMLET XES TO 5:00 ON 3. KING CONTINUES SPEECH IN SOFTER VEIN

XES TO ABOVE HAMLET ON 4

X CC AROUND·END AT ½ 7:00 JUST TO SEE QUEEN WHO IS
PRESSING HER CHEEK TO HAMLETS. CUE FEET JNON 3
SHARPLY, QUEEN XES TO HIS L, SHOWING PLEASURE AT HIS JEALOSY
THEY X UP TOGETHER

TURNING AT 3/4 10:30, HELMET AND BOUQUET ARE RETURNED

↑   ∧
     |
K   Q
⊕   ⊕

13

CLAUDIUS   For what we know must be, and is as common

As any the most vulgar thing to sense,

Why should we in our peevish opposition

Take it to heart? Fie, 'tis a fault to heaven,

A fault against the dead, a fault to nature,

To reason most absurd, whose common theme

Is death of fathers, and who still hath cried,

From the first corse till he that died to-day,

This must be so. We pray you throw to earth

This unprevailing woe, and think of us

As of a father, for let the world take note

You are the most immediate to our throne;

And with no less nobility of love

Than that which dearest father bears his son,

Do I impart toward you. For your intent

In going back to school in Wittenberg,

It is most retrograde to our desire,

And we beseech you bend to remain

Here in the cheer and comfort of our eye,

Our chiefest courtier, cousin, and our son.

GERTRUDE   Let not thy mother lose her prayers Hamlet,

I pray thee stay with us; go not to Wittenberg.

HAMLET   I shall in all my best obey you madam.

CLAUDIUS   Why 'tis a loving and a fair reply.

Be as ourself in Denmark. Madam come.

This gentle and unforced accord of Hamlet

Sits smiling to my heart, in grace whereof,

L #3A

M #3 (flash)

OUT UR
   OD, ROS
   HOR, MARCA
   FRAN
   MARCL, NYM
   POL, LAE   HOR ... OUT L POL

KING AND QUEEN TURN IN TO EACH OTHER, X AND EXIT UR. COURTIERS
FOLLOW.

(HAMLET XES SLOWLY TO 11.00 LOOKING AFTER THEM, THEN XES DOWN TO L OF C, SPEAKS
XES UP AFTER ROGO AND VAN X TO DL. XES UR SLOWLY. FOOTMEN SHUT DOORS AS HE
APPROACHES

   AT END FANFARE   MUSICIANS EXIT FROM ABOVE CLOSE DOORS AS THEY EXIT. DRUM TO
   R, OTHERS TO L

   TURN UPSTAGE VIAL

XES TO BENCH PLATFORM

   TURNS TO LOOK UR

FACED ONSTAGE LOOKING UR THEN TURNS, SITS US ON BENCH

Hop & Fors & Rogo & van out TUNL

RISES, X TO 3/4 9:00   _

14

CLAUDIUS   No jocund health that Denmark drinks to-day,

                But the great cannon to the clouds shall tell,

                And the king's rouse the heaven shall bruit again,

                Re-speaking earthly thunder. Come away.   (flash) M#3

                                    (Flourish, Exeunt all but Hamlet.   L#3A
                                    END OF FANFARE
HAMLET   T O that this too too solid flesh would melt, RED LITES ON

                Thaw and resolve itself into a dew,

                Or that the Everlasting had not fixed

                His canon 'gainst self-slaughter. O, God, God,

                How weary, stale, flat, and unprofitable

                Seem to me all the uses of this world".

                Fie on't, ah fie, 'tis an unweeded garden

                That grows to seed, things rank and gross in nature

                Possess it merely. That it should come to this--

take pix from   -But two months dead, nay not so much, not two---
vest pocket
                So excellent a King, that was to this

                Hyperion to a satyr, so loving to my mother,

                That he might not beteem the winds of heaven

                Visit her face too roughly. Heaven and earth,

                Must I remember? Why she would hang on him

                As if increase of appetite had grown

                By what it fed on, and yet within a month--

                Let me not think on't---frailty, thy name is woman.

                A little month or e'er those shoes were old

                With which she followed my poor father's body,

                Like Niobe all tears, why she, even she--

                O God, a beast that wants discourse of reason

X TO CENTER

X TO DS OF BENCH FACE OFF

TURNING BACK 4 AND 3 DS OF BENCH LOOKING UR

TURNS SITS ON DS END OF BENCH Face off

HAM SEATED FACING DS.   . PAUSE. MAR OPEN BOTH DOORS
                                    . PAUSE. MAR ENTER FROM L BELOW
THEN HOR, THEN BAR. HOR KES TO ½ 12:00. BAR TO ¾ 1:30 AND MAR TO 11:30 +
MAR OUT R BEL, HOR OUT C, BAR OUT L CLOSES DOORS.

/ RISING. HARDLY LOOKING AT THEM. TURNING TO EXIT TURN R ● TURNING BACK
  XING DS ON 3

       XING TOWARD HAMLET
X AND MEET ¼ 11:00

    TO HORATIO ● BERNARDO CLICK HEELS

    ¿TAKE HIM DS A COUPLE OF STEPS?

15

HAMLET   Would have mourned longer--married with my uncle,

My father's brother, but no more like my father

Than I to Hercules--within a month;

Ere yet the salt of most unrighteous tears

Had left the flushing in her galled eyes?

She married--o most wicked speed, to post

With such dexterity to incestous sheets.

It is not, nor it cannot come to good,

But break, my heart, for I must hold my tongue.

                Enter Horatio, Marcellus, and Barnardo.

HORATIO   Hail to your lordship.

HAMLET   I am glad to see you well.

Horatio--or do I forget my self.

HORATIO   The same my lord, and your poor servant ever.

HAMLET   Sir, my good friend, I'll change that name with you.

And what make you from Wittenberg Horatio?

Marcellus.

MARCELLUS   My good lord.

HAMLET   I am very glad to see you. (To Barnardo) -Good even sir.

But what in faith make you from Wittenberg?

HORATIO   A truant disposition good my lord.

HAMLET   I would not hear your enemy say so,

Nor shall you do my ear that violence

To make it truster of your own report

Against yourself. I know you are not truant.

But what is your affair in Elsinore?

We'll teach to to drink deep ere you depart.

? BACKING AWAY FROM HOR

TURNS, XES DOWN TO 7:30

HAMLET IS LOOKING RIGHT • HOR YES DR 2

VING TO BENCH PLAT

TURN TO HOR FROM CROTCH

SIT BENCH C — HOR LOOK TO HAM

X TO 3/4 9:00

GESTURING WIDE, BAR XES TO O AND I AT 7:30   HAM TO 3/4 10:00

16

HORATIO   My lord, I came to see your father's funeral.

HAMLET   I prithee do not mock me, fellow-student,

             I think it was to see my mother's wedding.

HORATIO   Indeed my lord it followed hard upon.

HAMLET   Thrift, thrift, Horatio. The funeral baked meats

             Did coldly furnish the marriage tables.

             Would I had met my dearest foe in heaven

             Or ever I had seen that day Horatio.

             My father--methinks I see my father.

HORATIO   Where my lord?

HAMLET   In my mind's eye Horatio.

HORATIO   I saw him, once, 'a was a goodly King.

HAMLET   'A was a man, take him for all in all,

             I shall not look upon his like again.

HORATIO   My lord, I think I saw him yesternight.

HAMLET   Saw? Who?

HORATIO   My lord, the King your father.

HAMLET   The king my father?

HORATIO   Season your admiration for a while

             With an attent ear till I may deliver

             Upon the witness of these gentlemen

             This marvel to you.

HAMLET   For God's love let me hear.

HORATIO   Two nights together had these gentlemen,

             Marcellus, and Barnardo, on their watch,

             In the dead waste and middle of the night,

             Been thus encountered--a figure like your father,

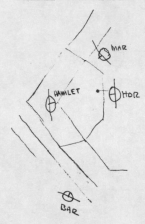

HAMLET RISES

HAM   X SLOWLY TO ½5.00 HOR COUNTER TO BEHIND HAMLET
____   MAR XES TOWARD C A FEW WATCHING HAMLET
PAUSE HOR LOOK TO MAR THEN BAR

17

HORATIO   Armed at point, exactly, cap-a-pe,

Appears before them, and with solemn march

Goes slow and stately by them; thrice he walked

By their oppressed and fear-surprised eyes,

Within his truncheon's lenght, whilst they distilled

Almost to jelly with the act of fear,

Stand dumb, and speak not to him. This to me

In dreadful secrecy impart they did.

And I with them the third night kept the watch,

Where, as they had delivered, both intime,

Form of the thing, each word made true and good,

The apparition comes. I knew your father;

These hands are not more like.

HAMLET   But where was this?

MARCELLUS   My lord, upon the platform where we watch.

HAMLET   Did you not speak to it?

HORATIO   My lord, I did,

But answer made it none; yet once methought

It lifted up it head, and did address

Itself to motion like as it would speak:

But even then the morning cock crew loud,

And at the sound it shrunk in haste away

And vanished from our sight:

HAMLET   "Tis very strange.

HORATIO   As I do live, my honoured lord, 'tis true;

And we did think it writ down in our duty

To let you know of it.

                                          + back
STOP^c 1/2 5:00 FACING DOWN @ HOR LOOK TO BAR AND MARR

· TURN TO THEM

MAR XES IN TO 1/2 10:00 . BAR UP ONTO 1 AND 2

X IN TO 1/2 6:00

X IN 1

TURN DC ✓ ⤵ 3

MAR XES TO L OF HOR

TURNING CC TO FACE THEM

(18)

HAMLET   ❡Indeed, indded sirs, but this troubles me❡

          ❡Hold you the watch to-night?

MARCELLUS
   and   Yes, my lord.
BARNARDO   We do my lord.

HAMLET   Armed say you?

MARCELLUS
   and
BARNARDO Armed my lord.

HAMLET   From top to toe?

MARCELLUS
   and
~~BARNARDO~~ My lord, from head to foot.

HAMLET   ❡Then saw you not his face.

HORATIO   ❡O yes my lord, he wore his beaver up.

HAMLET   What, looked he frowningly?

HORATIO   A countenance more in sorrow than in anger.

HAMLET   ❡Pale, or red?

HORATIO   Nay very pale.

HAMLET   And fixed his eyes upon you?

HORATIO   Most constantly.

HAMLET   I would I had been there.

HORATIO   It would have much amazed you.

HAMLET   ❡Very like, ver like ---stayed it long?

HORATIO   While one with moderate haste might tell a hundred.

MARCELLUS
   and
BARNARDO ❡Longer, longer.

HORATIO   Not when I saw't.

HAMLET   ❡His beard was grizzled--no?

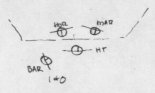

WITH AD LIBS

_TRIO MOVES QUICKLY TO HAMLET ↑ HOR TO UR OF HIM ON 4, MAR UL OF HIM
BAR XES ↳→ TO DR OF HAMLET ON 1 AND 0
   (AS THEY X IN

GROUP TIGHTENS AROUND HAMLET, HAMLET PUTS R HAND ON MARS
L SHOULDER. BAR XES TO 3 AND 2 DR OF HAMLET

ALL MURMUR ASSENT

_TRIO STARTS X STRAIGHT US

HAMLET STEPS ONTO 4, TRIO STOPPED BY HIS LINE AT X, HAMLET XES TO
C

SOLDIERS CLICK HEELS · HOR RAISES A HAND

_STOPPING THEM AGAIN AS THEY START MOVE UP ⓧ THEY TURN AND X, EXIT INTO BELOW
HOR & MAR OUT C BEL. BAR OUT R. HAMLET X UP , MAR, HOR THEN BAR OUT L DOORS,

  TURNS DC AT C

STARTS X, EXITS TUN L

1st VM
2nd ROSO

'2 SAILORS ENTER FROM BELOW WITH LUGGAGE X AND EXIT TUN R. LAE (R)
OPH (L) FOLLOW TO ½ 7:00. LAE CARRIES COAT HAT, OPH HAS 2 TENNIS RAQUETS
1 ST SAILOR HAS ONE END OF FOOT LOCKER AND SUITCASE, 2ND HAS REAR OF LOCKER AND UKULE CASE
ALL X THRU C BELOW, LAE-COAT L HAND, HAT R, OPH- RAQUETS L ARM.
_SPEAKING AS HE XES OUT OF BEL ⓧ STOPPING. EMBRACING ½ 8:00

19

WARN

L#4 AND HOUSE
L#4A AND HOUSE
C-LITE BELOW

HORATIO	It was as I have seen it in his life,
	A sable silvered.
HAMLET	I will watch to-night.
	Perchance 'twill walk again.
HORATIO	I warr'nt it will.
HAMLET	If it assume my noble father's person,
	I'll speak to it though hell itself should gape
	And bid me hold my peace. I pray you all,
	If you have hitherto concealed this sight,
	Let it be tenable in your silence still;
	And whatsoever else shall hap to-night,
	Give it an understanding/but no tongue.
	I will requite your loves--so fare you well.
	Upon the platform 'twixt eleven and twelve
	I'll visit you.
ALL	Our duty to your Honour.
HAMLET	Your loves, as mine to you. Farewell.

(Exeunt all but Hamlet.

My father's spirit--in arms--all is not well.
I doubt some foul play. Would the night were come. —
Till then sit still my soul. Foul deeds will rise,
Though all the earth o'erwhelm them, to men's eyes. L#4+HSE

(Exit)

HOUSE READY ■   L#4A+HSE

SCENE THREE (3) The house of Polonius. Enter Laertes & Ophelia.

CUE COMPLETE ■

LAERTES	My necessaries are embarked. Farewell. RED LITES OUT

And sister, as the winds give benefit,

N.B—If no break for latecomers, L#4 +4A
and BEL all go on "o'erwhelm".

EMBRACE AGAIN

STARTS XING TO PLAT WITH OPH PUTS HAT AND COAT DOWN ON US BENCH.

NOW ON PLAT, TAKES RACQUETS FROM HER PUTS THEM WITH COAT OPH SITS
PS BENCH

STARTING X C BENCH STOP 1st ON 3

X ON C BENCH TO UR OF OPH LEANING OVER BENCH

X ON TO ABOVE BENCH ON 2

20

LAERTES   And convoy is assistant, do not sleep,

            But let me hear from you.

OPHELIA   Do you doubt that?

LAERTES   For Hamlet and the trifling of his favour,

            Hold it a fashion, and a toy in blood;

            A violet in the youth of primy nature,

            Forward, not permanent, sweet, not lasting,

            The perfume and suppliance of a minute,

            No more.

OPHELIA   No more but so?

LAERTES   Think it no more.

            ~~For nature crescent does not grow alone~~

            ~~In thews and bulk, but as this temple waxes~~

            ~~The inward service of the mind and soul~~

            ~~Grows wide withal.~~ Perhaps he loves you now,

            And now no soil nor cautel doth besmirch

            The virtue of his will; but you must fear,

            His greatness weighed, his will is not his own,

            For he himself is subject to his birth.

            He may not as unvalued persons do,

            Carve for himself, for on his choice depends

            The safety and health of this whole state,

            And therefore must his choice be circumscribed

            Unto the voice and yielding of that body

            Whereof he is the head. Then if he says he loves you,

            It fits your wisdom so far to believe it

            As he in his particular act and place

X to OPH, SIT ABOVE HER ON BENCH

OPH TURNS AWAY TO FACE DL, SMILING

PUTS HAND ON HER ARM, TURNING HER BACK

RISE X TO C PLAT TURN BACK TO HER

OPH PUTS OUT HER HANDS TO HIM. LAE X TAKE THEM. AND SITS ABOVE HER
    AGAIN

THEY RISE X LEFT, SHE HOLDS HIS R HAND IN HER LEFT THEN SWINGS
IN FRONT OF HIM TO FACE HIM FROM L AT 1/4 8:00 AND TAKE R HAND

___ X TO BENCH TO PICK UP STUFF   OPH FOLLOWS TO EDGE OF PLAT
1st SAILOR X IN TO S BELOW BENCH

21

LAERTES   May give his saying deed, which is no further
           Than the main voice of Denmark goes withal.
           Then weigh what loss your honour may sustain,
           If with too credent ear you list his songs,
           Or lose your heart, or your chaste treasure open
           To his unmastered importunity.
           Fear it Ophelia, fear it my dear sister,
           And keep you in the rear of your affection,
           Out of the shot and danger of desire.
           The chariest maid is prodigal enough
           If she unmask her beauty to the moon;
           Virtue itself 'scapes not calumnious strokes.
           The canker galls the infants of the spring
           Too oft before their buttons be disclosed,
           And in the morn and liquid dew of youth
           Contagious blastments are most imminent.
           Be wary then, best safety lies in fear.
           Youth to itself rebels, though none else near.

OPHELIA   I shall the effect of this good lesson keep
           As watchman to my heart. But good my brother,
           Do not as some ungracious pastors do,
           Show me the steep and thorny way to heaven,
           Whiles like a puffed and reckless libertine
           Himself the primrose path of dalliance treads,
           And recks not his own rede.

LAERTES   O fear me not.
           I stay too long.

POL THEN REY ENTER L BEL, POL HAS SINGLE SHEET, REY SEVERAL
AND PEN. POL XES OUT R BEL, REY OUT C

STOPPING SEEING POL.

GIVE RACQUETS TO SAILOR WHO DROPS DOWN TO 2

XING UP TO MEET POL AT ½ 10:00. OPH COUNTERS TO DR BENCH

GIVING DOCUMENT TO REY AT BELOW DR POST AND XING TO MEET LAE
DURING POL'S SPEECH TO LAE REY COUNTERS TO ABOVE LAE TO BE AT
POL'S R WHEN LAE XES OUT   ├ ┤ POL

EMBRACING ● XING QUICKLY DS, KISSES OPH AND XES DOWN STEPS TOWARD
TUN R, SAILOR XES AT HIS R

REY
—⊖—
▭   ⊖ POL

(STOPPING HIM WITH VOICE ON O, REY IS NOW R OF POL GIVES POL PEN, POL LOOKS
OVER ANOTHER DOCUMENT. ONLY OCCASIONALLY LOOKS AT LAE DURING FOLLOWING.
LAE RETURNS TO 1 AT 8:00. SAILOR HOLDS AT O. OPH SITS DS BENCH.

LOOKING OVER DOCUMENT. REY HOLDS DOCUMENTS SO THAT THEY FACE POL, SUPPORTS
THEM WHEN POL SIGNS, THEN PUTS SIGNED DOCUMENT UNDER OTHERS. POL TAKES DOC-
UMENTS UP TO LOOK THEM OVER.

SIGNING DOCUMENT

TAKING ANOTHER

XING DOWN TO ½ 9:00 LEAVING REY, LOOKING AT LAE'S ATTIRE, STILL HAS
DOCUMENT. REY COUNTERS L SLIGHTLY
LAE OPENS JACKET, OVERLOOKING HIS MODEST VEST

RETURNING TO R OF REY TO SIGN FINAL DOCUMENT

22

Enter Polonius

LAERTES   But here my father comes.
           A double blessing is a double grace;
           Occasion smiles upon a second leave.

POLONIUS   Yet here Laertes? Aboard, aboard, for shame;
           The wind sits in the shoulder of your sail,
           And you are stayed for. There - my blessing with thee
           And these few precepts in they memory
                        cut
           Look thou character. Give thy thoughts no tongue,
           Nor any unproportioned thought his act.
                TAKE
           Be thou familiar, but by no means vulgar.
           Those friends thou hast, and their adoption tried,
           Grapple them unto thy soul with hoops of steel;
           But do not dull thy palm with entertainment
                                          comrade
           Of each new-hatched, unfledged courage.
                TAKE
           Beware
           Of entrance to a quarrel, but being in,
           Bear't that th'opposed may beware of thee.
           Give every man thy ear, but few thy voice;
                TAKE
           Take each man's censure, but reserve they judgement.
           Costly thy habit as thy purse can buy,
           But not expressed in fancy; rich, not gaudy;
           For the apparel oft proclaims the man;
           And they in France of the best rank and station,
           Or of a most select and generous, chief in that.
           Neither a borrower nor a lender be,

HANDS LAST NOTE TO REY · DISMISSES HIM · REY EXIT L BELOW , ALSO RETURN PEN,
REY OUT C BEL , EXIT L

HUG DOWN, LAE XES TO MEET HIM AT 1/2 8:00 . POL PUTS R ARM OVER
LAE'S SHOULDERS AND THEY X DOWN TO 6:00

                       ↑ ↑ POL

TAKING OUT WALLET, GIVING BILL TO LAE ON 'THIS' ,

    POCKETING BILL .

OPH RISES , XES TO LAE WHO XES TO HER, MEET EMBRACE 3/4 8:00

     OPH XES TO 1/2 8:00 POL MOVES TO L CF HER

KISSES OPH
LAE TURN FROM OPH XIT OUT TUN R .

STARTS OUT TUN R , LINE TO POL AS HE GOES ● XES OUT TUN L VIA L OF SAILOR WHO
FOLLOWS HIM OUT, OPH X TO 7:30 LOOKING AFTER HIM

     POL XES TO SIT C ON BENCH VIA ABOVE OPH

     X ↝ TO 1/2 12:00

23

POLONIUS   For loan oft loses both itself and friend,

And borrowing dulls the edge of husbandry.

This above all, to thine own self be true.

And it must follow, as the night the day,

Thou canst not then be false to any man.

Farewell, my blessing season this in thee.

LAERTES   Most humbly do I take my leave my lord.

POLONIUS   The time invites you; go, your servants tend.

LAERTES   Farewell Ophelia, and remember well

What I have said to you.

OPHELIA   'Tis in my memory locked.

And you yourself shall keep the key of it.

LAERTES   Farewell. (Exit.

POLONIUS   What is't Ophelia he hath said to you?

OPHELIA   So please you, something touching the Lord Hamlet.

POLONIUS   Marry well bethought.

'Tis told me hath very oft of late

Given private time to you, and you yourself

Have of your audience been most free and bounteous.

If it be so, as so 'tis put on me,

And that in way of caution, I must tell you,

You do not understand yourself so clearly

As it behoves my daughter, and your honour.

What is between you? Give me up the truth.

OPHELIA   He hath my lord of late made many tenders

Of his affection to me.

PAT SEAT US OF HIM · OPHELIA XES SITS BELOW HIM ☐ AS OPH SITS

RISES XES TO 3/4 |1 00

TURN TO FACE POL at 3/4 12:00

RISE X TO OPH

TAKE HER HAND THEY X DL TO 1/4 3:00

STOPPING SWINGING BELOW OPH 1 POL

XING BACK TO BENCH

24

POLONIUS   Affection? Pooh, you speak like a green girl

                Unsifted in such perilous circumstance.

                Do you belive his tenders as you call them?

OPHELIA   I do not know my lord what I should think.

POLONIUS   Marry I will teach you; think yourself a baby,

                That you have ta'en these tenders for true pay

                Which are not sterling. Tender yourself more dearly.

                Or--not to crack the wind of the poor phrase--

                Tend'ring it thus you'll tender me a fool. **WARN**

OPHELIA   My lord, he hath importuned me with love   ~~L#5,5A~~

                In honourable fashion.   **L#5,5A**

POLONIUS   Ay, fashion you may call it; go to, go to. **M#4,4A,4B**

OPHELIA   And hath given countenance to his speech, my lord, **(TRAP LITE)**

                With almost all the holy vows of heaven,

POLONIUS   Ay, springes to catch woodcocks. I do know,

                When the blood burns, how prodigal the soul

                Lends the tongue vows. These blazes daughter,

                Giving more light than heat, extinct in both,

                Even in their promise, as it is a-making,

                You must not take for fire. From this time

                Be something scanter of your maiden presence.

                Set your entreatments at a higher rate

                Than a command to parley. For Lord Hamlet,

                Believe so much in him that his young

                And with a larger tether may he walk

                Than may be given yOu. In few Ophelia,

                Do not believe his vows, for they are brokers,

<u>XING BACK TO R OF OPH</u>

X UP TO ¾ 12:15. OPH FACES DS ●TAKING SUSPICIOUSLY ON OPH AS
SHE XES UP TO WIDE R OF POL.
(OPH XES INTO R BEL OUT L, POL FOLLOWS

ENT TUNNEL R: MAR 1st XES TO DR OFC, STOPS THEN XES ON TOWARD 11:00. THEN
HOR X TO C BLOWING HANDS. WHEN HE IS ON 4 MAR AT UR OFC TURNS TO HIM CLICKS
HEELS. HOR XES ON TO ½ 3:00 THEN HAMLET ENTER SLOWLY STOP AT 7:30. MAR CLICK AGAIN
STOPPING AT ½ 7:30   THEN XING ON SLOWLY TOWARD 2:00   NOW AT 11:00

<u>XING TOWARD 2:00</u>

AT 10:30   ● STEPS DOWN ON 3 AT 10:00

<u>HAMLET AT 2:00 LOOKS OFF AND DOWN AS IF PEERING OVER BATTLEMENTS</u>
XING TO UR OFC LOOKING DS

25

POLONIUS   Not of that dye which their investments show,

But mere implorators of unholy suits,

Breathing like sanctified and pious bonds

The better to beguile. This is for all--

I would not in plain terms from this time forth

Have you so slander any moment leisure

As to give words or talk with the Lord Hamlet.

Look to't I charge you; come your ways.

OPHELIA   I shall obey, my lord.   L#5

(Exeunt.

SCENE FOUR (4) The battlements of the Castle. Enter Hamlet,

Horatio, and Marcellus.

HAMLET   The air bites shrewdly, it is very cold.   L#5A

HORATIO   It is a nipping and an eager air.

HAMLET   What hour now?

HORATIO   I thihk it lacks of twelve.

MARCELLUS No, it is struck.

HAMLET   Indeed? I heard it not; it then draws near the season

Wherein the spirit held his wont to walk.   M#4

(A flourish of trumpets, and two cannon shot within.

What does this mean my lord?

HAMLET   The King doth wake to-night and takes his rouse,

Keeps wassail, and the swaggering upspring reels;

And as he drains his draughts of Rhenish down,

The kettle-drum and trumpet thus bray out

The triumph of his pledge.

HORATIO   Is it a custom?

XES DS

XING TO 1/2 5:00 · HOR UR OFC   MAR ABOVE BENCH ON 3

HAMLET STARTS, AS IF HEARING SOMETHING, LOOKS UR, MAR + HOR
FOLLOW GAZE. IT IS NOTHING. MAR AND HOR TURN TO LOOK CURIOUSLY
AT HAMLET AND HE RESUMES HIS UNEASY DISCOURSE TURNING ⌐
TO LOOK OUT L TUN

STARTING AGAIN, LOOKING DR THEN LOOK AT HOR AND LAUGHS UNEASILY, MAR→3
XING TO 1/2 7:30 TO LOOK OUT R TUN

GHOST STARTS IN · SLOWLY TUN L

TURNING AND XING US STOPPING AT END OF SPEECH AT 1/2 9:00

26

HAMLET   Ay marry is't,

        But to my mind, though I am native here,

        And to the manner born, it is a custom

        More honoured in the breach than the observance.   M4A

        This heavy-headed revel east and west

        Makes us traduced, and taxed of other nations.

        They clepe us drunkards, and with swinish phrase   M4B

        Soil our addition, and indeed it takes

        FRom our achievements, though performed height,   WARN

        The pith and marrow of our attribute.   GHOST

                                                 L RAMP LITE

        So, oft it chances in particular men,

        That for some vicious mole of nature in them,

        As in their birth, wherein they are not guilty,

        Since nature cannot choose his origin,

        ~~By the o'ergrowth of some complexion,~~

        ~~Oft breaking down the pales and forts of reason~~,

        Or by some habit, that too much o'er-leavens

        The form of plausive manners—that these men,

        Carrying I say, the stamp of one defect,

        Being nature's livery, or fortune's star,

        His virtues else be they as pure as grace,

        As infinite as man may undergo,   L RAMP

        Shall in the general censure take corruption

        From that particular fault. ~~The dram of evil~~

        ~~Doth all the noble substance to a doubt~~

        ~~Of his own scandal.~~

                 Enter Ghost.

GHOST STOPS ON O · HOR SEEING GHOST BACKS FACING IT TO ABOVE HAMLET
TOUCHES HIM WITH EXTENDED R ARM AS HE BACKS

* HAMLET TURNS CW, FALLS TO KNEES AT HORATIOS SIDE HOLDS ONTO HIM
MARCELLUS CROSSES SELF · THEY ARE AT 3/4 10:00 · GHOST IS SCANNING
THE SKY ABOVE THEM

HAMLET RISES · HOR YES US 2

XING TO DL OF C GHOST LOOKS AT HAMLET FOR 1st TIME

*

GHOST SLOWLY RAISES R HAND THEN BECKONS HAMLET INDICATING
L TUNNEL, HOLDS TRUNCHEON

XING TO WIDE R OF HAMLET

YES IN 2 TOWARD HAMLET

27

HORATIO   Look my lord, it comes.

HAMLET   Angels and ministers of grace defend us.

          ·Be thou a spirit of health, or goblin damned,

          Bring with thee airs from heaven, or blasts from hell,

          Be thy intents wicked, or charitable,

          Thou com'st in such a questionable shape,

          That I will speak to thee. I*ll call thee Hamlet,

          King, [Father] royal Dane--o answer me.

          Let me not burst in ignorance, but tell

      Why thy canonized bones, hearsèd in death,

          Have burst their cerements; why the sepulchre,

          Wherein we saw thee quietly inurned ~~interred~~,

          Hath oped his ponderous and marble jaws

          To cast thee up again, What may this mean,

          That thou, dead corse, again in complete steel

          Revisits thus the glimpses of the moon,

          Making night hideous, and we fools of nature

          So horridly to shake our disposition

          With thoughts beyond the reaches of our souls?

          Say, why is this? Wherefore? What should we do?

HORATIO   It beckons you to go away with it,

          As if some impartment did desire

          To you alone.

MARCELLUS Look with what courteous action

          It waves you to a more removed ground.

          But do not go with it.

HORATIO   No, by no means.

STARTING TO X TOWARD GHOST

XING TO L OF HAMLET

GHOST XES OUT TUNL

XING AFTER GHOST

HOR RUNS TO US OF HAMLET, PUTS BOTH HANDS ON HIS SHOULDERS AND TURNS HAMLET TOWARDS HIM. HOR IS ON 4; HAMLET ON 3 AND 4. MAR MOVED IN TO 6:00 WHEN HAMLET MADE MOVE

FREEING R ARM GESTURING AFTER GHOST

X QUICKLY TO HIM, HOLD HIM BY R ARM, HOR NOW HAS L AND THEY DRAG HIM BACK TO C

GRAPPLING WITH HOR AND MAR AND TURNING THEM AND HIMSELF IN A HALF CIRCLE. SO THAT HE NOW FACES UR

FORCING FREE AND GETTING MAR'S SWORD AS HE PULLS AWAY TO UR OF C AND TURNING BACK TO FACE THEM. MAR CLEARS TO 3:00 AND HOR TO 6:00

MAR MAKES MOVE FOR HIM AND HAMLET QUICKLY THREATENS HIM WITH SWORD XING TO ½ 4:30 AS HE DOES SO. THEN TURNS EXITS TUNL

28

HAMLET   It will not speak; then I will follow it.

HORATIO   Do not my lord.

HAMLET   Why, what should be the fear?

I do not set my life at a pin's fee,

And for my soul, what can it do to that

Being a thing immortal as itself?

It waves me forth again. I'll follow it.

HORATIO   What if it tempt you toward the flood my lord,

Or to the dreadful summit of the cliff

That beetles o'er his base into the sea,

And thre assume some other horrible form

Which might deprive your sovereignty of reason,

And draw you into madness? Think of it.

The very place puts toys of desperation,

Without more motive, into every brain

That looks so many fathoms to the sea,

And hears it roar beneath.

HAMLET   It waves me still.

Go on; I'll follow thee.

MARCELLUS   You shall not go my lord.

HAMLET   Hold off your hands.

HORATIO   Be ruled, you shall not go.

HAMLET   My fate cries out.

And makes each petty artery in this body

As hardy as the Nemean lion's nerve.

Still am I called. Unhand me gentlemen--

By heaven I'll make a ghost of him that lets me.

I say, away! -- Go on, I'll follow thee.

(Exeunt Ghost and Hamlet.

WARN

L #5B

XING DL 2

    XING : TOWARD L TUN

KING TO EDGE ● L HAND OUT TO STOP MAR , STOPPING MAR ON 3 , HOR DR OF HIM ONLY

RACING OUT TUN L THEN HORATIO FOLLOWS

GHOST ENTERS TUN R XES BRISKLY TOWARD 12:00

GHOST WAITS 5 BEATS BEFORE ENTRANCE , HAMLET SPEAKS AS GHOST XES UP STEPS
ENTERS FOLLOWING GHOST , XES TO 0 , STOPS , HIS LINE STOPS GHOST
AT CENTER GHOST TURNS TO HIM SLOWLY , HAMLET SPEAKS IN TUNNEL

(TURNS SLOWLY TO FACE HAMLET THEN SPEAKS SOFTLY

XING ONTO 1 + 2 AT 7:00

GHOST STARTS SLOW CURVING X) TO HAMLET

29

HORATIO   He waxes desperate with imagination.

MARCELLUS   Let's follow, 'tis not fit to obey him.

HORATIO   Have after. To what issue will this come?

MARCELLUS   Something is rotten in the state of Denmark.

HORATIO   Heaven will direct it.

MARCELLUS   Nay, let's follow him.   L*5B

                                    (Exuent.

        SCENE FIVE (5) At the foot of the battlements. Enter
                        Ghost and Hamlet.

HAMLET   Whither wilt thou lead me? Speak, I*ll go no further.

GHOST   Mark me.

HAMLET   I will.

GHOST   My hour is almost come

                 When I to sulphurous and tormenting flames

                 Must render up myself.

HAMLET   Alas poor ghost!

GHOST   Pity me not, but lend they serious hearing

                 To what I shall unfold.

HAMLET   Speak, I am bound to hear.

GHOST   So art thou to revenge, when thou shalt hear.

HAMLET   What?

GHOST   I am thy father's spirit,

                 Doomed for a certain term to walk the night,

                 And for the day confined to fast in fires,

                 Till the foul crimes done in my days of nature

                 Are burnt and purged away. But that I am forbid

                 to tell the secrets of my prison-house,

IMPORTANCE OF EAR, HEARING TO PLAY

STOPPING AT   6:00 ON WAY TO HAMLET _____

XING OU TO ABOVE HEMLET   AT 7:00

TURNING ↻ SLOWLY TO FACE DL _____

TURN BACK TO FACE HAMLET (CW) _____

XING OUTD 3 AT 7:00

GHOST MOVES CLOSER TO HAMLET. HAMLET PUTS R FOOT ONTO 4. GHOST
TALKS INCHES FROM HAMLET'S L EAR HAMLET TILTS HEAD TOWARD R SHOULDER
AS GHOST CONTINUES.

30

GHOST   I could a tale unfold whose lightest word
Would harrow up thy soul, freeze they young blood,
Make thy two eyes like stars start from their spheres,
Thy knotted and combined locks to part,
And each particular hair to stand an end,
Like quills upon the fretful porpentine.
But this eternal blazon must not be
To ears of flesh and blood. List, list, o list!
If thou didst ever thy dear father love---

HAMLET   O God!

GHOST   Revenge his foul and most unnatural\ murder.

HAMLET   Murder?

GHOST   Murder most foul, as in the best it is,
But this most foul, strange and unnatural.

HAMLET   Haste me to know't, that I with wings as swift
As meditation or the thoughts of love,
May sweep to my revenge.

GHOST   I find thee apt,
And duller shouldst thou be than the fat weed
That roots itself in ease on Lethe wharf,
Wouldst thou not stir in this. Now Hamlet, hear.
"Tis given out that sleeping in my orchard
A serpent stung me, so the whole ear of Denmark
Is by a forged process of my death
Rankly abused; but know, thou noble youth,,
The serpent that did sting thy father's life
Now wears his crown.

BACKING TO 6:00 ON 3, HAND TO L EAR

TURNING DS

XING TO ABOVE HAMLET (3/4 6:00)

CIRCLING CW TO C

HAVING TURNED, FACING HAMLET

SINKING DOWN SITTING ON 4 FACING L

X TO 1/2 4:00

TURNING CW GESTURING WIDE WITH R HAND - TO FACE UL

XQ TO ABOVE HAMLET (4:00)

XING TO 1/4 3:00

HAMLET KNEELS ON 3 · GHOST AT 1/2 3:00 LOOKS APPRHESIVELY UR BACKS THEN
CROSSES DOWN ONTO 3 AT L OF HAMLET

BENDING OVER HIM R FOOT ON 4, L ON 3 HAMLET INCLINES HEAD AGAIN
HAMLET ON KNEES

31

HAMLET   O my prophetic soul!

My uncle?

GHOST   Ay, that incestous, that adulerate beast,

With witchcraft of his wits, with traitorous g...

O wicked wit and gifts that have the power

So to seduce--won to his shameful lust

HAMLET   The will of my most seeming virtuous Queen.

Ohh!

O Hamlet, what a falling off was there,

From me whose love was of that dignity,

That it went hand in hand even with the vow

I made to her in marriage, and to decline

Upon a wretch whose natural gifts were poor

To those of mine.

But virtue, as it never will be moved,

Though lewdness court it in a shape of heaven;

So lust, though to a radiant angel linked,

Will sate itself in a celestial bed,

And prey on garbage.

But soft, methinks I scent the morning air;

Brief let me be. Sleeping within my orchard,

My custom always of the afternoon,

Upon my secure hour thy uncle stole,

With juice of cursed hebona in a vial,

And in the porches of my ears did pour

The leperous distilment, whose effect

Holds such an enmity with blood of man,

That swift as quicksilver it courses through

CIRCLING BELOW HAMLET DOWN TO 1   ARM WRITHING OVER HIS
BODY.

GETTING BACK ONTO 4 AT R OF HAMLET...
CONTINUING US TO ½ 12:00

HANDS OUT TO SIDE, FACING US
    HAND WRITHING, FACING US   + β

XING ON US

TURNING BACK TO HAMLET WITH JOVIAN RAGE, POINTING FROM ½ 12:00

CRINGING TURNING TO FACE DL, SITTING ON 4
GHOST XES ↓ TO 4:00   SOFTENING ATTACK

HAMLET TURNS TO LOOK AT GHOST OVER R SHOULDER

XING UP TO UR OF C

RAISES HANDS AS IF IN DEFENSE, L TO FACE, R EXTENDED. MAKES SEMI-
CIRCULAR X, BACKING TO EXIT TUN L. HAMLET RISES XES ↷ TO FOLLOW GHOST
L HAND EXTENDED TO GHOST

GHOST BACKING ONTO 3, HAMLET REACHING XING AFTER HIM ALMOST TOUCHING
● HAMLET SPRAWLS ON FLOOR REACHING FOR GHOST. GHOST EXIT TUN L

RETURN TO CONSCIOUSNESS AFTER DELIRIUM

32

GHOST   The natural gates and alleys of the body,

And with a sudden vigour it doth posset

And curd, like eager droppings into milk,

The thin and wholesome blood; so did it mine,

And a most instant tetter barked about,

Most lazar-like, with vile and loathsome crust

All my smooth body.

Thus was I sleeping by a brother's hand

Of life, of crown, of Queen, at once dispatched;

Cut off even in the blossoms of my sin,

Unhouseled, disappointed, unaneled, (unanealed)

No reckoning made, but sent to my account

With all my imperfections on my head--

HAMLET: O horrible! O horrible, most horrible!

GHOST: If thou hast nature in thee bear it not,

Let not the royal bed of Denmark be

A couch for luxury and damned incest.

HAMLET: Ohhh.

But howsoever thou pursued this act,

Taint not thy mind, nor let thy soul contrive

Against thy mother|aught; leave her to heaven,

And to those thorns that in her bosom lodge

To prick and sting her. Fare thee well at once.

The glow-worm shows the matin to be near

And 'gins to pale his uneffectual fire.

Adieu, adieu, adieu. Remember me.

                                  (Exit)

HAMLET   O all you host of heaven! O earth! What else?

And shall I couple hell? O fie! Hold, hold my heart,

RISING WITH DIFFICULTY · LEAVES SWORD ON STAGE   THEN TURNING CW
LOOKING OUT L TUN OVER R SHOULDER

RIGHT HAND TO TEMPLE, ELBOW HIGH

XING S TO C   THEN LOOKING DL

LOOKING DL OVER L SHOULDER

LOOKING DC   X TO ½ G. 00

BOTH HANDS TO BROW

X TO SWORD PICK IT UP THEN STANDING POINTING OUT TUNNEL WITH
SWORD AT ¾ 4. 00

KNEELS FACING DL HOLDING UPRIGHT SWORD IN BOTH HANDS BEFORE HIM

THIS AND FOLLOWING LINES FROM OFF TUN R

HAMLET RISES, THE CALL IS FALSETTO

33

WARN

L#6

HAMLET   And you my sinews, grow not instant old,

But bear me stiffly up. Remember thee?

Ay thou poor ghost, whiles memory holds a seat

In this distracted globe. Remember thee?

Yea, from the table of my memory

I'll wipe away all trivial fond records,

All saws of books, all forms, all pressures past

That youth and observation, copied there,

And thy commandment all alone shall live

Within the book and volume of my brain,

Unmixed with baser matter--yes, by heaven!

O most pernicious woman!

O villain, villain, smiling damned villain!

My tables--meet it is I set it down

That one may smile, and smile, and be a villain;

At least I am sure it may be so in Denmark.

                              (Writes.

So uncle, there you are. Now to my word;

It is, adieu, adieu, remember me.

I have sworn't.   L#6

                 Enter Horatio and Marcellus

HORATIO   My lord, my lord!

MARCELLUS   Lord Hamlet!

HORATIO   Heavens secure him.

HAMLET   So be it.

HORATIO   Illo, ho, ho, my lord!

HAMLET   Hillo, ho, ho, boy! Come bird, come.

HOR AND MAR ENT TUN R. HOR ENTER FIRST. THEY X ACROSS STAGE
TO HIM. HOR TO 3/4 4:00. MAR TO ½ 7:00. LINE ON STEPS

YES TO MAR

KING TO 6:00 ● CHECKING HIMSELF
  TURNS BACK TO FACE US
KING TO UL OF HAMLET

SHAKING HOR'S HAND THEN KING TO MAR. SHAKING HIS

STARTING TO EXIT TUN R

KING TO 3/4 5:00 HAMLET. STOPS ON 3 AND 2 ON WAY OUT

KING BACK ON STAGE TAKING HORATIO TO 3:00. XES UIA ABOVE HOR
ARM AROUND R SHOULDER

34

MARCELLUS   How is't my noble lord?

HORATIO   What news my lord?

HAMLET   O wonderful!

HORATIO   Good my lord tell it.

HAMLET   No; you will reveal it.

HORATIO   Not I my lord by heaven.

MARCELLUS   Nor I my lord.

HAMLET   How say you then, would heart of man once think it---
        But you'll be secret?

HORATIO &
MARCELLUS   Ay by heaven my lord.

HAMLET   There's never a villain dwelling in Denmark s
        But he's an arrant knave.

HORATIO   There needs no ghost, my lord, come from the grave
        To tell us this.

HAMLET   Why right, you are in the right,
        And so without more circumstance at all
        I hold it fit that we shake hands and part;
        You as your business and desire shall point you,
        For every man hath business/ and desire,
        Such as it is, and for my own poor part'
        I will go pray.

HORATIO   These are but wild and whirling words, my lord.

HAMLET   I am sorry they offend you, heartily,
        Yes faith heartily.

HORATIO   There's no offence my lord.

HAMLET   Yes by Saint Patrick but there is, Horatio,
        And much offence too. Touching this vision here----

MARCELLUS AND HORATIO DON'T HEAR GHOST

MAR XES OVER TO LISTEN · XES TO 3 30 ON 3+2 , HAMLET CHECKS HIMSELF

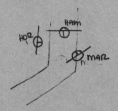

HOLD OUT HILT OF SWORD FOR THEM

HAMLET XES TO 11:00 , MAR XES UP TO 2:00 ON 3

HOR → ½ 3:00

XING TO 12:00 HOLDING OUT SWORD

HOR AND MARCELLUS X IN TO HAMLET *

THEY PUT HANDS ON SWORD

XES TO 8:00

* HAM ⌀╌╌⊘ MAR   THEY X DOWN TO HAMLET
           ⊘ HOR

35

WARN

HAMLET	It is an honest ghost, that let me tell you--

GHOST
TRAP LITE

For your desire to know what is between us

O'ermaster't as you may. And now good friends,

As you are friends, scholars, and soldiers,

Give me one poor request.

HORATIO   What is't my lord? We will.

HAMLET   Never make known what you have seen to-night.

HORATIO &
MARCELLUS   My lord we will not.

HAMLET   Nay but swear't.

HORATIO   In faith

My lord not I.

MARCELLUS   Nor I my lord in faith.

HAMLET   Upon my sword.

MARCELLUS   We have sworn my lord already.

HAMLET   Indeed, upon my sword indeed.   TRAP LITE

GHOST(beneath) Swear

HAMLET   Ha, ha, boy, sayst thou so? Art thou there truepenny?

Come on--you hear this.fellow in the cellarage--

Consent to swear.

HORATIO   Propose the oath, my lord.

HAMLET   Never to speak of this that you have seen,

Swear by my sword   TRAP LITE

GHOST(beneath) Swear.

HAMLET   Hic et ubique? Then we'll shift our ground.

Come hither gentlemen.

And lay your hands again upon my sword

Swear by my sword,

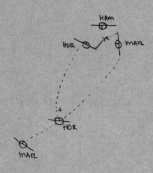

KNEELING TO PAT EARTH AT 7:30 _____

    RISING , XING U/A R OF HOR AND MAR TO ³/4 12:30 _____

    XING UP TO BELOW C _____

HOR AND MAR X TO HAMLET. HOR TO DR, MAR TO DL OF HIM. MAR GRABS HILT
TESTILY . HOR XES FIRST _____

LETTING GO OF SWORD TO DEMONSTRATE _____

TURNING KING ⌢ ⏀ 11:00 ● XING BACK TO THEM AFTER PAUSE _____

    PAUSE, MAR LOOKS DISGRUNTLED _____

XING TOWARD DR U/A BETWEEN THEM ● STOPS AT ¼ 7:30 TURNS BACK TO THEM
HOR XES. TO L OF HAMLET, MAR TO R OF HIM. THEY TOWARD DR

36

HAMLET   Never to speak of this that you have heard.   TRAP LITE
           Swear by my [sword]

GHOST (beneath)   Swear ~~by his sword~~.

HAMLET   Well said old mole, canst work i'th' earth so fast?

           A worthy pioneer. Once more remove, good friends.

HORATIO   O day and night, but this is wondrous strange.

HAMLET   And therefore as a stranger give it welcome.

           There are more things in heaven and earth, Horatio,

           Than are dreamt of in your philosophy.

           But come---   **WARN**

           Here as before, never, so help you mercy,   L #7

           How strange or odd some'er I bear myself--   GHOST

           As I perchance hereafter shall think meet   (TRAP LITE)

           To put an antic disposition on--

           That you at such times seeing me never shall,

           With arms encumbered thus, or this head-shake,

           Or by pronouncing of some doubtful phrase,

           As, well, well, we know--or, we could an if we would--

           Or, if we list to speak--or, there be an if they might,

           Or such ambigous giving out, to note

           That you know aught of me-- this not to do ~~this do swear~~,

           So grace and mercy at your most need help you. [Swear]   TRAP LITE

GHOST (beneath)   Swear   They swear.

HAMLET   Rest, rest, perturbed spirit. So gentlemen,

           With all my love I do commend me to you,

           And what so poor a man as Hamlet is

           May do t' express his love and friending to you,

           God willing, shall not lack. Let us go in together.

STOPPING ON EDGE OF 4, SPEAKING TO HOR AS HE PASSES VIA L OF HAMLET

STOPPING ON 4 AND 3 LOOKING BACK ON STAGE. HOR AND MAR STOP 3 AND 2

HE FALTERS, MAR AND HOR HAVING XED DOWN A STEP MOVE BACK UP TO SUPPORT HIM

EASING THEM ASIDE EXITING TUNL · MAR AND HOR FOLLOW. ● POL THEN
REY ENTER BEL L, POL HAS RUG, 2 BOOK AND ENVELOPES. REY HAS COAT AND SUITCASE, POL
SPEAKS AT C BEL XING TO DOWN RIGHT OF BEL; REY CLOSES DOOR XES OUT C BEL

HANDING ENVELOPES TO REY WHO IS L OF HIM, THEN CONTINUES TO BENCH

PUTTING NOTES INTO POCKET OF OVERCOAT THEN XES TO 10:00 ON 3

PUTTING DOWN CANE AND BOOKS DS ON BENCH THEN OPENING RUG SITTING
C ON BENCH PUTTING RUG ABOUT KNEES

PUTTING DOWN SUITCASE ON US BENCH, OVERCOAT ON TOP OF IT.

REY TAKES OUT NOTEBOOK AND PEN. POL NOW SITS.

37

HAMLET   And still your fingers on your lips I pray.

The time is out of joint; o cursed spite,

That ever I was born to set it right. STUMBLE   L#7

Nay come, let's go together.

                            (Exeunt.

ACT TWO SCENE ONE (6) Elsinore, The house of Polonius. Enter

                          Polonius and Reynaldo.

POLONIUS   Give him this money, and these notes Reynaldo.

REYNALIO   I will my lord.

POLONIUS   You shall do marvellous wisely, godd Reynaldo,

Before you visit him, to make enquire

Of his behaviour.

REYNALDO   My lord, I did intend it.

POLONIUS   Marry well said, very well said. Look you sir,

Enquire me first what Ianskers are in Paris,

And how, and who, what means, and where they keep,

What company, at what expense; ~~and finding~~ and then

~~By this encompassment and drift of question,~~

~~That they do know my son, come you more nearer~~

~~Than your particular demands will touch it.~~

TAke you as 'twere some distant knowledge of him,

As thus, I know his father and friends,

And in part him--do you mark this Reynaldo?

REYNALDO   Ay, very well my lord.

POLONIUS   And in part him--but, you may say, not well,

But if't be he I mean, he's very wild,

Addicted so and so; and there put on him

REY START X √ BENCH ON 2 , TAKING NOTES

STOPPING UTL OF POL ON 2 ● XING ON

REY STOPS TURNS TO POL FROM DIR OF HIM

XING ONTO 3 BELOW BENCH

POLONIUS What forgeries you please, marry none so rank

    As may dishonour him, take heed of that;

    But sir, such wanton, wild, and usual slips

    As are companions noted and most known

    To youth and liberty.

REYNALDO As gaming my lord?

POLONIUS Ay, or drinking, fencing, swearing,

    Quarrelling, drabbing—you may go so far.

REYNALDO My lord, that would dishonour him.

POLONIUS Faith no, as you may season it in the charge.

    You must not put another scandal on him,

    That he is open to incontinency;

    That's not my meaning. But breathe his faults so quaintly,

    That they may seem the taints of liberty,

    The flash and outbreak of a fiery mind,

    A savageness in unreclaiméd blood,

   n. Of general assault.

REYNALDO But my good lord--

POLONIUS Wherefore should you do this?

REYNALDO Ay my lord,

    I would know that.

POLONIUS Marry sir, here's my drift,

    And I believe it is a fetch of warrant,

    You laying these slight sullies on my son

    As 'twere a thing a little soiled wi' th' working,

    Mark you.

    Your party in converse, him you would sound,

RISES

XING TO DL OF REY

READING FROM THE NOTES HE HAS BEEN TAKING

X TO 1/2 9:00

REY X TO SUITCASE, REPLACE PEN, XES VIA R OF POL

XING TO C OF PLAT

SHOWING NOTE PAD

39

POLONIUS   ~~Having ever seen in the prenominate crim~~es

~~The youth you breathe guilty, be assure~~d

He closes with you in this consequence;

Good sir, or so, or friend, or gentleman,

According to the phrase or the addition

Of man and country.

REYNALDO   Very good my lord.

POLONIUS   And then sir does 'a this; 'a does--what was I

about to say? By the mass I was about to say

something. Where did I leave?

REYNALDO   At, closes in the consequence, at, friend or so,

and, gentleman.

POLONIUS   At, closes in the consequence, ay marry.

He closes thus; I know the gentleman;

I saw him yesterday, or th} other day,

Or then, or then; with such, or such; and as you say,

There was 'a gaming, there o'ertook in's rouse,

There falling out at tennis, or perchance,

I saw him enter such a house of sale,

(viz)   REYNALDO: Oh, my lord!

Videlicet a brothel or so forth. ~~See you now,~~

~~Your bait of falsehood takes this carp of trut~~h.

And thus do we of wisdom, and or reach,

~~With windlasses, and with assays of bia~~s,

By indirections find directions out;

~~So by my former lecture and advice~~

~~Shall you my son.~~ You have me, have you not?

REYNALDO   My lord, I have.

REPLACING PAD, PICKING UP COAT AND CASE

SITTING BENCH C, PUTTING RUG ABOUT LEGS, TAKES UP BOOK

XING ↓ TO EXIT TUN R

XING DOWN STEPS AT 8:00 , THEN CONTINUES OUT R TUN

OPHELIA RACES IN FROM BELOW L RUNS TO KNEEL BEFORE POL

RISING THROWING DOWN BLANKET

XING ↑ SLOWLY TO UL OF PLAT

POL XES SLOWLY DOWN TO DL OF PLAT

40

POLONIUS   God buy ye, fare ye well.

REYNALDO   Good my lord

POLONIUS   Observe his inclination in yourself.

REYNALDO   I shall my lord.

POLONIUS   And let him ply his music.

REYNALDO   Well, my lord

POLONIUS   Farewell.   (Exit Reynaldo) Enter Ophelia.

How now Ophelia, what's the matter?

OPHELIA   O my lord, my lord, I have been so affrighted.

POLONIUS   With what, i' th' name of God?

OPHELIA   My lord, as I was sewing in my closet,

Lord Hamlet with his doublet all unbraced

No hat upon his head, his stockings fouled,

Ungartered, and down-gyved to his ankle,

Pale as his shirt, his knees knocking each other,

And with a look so piteous in purport

As if he had been loosed out of hell

To speak of horrors he comes before me.

POLONIUS   Mad for thy love?

OPHELIA   My lord I do not know,

But truly I do fear it.

POLONIUS   What said he?

OPHELIA   He took me by the wrist, and held me hard;

Then goes he to the length of all his arm,

And with his other hand thus o'er his brow,

He falls to such perusal of my face

As he would draw it. Long stayed he so;

RISES XES TO ¼ 12:00, THEN OPH RISES ● OPH XES QUICKLY TO HIM ⌐ ⌐

TURN BACK TO HER ● X ON TO ½ 3:00

X TO ½ 3:30

TURN BACK TO HER

X TO ABOVE CENTER

X UP TO ½ 10:00

HOLDING ARMS OUT, OPH XES INTO HIS EMBRACE

X TO HER ● PUTS ARM AROUND HER

OPH LOOKS SHARPLY UP AT HIM BUT HE STARTS X BACK TO BENCH STOPS
IN FRONT OF PLATFORM

TURNS XES TO BENCH TO GET PROPS ● OPH XES TO ¾ 9:00 PROTESTING

41

OPHELIA   At last, a little shaking of mine arm,

And thrice his head thus waving up and down,

He raised a sigh so piteous and profound

As it did seem to shatter all his bulk,

And end his being; that done, he lets me go,

And with his head over his shoulder turned,

He seemed to find his way without his eyes,

For out o' doors he went without their helps,

And to the last bended their light one me.

POLONIUS   Come, go with me, I will go seek the King.
OPHELIA   No, my Lord
      This is the very ecstasy of love,

Whose violent property fordoes itself,

And leads the will to desperate undertakings

As oft as any passion under heaven

That does afflict our natures. I am sorry.

What, have you given him any hard words of late?

OPHELIA   No my good lord, but as you did command,

I did repel his letters, and denied

His access to me.

POLONIUS   That hath made him mad.

I am sorry that with better heed and judgement

I had not quoted him. I feared he did but trifle,

And meant to wreck thee, but beshrew my jealousy.

By heaven it is as proper to our age

To cast beyond ourselves in our opinions,

As it is common for the younger sort

To lack discretion. Come, go we to the King.
OPHELIA   No, my lord.

WARN

L #8

XING TO L BELOW EXIT, OPHELIA A† HIS R

⌀ NYM

⊘ BAR

SLING

(TROLLEY OF DRINKS WHEELED IN TO ½ 9:00 ▱) /

ROS(L) AND GUI SHOWN ON UR. BAR AT UR DOOR. THEY X OVER TO 12:00 LOOKING
ABOUT, PRIMPING. ROS SEES TROLLEY XES TO DL OF IT. STARTS TO PICK UP GLASS, GUI COUGHS,
ROS REPLACES GLASS. GUI XES ON TO ¾ 2:00. ROS TO ½ 4:00. KING (R) AND QUEEN ENTER
UR. KING XES BRISKLY TO ROS SHAKING HANDS THEN TO GUI, STANDS R OF HIM. QUEEN
GOES TO ROS FOLLOWING KING SHAKES HANDS, THEN UP TO GUI, SHAKES, FROM DL OF GUI.

XING VIA ABOVE TROL TO ROS ● X TO GUI, QUEEN X TO ROS
½ 12:30 (top of ramp)
(TURNING TO FACE ROS FROM R OF GUI, QUEEN XES TO DL OF GUI THEN TO L OF KING

LAUGHS, XES TO R OF TROL TO POUR DRINKS, QUEEN XES TO ½ 12:00

POURING BUT WATCHING THEIR REACTIONS.

GIVE DRINK TO QUEEN THEN XES AROUND ↘ TROL TAKING DRINK
FIRST TO ROS THEN GUI THEN BACK TO TROL · UR OF IT.

BACK AT TROLLEY GETTING OWN DRINK. UR OF TROL

XING DOWN HOOK AROUND AT ½ 3:30, GUI MOVES IN TO
ABOVE HER

42

POL AND OPH ON BEL PLAT III   L #8

POLONIUS   This must be known, which being kept close might move

More grief to hide, than hate to utter love.

Come

(Exeunt.

II, SCENE TWO (7) The Castle. Flourish. Enter Claudius,
                   Gertrude, Rosencrantz, Guildenstern,
                   and Attendants.

CLAUDIUS   Welcome dear Rosencrantz and Guildenstern.

Moreover, that we much did long to see you,

The need we have to use you did provoke

Our hasty sending. Something have you heard

Of Hamlet's transformation; so call it,

Sith nor th' exterior nor the inward man

Resembles that it was. What it should be,

More than his father's death, that thus hath put him

So much from the understanding of himself,

I cannot dream of. I entreat you both,

That being of so young days brought up with him,

And sith so neighboured to his youth and haviour,

That you vouchsafe your rest here in our Court

Some little time, so by your companies

To draw him on to pleasures, and to gather

So much as from occasion you may glean,

Whether aught to us unknown afflicts him thus

That opened lies within our remedy.

GERTRUDE   Good gentlemen, he hath much talked of you,

And sure I am, two men there is not living

To whom he more adheres. If it will please you

To show us so much gentry and good will,

EXIT OF <u>ROS</u> AND <u>GUI</u>.

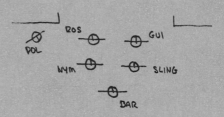

CUTTING OFF <u>ROS</u>

ABOVE <u>TROL</u> · CONFUSING <u>ROS</u> & <u>GUI</u>

CORRECTING HIM MOVE INT

TURNING TO <u>ROS</u>

BAR X IN TO 10:30 CLICK HEELS <u>NYM</u> & <u>SLING</u> X IN 2

(RAISING GLASS AS IN TOAST

XES TO TROL, PUTS DN GLASS UL ON IT. BOWS. AT SAME TIME <u>ROS</u> X TO BELOW TABLE PUT DOWN DRINK
BOW, BOTH EXIT UR. <u>ROS</u> VIA R OF TROL.

POL ENTERS UR, HOLDS. KING AND QUEEN MEET ON L SIDE OF TROL, NUZZLE
POL COUGHS DISCREETLY AND THEY BREAK.

XES TO 11:00 3/4 11:00

QUEEN XES VIA BELOW TROL, SITS AT CROTCH, PUTS UP PARASOL

XING IN TWO TOWARD <u>KING</u>

GERTRUDE As to expend your time with us awhile,

For the supply and profit of our hope,

Your visitation shall receive such thanks

As fits a King's remembrance.

ROSENCRANTZ Both your Majesties

Might by the sovereign power you have of us,

Put your dread pleasures more into command

Than to entreaty.

GUILDENSTERN But we both obey,

And here give up ourselves in the full bent,

To lay our service freely at your feet

To be commanded.

CLAUDIUS Thanks Rosencrantz and gentle Guildenstern.

GERTRUDE Thanks Guildenstern, and gentle Rosencrantz.

And I beseech you instantly to visit

My too much changed son. Go some of you.

And bring these gentlemen where Hamlet is

GUILDENSTERN Heavens make our presence and our practices

Pleasant and helpful to him

GERTRUDE Ay, amen.
   (Exeunt Rosencrantz, Guildenstern, and
   some attendants.

Enter Polonius

POLONIUS Th' ambassadors from Norway, my good lord,

Are joyfully returned.

CLAUDIUS Thou still hast been the father of good news.

POLONIUS Have I my lord? I assure you my good liege,

I hold my duty as I hold my soul,

CLEARS THROAT SIGNIFICANTLY XES ABOVE KING WHO FOLLOWS FOR CONFERENCE
AT 3/4 4:00 ⊘ ⊘POL

POL TURNS, XES, EXITS UR

XING TO L OF TROL POURING DRINK

XING TO QUEEN, STANDS BELOW HER ON BENCH PLAT

RISING ~ Split parasol

VOLT AND CORN ENTER U R X DOWN TO KING. VOLT TO 3/4 8:00, CORN
TO 1/2 9:00. POL XES AROUND TO 5:00, OBSERVING

UNUTTERABLY EAGER, THROUGHOUT SPEECH, CLAUDIUS TRIES TO GET A WORD
IN. QUEEN SITS

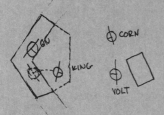

GIVES IT UP, SITS DS ON QUEEN WAITING FOR BREAK

44

POLONIUS   Both to my God, and to my gracious King,
            And I do think-or else this brain of mine
            Hunts not the trail of policy so sure
            As it hath used to do--that I have found
            The very cause of Hamlet's lunacy.

CLAUDIUS   O speak of that, that do I long to hear.

POLONIUS   Give first admittance to th' ambassadors;
            My news shall be the fruit to that great feast.

CLAUDIUS   Thyself do grace to them, and bring them in.

                        (Exit Polonius.

            He tells me, my dear Gertrude, he hath found
            The head and source of all your son's distemper

GERTRUDE   I doubt it is no other but the main,
            His father's death, and our o'erhasty marriage.

CLAUDIUS   Well, we shall sift him.

                        (Enter Polonius, Voltemand & Cornelius.

            Welcome my good friends,
            Say Voltemand, what from our brother Norway?

VOLTEMAND   Most fair return of greetings and desires.
CLAUDIUS   Yes
            Upon our first, he sent out to suppress
            His nephew's levies, which to him appeared

            To be preparation 'gainst the Polack;
CLAUDIUS   Yes
            But better looked into, he truly found
            It was against your Highness, whereat grieved
            That so his sickness, age, and impotence
            Was falsely borne in hand, sends out arrests
            On Fortinbras; which he in brief obeys,
            Receives rebuke from Norway, and in fine,

KING STARTS TO RISE BUT VOLT RUNS ON, HE SITS.

KING STARTS TO SPEAK, BUT CORN STARTS SPEAKING, KING ALSO ATTEMPTS RISE
HOLDING OUT DISPATCH & IN BIT TO EDGE

KING HOLDS A BEAT TO BE SURE THEY ARE FINISHED THEN RISES TAKES
DISPATCH FROM CORN

HOLDS OUT DISPATCH POL XES IN TAKES IT FROM HIM AND XES 7:30 ON 3

SHAKES HAND FIRST OF CORN THEN VOLT, WITH EACH SHAKE LAUNCHES THEM ON
WAY UR, THEY BACK BOW AND EXIT UR. CORN AND VOLT REMOVE GLOVES TO SHAKE.

A LOOK TO POL THEN XES TO R OF TROL TO POUR DRINK FOR POL

XING QUICKLY UP TO L OF TROLLY PUTS DOWN DISPATCH USON IT.

X TO WIDE UR OF TROLLEY

HAVING POURED DRINK XES, GIVES IT TO POL THEN XES TO BELOW QUEEN ON PLAT

SIPS WINE · QUEEN RISES · KING XES TO DS OF QUEEN

45

VOLTEMAND   Makes vow before his uncle never nore

To give th' assay of arms against your Majesty.

Whereon old Norway, overcome with joy,

Gives him threescore thousand crowns in annual fee,

And his commission to employ those soldiers,

So levied, as before, against the Polack,

CORNELIUS,   With an entreaty, herein further showne

                                    (Gives a paper.

That it might please you to give quiet pass

Through your dominions for this enterprise,

On such regards of safety and allowance

As therein are set down.

CLUADIUS   It likes us well;

And at our more considered time, we'll read,

Andwer, and think upon this business.

Meantime, we thank you for your well-took labour.

Go to your rest, at night we'll feast together.

Most welcome home.
                        (Exent Voltemand and Cornelius.

POLONIUS   This business is well ended.

My liege, and madam, to expostulate

What majesty should be, what duty is,

Why day is day, night night, and time is time,

Were nothing but to waste night, day, and time.

Therefore since brevity is the soul of wit,

And tediousness the limbs and outward flourishes,

I will be brief--your noble son is mad.

Mad call I it, for to define true madness

QUEEN XES TO ½ 4:00

POL XES TO R OF TROL PUTS DOWN WINE

TAKING OUT LETTER, QUEEN XES TO UL OF TROL, PUTS DOWN DRINK
SHE APPROACHES HIM, POL XES TO KING.

QUEEN STIRS IMPATIENTLY
KING IN 1 TO ABOVE TROL

FINDING WAY TO PASSAGE HE WANTS TO REHD ● POL AND KING SHARE CHORTLE
OVER SOME BLUE PASSAGE.

46

POLONIUS   What is't but to be nothing else but mad?

But let that go.

GERTRUDE   More matter with less art.

POLONIUS   Madam, I swear I use no art at all.

That he's mad 'tis true; 'tis true 'tis pity,

And pity 'tis 'tis true—a foolish figure,

But farewell it, for I will use no art.

Mad let us grant him then, and now remains

That we find out the cause of this effect,

Or rather say, the cause of this defect,

For this effect defective comes by cause.

Thus it remains, and the remainder thus.

Perpend;

I have a daughter--have while she is mine--

Who in her duty and obedience, mark,

Hath given me this. Now gather and surmise.

                             (Reads.

To the celestial and my soul's idol, the most
beautified Ophelia.

That's an ill phrase, a vile phrase; beautified is a

vile phrase, but you shall hear. Thus--

In her excellent white bosom, these, & c.-

GERTRUDE   Came this from Hamlet to her?

POLONIUS   Good madam stay awhile; I will be faithful
             Da,dum, da dum, da dum
             Doubt thou 'the stars are fire;

             Doubt that the sun doth move;

             Doubt truth to be a liar;

             But never doubt I love.

GIVE NOTE TO KING, XES TO ¾ 3:30 , KING XES OFF PLAT THEN TURNS D LOOKING AT NOTE, QUEEN XES TO ABOVE KING

Ø QUEEN ✓

Ø KING

TURNING FROM ¾ 3:30

AFTER A GLANCE AT THE QUEEN WHO XES DOWN TO ¾ 7:00, KING XES ↱ TO R OF TROLLEY PUTS DOWN LETTER DS ON IT, POURS ANOTHER DRINK FOR SELF. (KING X FIRST)

XING IN TO L OF TROL

QUEEN XES TO 6:00, KING WATCHES HER, MOVES OUT TO WIDE R OF TROL (¾ 9:00)

QUEEN XES R TO ¾ 8:00

47

POLONIUS(reading)   O dear Ophelia, I am ill at these numbers, I

                   have not art to reckon my groans, but that I love

                   thee best, o most best, believe it. Adieu.

                   Thine evermore most dear lady, whilst this

                   machine is to him, Hamlet.

              This in obedience my daughter shown me,

              And more above hath his solicitings,

              As they fell out by time, by means, and place,

              All given to mine ear.

CLAUDIUS   But how hath she

              Received his love?

POLONIUS   What do you think of me?

CLAUDIUS   As of a man faithful and honourable.

POLONIUS   I would fain prove so. But what might you think,

              When I had seen his hot love on the wing,

              As I perceived it, I must tell you that,

              Before my daughter told me, what might you,

              Or my dear Majesty your Queen here think,

              If I had played the desk, or table-book,

              Or given my heart a winking, mute and dumb,

              Or looked upon this love with idle sight;

              What might you think? No, I went round to work,

              And my young mistress thus I did bespeak--

              Lord Hamlet is a Prince out of thy star:

              This must not be--and then I prescripts gave her

              That she should lock herself from his resort,

              Admit no messengers, receive no tokens,

QUEEN MOVES IMPATIENTLY

SEEING QUEEN, SOFTENING ATTACK

X IN ONE TOWARD QUEEN

AT TROLLEY, GETS DRINK

HAMLET STARTS IN FROM R ABOVE

KING TO CROTCH, SITS   HAMLET STOP C ABOVE LISTENING

POL XES   TO 3/4 9:30

QUEEN XES TO DL OF PLAY

HAMLET XES BACK TO R ABOVE DOOR, RE-ENTERS, XING ACROSS ABOVE READING

QUEEN XES TO UR OF TROLLEY, PRECEDES KING OUT

48

POLONIUS   Which done, she took the fruits of my advice;

And he repelled, a short tale to make,

Fell into a sadness, then into a fast,

Thence to a watch, thence into a weakness,

Thence to a lightness, and by this declension,

Into the madness wherein now he raves,

And all we mourn for.

CLAUDIUS   Do you think 'tis this?

GERTRUDE   It may be, very like.

POLONIUS   Hath there been such a time--I would fain know that--

That I have postively said, 'tis so,

When it proved otherwise?

CLAUDIUS   Not that I know.

POLONIUS   (Points to his head and shoulder)

Take this, from this, if this be otherwise

If circumstances lead me, I will find

Where truth is hid, though it were hid indeed

Within the centre.

CLAUDIUS   How may we try it further?

POLONIUS   You know sometimes he walks four hours together

Here in the lobby.

GERTRUDE   So he does indeed.

POLONIUS   At such a time, I'll loose my daughter to him.

Be you and I behind an arras then;

Mark the encounter, if he love her not,

And be not from his reason fall'n thereon,

Let me be no assistant for a state,

But keep a farm and carters,

RISING, KING OUT

KING UP TO ½ 12:00

KING ↰ TO BELOW KING ● KING XES TO TROL PUTS DOWN DRINK, THEN XES
TO R OF QUEEN AND THEY EXIT UR, QU 1st ↰↰

HAMLET ENTERS BELOW L XING SLOWLY DOWN L SIDE OF STAGE. POL HEMS. NO
RESPONSE. POL XES ↰ TO ½ 3:00 THEN LINE

(HAMLET TURNS STARTS XING↰ ABOVE TROL

(XING AROUND BELOW TROL TO MEET HAMLET AT UR OF IT

(HAMLET BARELY LOOKS AT POL DURING FOLLOWING. LOOKS AT TROL

NOW REALLY SEEING HIM FOR 1st TIME

TURNS TO FACE L

TURNING XING ↰ TO ½ 4:00 AND THEN TO R DURING ASIDE, ADDRESSING
DS HOUSE.

HAMLET (WHO HAS BEEN WATCHING THIS NOW TURNS XES L

XING ↑ TROL TO ½ 10:30

STOPPING AT ½ 2:00

49

CLAUDIUS   We will try it.

(Enter Hamlet)

GERTRUDE   But look where sadly the poor wretch comes reading.

POLONIUS   Away, I do beseech you both, away.

I'll board him presently. O give me leave.

(Exeunt Claudius, Gertrude & Attendants)

How does my good Lord Hamlet?

HAMLET   Well, God-amercy.

POLONIUS   Do you know me my lord?

HAMLET   Excellent well, you are a fishmonger.

POLONIUS   Not I my lord.

HAMLET   Then I would you were so honest a man.

POLONIUS   Honest, my lord?

HAMLET   Ay sir; to be honest as this world goes is to be one
man picked out of ten thousand.

POLONIUS   That's very true my lord.

HAMLET   For if the sun breed maggots in a dead dog, being
a god kissing carrion--have you a daughter ?

POLONIUS   I have my lord.

HAMLET   Let her not walk i' th' sun. Conception is a blessing,
but as your daughter may conceive--friend look to't.

POLONIUS(aside)
How say you by that? Still harping on my daughter.
Yet he knew me not at first; 'a said I was a fishmonger;
'a is far gone, far gone, and truly in my youth I suffered
such extremity for love, very near this. I'll speak to
him again.-- What do you read my lord?

HAMLET   Words, words, words.

XING TO DR OF POL VIA ABOVE TROL   HT
                                                                     Ø

                                                                ⊘ POL

_____

TURNING FROM POL XING TO 3/4 3:30

XING ↳ TROL TO FACE HAMLET, XES TO 1/2 4:30,

TURNS, STARTS SLOW X UP TO UL

  TURNING DS FOR ASIDE

  HAMLET TURNS AT UL STARTS PACE DS

XES AROUND PICKS UP DISPATCH FROM TROL XES TO 3/4 11:00, TURNS TO HAMLET

  STOPPING

  CONTINUING X DS

  XING QUICKLY TO UR

  XING ONTO 3 AT 4:00 ● POL TURNS BACK SHARPLY HAVING HEARD.
  ROS AND GUI ENTER UR X TO POL

        RO   ⊘ POL
        Ø
     GU
     Ø

50

POLONIUS   What is the matter my lord?

HAMLET   Between who?

POLONIUS   I mean the matter that you read, my Lord.

HAMLET   Slanders sir, for the satirical rogue says here, that old
            men have grey beards, that their faces are wrinkled, their
            eyes purging thick amber and plum-tree gum, and that they
            have a plentiful lack of wit, together with most weak hams
            all which sir though I most powerfully and potently
            believe, yet I hold it not honestly to have it thus set
            down; for yourself sir shall grow old as I am, if like
            a crab you could go backward.

POLONIUS (aside) Though this be madness, yet there is method in't.
            --Will you walk out of the air my lord?

HAMLET   Into my grave?

POLONIUS   Indeed that's out o' th' air. (Aside) How pregnant
            sometimes his replies are; a happiness that often
            madness hits on, which reason and sanity could not so
            prosperously be delivered of. I will leave him, and
            suddenly contrive the means of meeting between him and
            my daughter. --- My honourable lord, I will most humbly
            take my leave of you.

HAMLET   You cannot sir take from me anything that I will more
            willingly part withal--except my life, except my life,
            except my life.

POLONIUS   Fare you well my lord.

HAMLET   These tedious old fools

                    Enter Rosencrantz and Guildenstern.

FACING R, POINTING BACK OVER HIS HEAD

LINE TO POL ● POL EXITS UR VIA ABOVE THEM ● ROS AND GUI X TOWARD
HAMLET

STOPPING AT Y4 12:00 ROS STOPS ABOVE HIM

XING ON STOPPING ½ 1:00

PAUSE THEN HAMLET TURNS TO FACE THEM ● XES DELIGHTEDLY UP TO THEM
SHAKES HANDS, THEY AD LIB RESPONSES

PAT GUI ON SHOULDER AND XES TOWARD BENCH ● GUI XES AT HIS R, ROS
BEHIND GUI

XING ON TO PLAT

TURNING BACK TO THEM, SITTING C ON BENCH

X IN 2 TO BEFORE BENCH PLATFORM ON 9:00 LINE ● GUI IS UL OF
PLATFORM

State

51

POLONIUS   You go to seek the Lord Hamlet, there he is.

ROS$NCRANTZ God save you sir.

(Exit Polonius.

GUILDENSTERN My hornoured lord.

ROSENCRANTZ My most dear lord.

HAMLET   My excellent good friends. How dost thou Guildenstern?

Ah Rosencrantz. Good lads how do ye both?

ROSENCRANTZ As the indifferent children of the earth.

Guildenstern Happy, in that we are not overhappy.

Oh Fortune's cap we are not the very button.

HAMLET   Nor the soles of her shoe?

ROSENCRANTZ Neither my lord.

HAMLET   Then you live about her waist, or in the middle of her

favours?

Guildenstern Faith her privates we.

HAMLET   In the secret parts of Fortune? O most true, she is

a strumpet. What news?

Rosencrantz   None my lord, but that the world's grown honest.

HAMEET   Then is doomsday near--but your news is not true. Let

Me question more in particular. What have you, my good

friends, deserved at the hands of Fortune, that she sends

you to prison hither?

GUILDENSTERN Prison my lord?

HAMLET   Denmark's a prison.

ROSENCRANTZ Then is the world one.

HAMLET   A goodly one, in which there are many confines, wards,

and dungeons, Denmark being one o' th' worst.

ROSENCRANTZ   We think not so my lord.

XES AROUND TO END OF DS BENCH, SITS ON IT WITH LEGS OFF-STAGE, FACING HAMLET.

X IN 1, ONTO PLAT

HAMLET RISES XES TO 3/4 12:00 ROS, RISES AND ROS AND GUI X AFTER HIM. ROS VIA L OF TROL

KING AFTER- ROS TO DL OF TROLLEY, GUI TO 3/4 11:00

TURNING FROM 3/4 12:00, ROS IS L OF TROL, GUI AT 3/4 11:00

TURNS TO START X OUT THEN TURNS BACK TO THEM

52

HAMLET   Why then 'tis none to you; for there is nothing either

             godd or bad but thinking makes it so. To me it is a

             prison.

Rosencrantz Why then your ambition makes it one; 'tis too narrow

             for your mind.

HAMLET   O God, I could be bounded in a nutshell, and count

             myself a king of infinite space, were it not that I have

             bad dreams.

GUILDENSTERN Which dreams indeed are amibition, for the very substance

             of the ambitious is merely the shadow of a dream.

HAMLET   A dream itself is but a shadow.

ROSENCRANTZ Truly, and I hold ambition of so airy and light a

             quality, that it is but a shamdow's shadow.

HAMLET   Then are our beggars bodies, and our monarchs and

             outstretched heroes the beggars' shadows. Shall we

             to th' Court for by fay I cannot reason?

ROSENCRANTZ &
GUILDENSTERN We*ll wait upon you.

HAMLET   No such matter. I will not sort you with the rest of my

             servants; for to speak to you like an honest man I am

             most dreadfully attended. But, in the beaten way of

             friendship, what make you at Elsinore?

ROSENCRANTZ To visit you my lord, no other occasion.

HAMLET   Beggar that I am, I am even poor in thanks, but I thank

             you; and sure, dear friends, my thanks are too dear a

             halfpenny. Were you not sent for? Is it your own

             inclining? Is it a free visitation? Come, deal justly

             with me. Come, come -- nay, speak.

KING TO GUI, R HAND TO SHOULDER, THEY X TOWARD PLAT. GUI SLIGHTLY
IN ADVANCE, NOT LOOKING AT HAMLET, AT SAME TIME ROS XES ← TROL
TO FOLLOW THEM, HAMLET X TO 3/4 9'00

GUI TURNS BACK TO FACE HAMLET FROM C OF BENCH · HAMLET IS
ABOVE HIM BY BENCH

AT R OF TROL

KING TO ROS,

TURNS XES TO GUI, UL OF HIM GUI ⊗ ⊘HT

XING IN TO 3/4 8'00 ● GUI SITS

HAMLET X US 2 LOOKING OFF UR, THEN TURN BACK THEN X TO SIT
ROS X TO 1/2 9'00

SIT US ON BENCH,

ROS AND GU EXCHANGE GLANCE,

RISES, FACING ROS

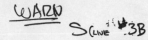

53

GUILDENSTERN   What should we say my lord?

HAMLET   Why, anything but to th' purpose. You were sent for, x
                and there is a kind of confession in your looks, which
                your modesties have not craft enough to color. I know
                the good King and Queen have sent for you.

ROSENCRANTZ   To what end my lord?

HAMLET   That you must teach me. But let me conjure you, by the
                rights of our fellowship, by the consonancy of our youth,
                by the obligation of our ever-preserved love, and by what
                more dear a better proposer can charge you withal, be even
                and direct with me, whether you were sent for or no.

ROSENCRANTZ (aside to Guildenstern)
                What say you?

HAMLET(aside) Nay then I have an eye on you. -- If you love me, hold
                not off.

GUILDENSTERN   My lord, we were sent for.

HAMLET   I will tell you why; so shall my anticipation prevent
                your discovery, and your secrecy to the King and Queen
                moult no feather. I have of late, but wherefore I know
                not, lost all my mirth, forgone all custom of exercises;
                and indeed it goes so heavily with my disposition, that
                this goodly frame the earth, seems to me a sterile
                promontory, this most excellent canopy the air, look
                you, this brave o'erhanging firmament, this majestical r
                roof fretted with golden fire, why, it appeareth
                nothing to me but a foul and pestilent congregation
                of vapours. What a piece of work is a man, how noble
                in reason, how infinite in faculties, in form and

X DS TO 3/4 7:45

TURN BACK TO THEM CW

RISING

XING L TO 4:00

HAMLET STOPS 3/4 4:00   TURNS BACK TO THEM

TURNING STARTING OUT DL AGAIN JUST AS POL ENTERS TUN L

ENTERING DL ● HAMLET XES DOWN TAKES ROS & GUI TO 7:00. ARM ON SHOULDERS
POL XES TO UR DOOR TAPS WITH CANE XES BACK TO TROLLEY. WOODY OPENS UR
DOOR, POL SIGNALS THAT TROLLEY SHOULD BE REMOVED, WOODY
STRIKES IT OUT UR.

54

HAMLET   moving, how express and admirable in action, how like an

angel in apprehension, how like a god—the beauty of the

world; the paragon of animals; and yet to me, what

is this quintessence of dust? Man delights not me, no

nor woman neither, though by your smiling you seem to

say so.

ROSENCRANTZ   My lord, there was no such stuff in my thoughts.

HAMLET   Why did ye laugh then, when I said man delights not me?

ROSENCRANTZ   To think, my lord, if you delight not in man, what

lenten entertainment the players shall receive from

you. \We coted them on the way, and hither are they

coming to offer you service.
HAMLET   He that plays the king shall be welcome. His majesty shall have tribute of me   S*3B

(Enter players)

Flourish of trumpets within)

GUILDENSTERN   There are the players.

HAMLET   Gentlemen, you are welcome to Elsinore. ~~Your hands.~~

~~Come them th' appurtenance of welcome is fashion and~~

~~ceremony; let me comply with you in this garb; lest my~~

~~extent to the players, which I tell you must show~~

~~fairly outwards, should more appear like entertainment~~

~~than yours.~~ You are welcome; but my uncle-father, and

aunt-mother, are deceived.

GUILDENSTERN   In what my dear lord?

HAMLET   I am but mad north-north-west; when the wind is

southerly, I know a hawk from a handsaw

Enter Polonius

POLONIUS   Well be with you, gentlemen

HAMLET   Hark you Guildenstern, and you too, at each ear a

ALOUD, FOR POL'S BENEFIT

  XING DOWN TO ½ 6:00

  TURN TO ROS AND GUI

ENTHUSIASTICALLY, 'THAT'S JUST WHAT I'VE COME TO TELL YOU ABOUT'

  GUI AND ROS TURN AWAY 'BREAKING UP', HAMLET XES TO PLATFORM, ROS XES
  ↳ GUI LAUGHING

POL XES PLAYFULLY TO ROS AND GUI ABOVE THEM AT 7:00. POL CLOWNING
GUI AND ROS LAUGHING AT HIM

PLAYERS START IN TUN L, FIRST P KING, THEN P QUEEN THEN RPS THEN PRO AND LUC
THEN OTHERS PER DIAGRAM.

INDICATING DL AS P KING XES UP STEPS REMOVING GLOVE AD LIBBING "MY LORD" HAMLET
XES TO SHAKE WITH HIM AT ½ 4:00

55

HAMLET   a hearer--that great baby you see there is not yet out
of his swaddling-clouts. ^{hit door}

ROSENCRANTZ   Happily he is the second time come to them, for they say
an old man is twice a child.

HAMLET   I will prophesy, he comes to tell me of the players;
mark it. You say right sir, a Monday morning, 'twas
then indeed.

POLONIUS   My lord, I have news to t411 you.

HAMLET   My lord, I have news to tell you. When Roscius was an
actor in Rome--

POLONIUS   The actors are come hither my lord.

HAMLET   Buz, buz!

POLONIUS   ~~Upon my honour---~~

HAMLET   ~~Then came each actor on his ass--~~

POLONIUS   The best actors in the world, either for tragedy, comedy,
history, pastoral, pastoral-comical, historical-pastoral,
tragical-histornal, tragical-comical-historical-pastoral,
scene individable, or poem unlimited. Senecal cannot be
too heavy nor Plautus too light, for the law of writ and
the liberty. These are the only men.

~~HAMLET O Jephtha, judge of Israel, what a treasure hadst thou!~~

~~POLONIUS What a treasure had he my lord?~~

~~HAMLET Why~~
~~One fair daughter, and nor more.~~
~~The which he loved passing well.~~

~~POLONIUS (aside) Still on my daughter.~~

~~HAMLET Am I not i' th' right old Jephtha?~~

~~POLONIUS If you call me Jephtha my lord, I have a daughter that~~
~~I love passing well.~~

KING TO PLAY K AT ½ 4'. TAKING PLAY Q HAND SHE CURTSIES, THEN HOLDS AT
½ 4:00

KING TO RP'S, SHAKES HANDS WITH #1, ● KING TO SHAKE HANDS WITH PLAY K

KING TO LUC AND PRO CLAPPING THEM ON SHOULDERS

TURNING BACK TO FACE PLAY K

XES TO PLAY K. PRO AND LUC PUT DOWN BAGS. PRO XES DOWN TO 4 AND 3
AT 4:00. QUEEN XES UP TO BELOW CASES. LUC STANDS UL OF THEM, BAGS ARE
SET AT ½ 3:00. POL XES UP TO C PLAT. GUI BELOW BENCH ON 3. ROS XES TO 4:30
ON 1 + 2

KING DS TURN BACK AT 3/4 5:00

56

HAMLET ~~Nay that follows not.~~

POLONIUS ~~What follows then my lord?~~

HAMLET ~~Why~~

~~As by lot, God wot,~~

~~and then you know~~

~~It came to pass, as most like it was~~

~~the first row of the pious chanson will show you more,~~

~~for look where my abridgement comes.~~

Enter Players

You are welcome masters, welcome all, I am glad to see
thee well. Welcome good friends. O my old friend,
why thy face is valanced since I saw thee last; com's.
thou to beard me in Denmark? ~~What, my young lady and~~
~~mistress; by'r Lady your ladyship is nearer to heaven~~
~~than when I saw you last by the altitude of a chopine.~~
~~Pray God your voice like a piece of uncurrent gold~~
~~be not cracked within the ring.~~ Masters, you are all
welcome. We'll e'en to't like French falconers, fly at
any thing we see. We'll have a speech straight; come give
us a taste of your quality; come, a passionate speech.

FIRST PLAYER What speech my good lord?

HAMLET I heard thee speack me a speech once, but it was never
acted, or if it was, not above once, for the play I
remembered pleased not the million, 'twas caviare to the
general; but it was, as I received it, and others, whose
judgements in such matters cried in the top of mine, an
excellent play, well digested in the scenes, set down
with as much modesty as cunning. ~~I remember one said there~~

X TO PLAYER KING, TO L OF HIM

PLAY QUEEN EXCLAIMS DELIGHTEDLY

HAMLET XES DS TO 7:00. PLAY Q XES TO PLAY K WHISPERS THEN RETURNS TO PLACE
HAMLET TURNS TO FACE DS

TURNING BACK TO PLAY K

HAMLET DRIES UP · COMPANY AS ONE WHISPERS THE PROMPT. HAMLET TAKES IT AND CONTINUES
XING BACK UP VIA R OF PLAY K. RP#2 POINTS OUT BLACK ON COSTUME BY WAY OF
PROMPT
        XING ⌐ PLAY K AND L TOWARD LUC

HAMLET DRIES, LUC HELPFULLY MOVES HIS HANDS TO CHEEKS, HAMLET GETS IT, SAYS THE
WORD, LAUGHS THEN CONTINUES. HAMLET XES DOWN TO 5:00. FRAN XES IN AD LIBS TO
#2 AND THEY X TO WATCH FROM 3 ABOVE BENCH, FRAN US

                    ½ 6:00
XING WITH MANY STOPS TO 8:00, PROCLAIMING LINES AND SAWING THE AIR.

WARM APPLAUSE LED BY POL, HAMLET ENDS AT 8:00
XES TO R OF PLAY K ● XES TO SIT ON C BENCH. PLAY K XES TO PLAY Q' WHO
SITS ON DS CASE, GIVES HER OVERCOAT AND STICK. RP#1 & #2 X TO SIT ON US CASES
PLAY Q HOLDS BOOK DURING FOLLOWING. PRO SITS ON 4

    SITS ON DS BENCH. PLAY K XES TO C, STARTS FACING DS

57

HAMLET ~~were no sallets in the lines, to make the matter savoury,~~
~~nor no matter in the phrase that might indict the author~~
~~of affection, but called it an honest method, as whole-~~
~~some as sweet, and by very much more handsome than fine.~~
One speech in't I chiefly loved, 'twas Aeneas' tale to
Dido, and thereabout of it especially where he speaks
of Priam's slaughter. If it live in your memory, begin
at this line--let me see, let me see--

PLAYER   No, no   The rugged Pyrrhus like th' Hyrcanian beast.
'tis not so, it begins with pyrrhus--
         PLAYERS' "He whose -
The rugged Pyrrhus he whose sable arms,
Black as his purpose, did the night resemble,
When he lay couched in the ominous horse,
Hath now this dread and black complexion smeared
With heraldry more dismal; head to foot
Now is he total gules, horridly tricked
With blood of fathers, mothers, daughters, sons,
Baked and impasted with the parching streets,
That lend a tyrannous and a damned light
To their lord's murder. Roasted in wrath and
fire,
And thus o'er sized with coagulate gore,
With eyes like carbuncles, the hellish Pyrrhus
Old grandsire Priam seeks--

So proceed you.

POLONIUS   "Fore God my lord, well spoken, with good accent
and good discretion

FIRST PLAYER   anon he finds him
Striking too short at Greeks, his antique sword,

TURNING IN CIRCLE ↻

HAMLET REACTS ● DRAWING IMAGINARY SWORD UP OVER HEAD

ARMS RAISED ABOVE HEAD

XING DOWN TOWARD ROS

TURNING TOWARD HAMLET

XING TOWARD HAMLET, TO ½ 9:00, HAMLET STARTS ON 'VENGEANCE'.

TURNING ↻ TO FACE DS

COCKING L ARM ACROSS BODY. THEN POINTING OUT L TUN

58

FIRST PLAYER   Rebellious to his arm, lies where it falls,

Repugnant to command; unequal matched,

Pyrrhus at Priam drives, in rage strikes wide,

But with the whiff and wind of his fell sword

Th' unnerved father falls. Then senseless Ilium,

Seeming to feel this blow, with flaming top

Stoops to his base; and with a hideous crash

Takes prisoner Pyrrhus' ear; for lo his sword,

Which was declining on the milky head

Of reverend Priam, seemed i' th' air to stick;

So as a painted tyrant Pyrrhus stood,

And like a neutral to his will and matter,

Did nothing.

But as we often see against some storm

A silence in the heavens, the rack stand still,

The bold winds speechless, and the orb below

As hush as death, anon the dreadful thunder

Doth rend the region; so after pyrrhus' pause,

A roused vengeance sets him new awork,

And never did the Cyclops' hammers fall

On Mars's armour, forged for proof eterne,

With less remorse than Pyrrhus' bleeding sword

Now falls on Priam.

Out, out, thou strumpet Fortune! All you gods.

In general synod take away her power,

Break all the spokes and fellies from her wheel,

And bowl the round nave down the hill of heaven,

As low as to the fiends.

HAMLET GIVES QUICK SHH TO POL · PLAY Q GASPS · PLAY K SHOOTS POL A DIRTY LOOK AND XES
TO 3:00 ON 3. ALL PLAYERS X TO HIM. AD LIB BEGGING HIM TO GO ON. HE SULKS

RISING KING TO PLAY K LIVE TO POL AS HE XES ● AT ROF PK ON 4, HAND ON HIS
SHOULDER

PLAY·K RELENTS, HAMLET LEADS HIM TO C, XES TO HAND 3 AT 7:00
PLAYERS RETURN TO PLACES. ONLY CHANGE RP #2 NOW STANDS.
BEGINNING AFTER GLOWERING AT POL

BARKING FIRST PHRASE AT POL TO QUELL FURTHER INTERUPTION

PIVOTING CW AND REACHING AROUND END FACING DS ATC. HANDS
CROSSED OVER LOINS AS IT HOLDING BLANKET.

HAMLET XES SLOWLY UP TO 3/4 9:00 WATCHING PLAY K

KING TO ½ 6:00

XES 3 AT 4:30   ROS GIVES DS ● A PAUSE AS POL XES ↳ TO O BELOW PK

HAMLET XES TO L OF PLAY K. POL STARTS ↖ TO 4

TURNING TO FACE POL WHO STOPS AT 6:00 ON 2 ● PRO RISES
                    POL X → 7:00 WS

XING OUT O 4

59

POLONIUS   This is too long.

HAMLET   It shall to the barber's with your beard—prithee say on— *FIRST PLAYER: NO*

he's for a jig, or a tale of bawdry, or he sleeps—— *FIRST PLAYER: NO*

say on, come to Hecuba.

RST PLAYER   But who, o who, had seen the mobled queen---

HAMLET   The mobled queen?

POLONIUS   That's godd, mobled queen is good.

IRST PLAYER   Run barefoot up and down, threat'ning the flames

        With bisson rheum, a clout upon that head

        Where late the diadem stood, and for a robe,

        About her lank and all o'er-teemed loins,

        A blanket in the alarm for fear caught up--

        Who this had seen, with tongue in venom steeped,

        'Gainst Fortune's state would-treason have pronounced;

        But if the Gods themselves did see her then,

        When she saw Pyrrhus make malicious sport

        In mincing with his sword her husband's limbs,

        The instant burst of clamour that she made,

        Unless things mortal move them not at all,

        Would have made milch the burning eyes of heaven,

        And passion in the gods.

POLONIUS   Look whe'r he has not turned his colour, and his tears

        in's eyes--prithee no more.

HAMLET   'Tis well, I'll have thee speak out the rest of this soon.

        Good my lord, will you see the players well bestowed?

        Do youhear, let them be well used, for they are the

        abstract and brief chronicles of the time; after your

        death you were better have a bad epitaph than their ill

XING ONTO 3

XING TO UL OF POL

PRO LAUGH, PLAY K SILENCES HIM.

XING ONTO 4 AND TOWARD UR ● SEATED PLAYERS RISE

 PLAY K XES TO GET COAT AND CANE, OTHER PLAYERS START TO EXIT UR
 ● HAMLET XES OVER TO R OF PLAY K. GUI XES ↳ ON 3 TO ROS AT 3:30

   TAKING PLAY K L ARM THEY X DOWN TO 7:00 ON 3

 PLAY K XES ONTO 4 AND STARTS US. HAMLET STOPS HIM AT ½ 9:00 FOR
 REST OF LINE ● PLAY K BOWS GIVING HAMLET THE SLIGHTEST OF WINKS TURNS XES OUT UR

   HAMLET XES IN TO C   ● ALL REMAINING COURTIERS X IN
   TOWARD HIM

 ALL OUT NEAREST EXIT

 TURNING AROUND TO FACE DS

 XING TO CROTCH

 TURNING BACK TO LOOK ON STAGE

60

WARN ⌐ #9

HAMLET	report while you live.
POLONIUS	My lord, I will use them according to their desert.
HAMLET	God's bodkin man, much better. Use every man after his desert, and who shall 'scape whipping? Use them after your own honour and dignity; the less they deserve, the more merit is in your bounty. Take them in.
POLONIUS	Come sirs.
HAMLET	Follow him friends, we'll hear a play to-morrow.

(Exeunt Polonius and other players)

HAMLET(T First Player)

Dost thou hear me old friend, can you play the Murder of Gonzago?

FIRST PLAYER	Ay my lord.
HAMLET	We'll ha't to-morrow night. You could for need study a speech of some dozen or sixteen lines, which I would set down and insert in't, could you not?
FIRST PLAYER	Ay my lord.
HAMLET	Very well. Follow that lord, and look you mock him not.

(Exit First Player.

My good friends, I'll leave you till night. You are welcome to Elsinore.

ROSENCRANTZ	Good my lord.

soldiers turn to exit

(Exeunt Rosencrantz and Guildenstern.

HAMLET	Ay so God buy to you. Now I am alone.

O what a rogue and peasant slave am I!

Is it not monstrous that this player here
But in a fiction, in a dream of passion,
Could force his soul to his own conceit, ↓

SITTING US BENCH

XING TO C

XING C SLOWLY TO DR POLE

61

HAMLET   That from her working all his visage wanned;

Tears in his eyes, distraction in his aspect,

A broken voice, and his whole function suiting

With forms to his conceit? and all for nothing?

For Hecuba!

What's Hecuba to him, or he to Hecuba,

That he should weep for her? What should he do,

Had he the motive and the cue for passion

That I have? He would drown the stage with tears,

And cleave the general ear with horrid speech,

Made mad the guilty, and appal the free,

Confound the ignorant, and amaze indeed

The very faculties of eyes and ears; yet I,

A dull and muddy-mettled rascal, peak

Like John-a-dreams, unpregnant of my cause,

And can say nothing; no, not for a King,

Upon whose property and most dear life

A damned defeat was made. Am I a coward?

Who calls me villain, breaks my pate across,

Plucks off my beard, and blows it in my face,

Tweaks me by the nose, gives me the lie i' th' throat,

As deep as to the lungs—who does me this ha?

'Swounds, I should take it; for it cannot be

But I am pigeon-livered, and lack gall

To make oppression bitter, or ere this

I should ha' fatted all the region kites

With this slave's offal. Bloody, bawdy, villain,

Remorseless, treacherous, lecherous, kindless villain!

WARN

L#9A, 9B

9C, HOUSE,

L#10

RED LITES ON

GRASPING DR POLE, STANDING 12 OF IT.

XING ↓ TO ABOVE C

TURNS SEES CASES LEFT BY PLAYERS, STARTS TO X SLOWLY AROUND THEM

STOPPING DL OF CASES

XES ON~ STOPS DR OF CASES

XES TO 6:00 ON 3, SITS ON 4, LOOKING DR HIGH

RISES XES SLOWLY UP TO ½ 9:00

POINTING AT CASES

TURNS YES OUT UR

62

HAMLET   O vengeance!

Why, what an ass am I, This is most brave,

That I, the son of a dear father murdered,

Prompted to my revenge by heaven and hell,

Must like a whore unpack my heart with words,

And fall a-cursing like a very drab,

A scullion!

HAMLET x DS   L 9A

Fie upon't, foh! About, my brains. Hum, I have heard

That guilty creatures sitting at a play

Have by the very cunning of the scene

Been struck so to the soul, that presently

They have proclaimed their malefactions.

For murder, though it have no tongue, will speak

With most miraculous organ. I'll have these players

Play something like the murder of my father

Before mine uncle; I'll observe his looks.

I'll tent him to the quick; if 'a do blench,

I know my course. The spirit that I have seen

May be a devil, and the devil hath power

T' assume a pleasing shape; yea, and perhaps,

Out of my weakness and my melancholy,

As he is very potent with such spirits,

HAMLET RISES   L 9B

Abuses me to damn me. I*ll have grounds

More relative than this—the play's the thing.

Wherein I'll catch the conscience of the King.   L #9C

                                        (Exit.

INTERMISSION   COUNT 5   HOUSE, L#10

                      HOUSE UP   RED LITES OFF

Check List

chair in above
stand in above
R above door closed
L above door opened
All other doors except Andrei closed.
Skene set
Curtains in below closed

STARTERS READY
MUSICIANS READY

WARN

HOUSE
L #11

M# 4c

SLING AND GUARDS ENT UR PER DIAGRAM

QUEEN, INDIGNANT ENTERS UR FIRST XES DOWN AND ⌣ TO 7:00, STOP BRIEFLY THEN
UP TO ½ 10:00 KING ENTERS NEXT BACKING PROTESTING ROS AND GUI BEFORE
HIM HIM. ROS BACKS STAGE R OF GUI. KING STARTS SPEAKING AT
11:00. EVERYTHNG IS FAST AND ANGRY. FOLLOWING THEM POL ENTERS WITH
OPHELIA. TAKES HER TO DR POST, STAND R OF HER.

XING THRU ROS AND GUI WHO HAVE BACKED ASIDE FROM HIS PATH
TURNING BACK TO FACE THEM AT ¾ B 30. ROS AT ½ 6:00. GUI AT ½ 3:00

KING SNORTS XES TO CROTCH, SITS

XING AFTER KING ½ 10', ROS XES TO '8:00

KING SITS C ON BENCH

XING FROM ½ 10:00 IN A FEW TOWARDS THEM

XING TOWARD HER, TO ½ 8:00

LINE TO KING XING TO DL OF PLAT

XING TO 10:00

ALL LOOK TO KING APPREHENSIVELY WAITING FOR THE STORM TO BURST
GUI X IN ONE

actors ready HOUSE

ACT THREE SCENE ONE (7) Elsinore, The Castle. Enter Claudius,
                        Gertrude, Polonius, Ophelia, Rosencrantz,
                        and Guildenstern.

CLAUDIUS - And can you, by no drift of conference, house out L#11m

          Get from him why he puts on this confusion,

          Grating so harshly all his days of quiet

          With turbulent and dangerous lunacy?

ROSENCRANTZ He does confess he feels himself distracted,

          But from what cause 'a will by no means speak.

GUILDENSTERN Nor do we find him forward to be sounded,

          But with a crafty madness keeps aloof,

          When we would bring him on to some confession

          Of his true state.

GERTRUDE Did he receive you well?

ROSENCRANTZ Most like a gentleman.

GUILDENSTERN But with much forcing of his disposition.

ROSENCRANTZ Niggard of question, but of our demands

          Most free in his reply.

GERTRUDE Did you assay him

          To any pastime?

ROSENCRANTZ Madam, it so fell out that certain players

          We o'er-raught on the way; of these we told him.

          And there did seem in him a kind of joy

          To hear of it. They are about the Court,

          And as I think they have already order

          This night to play before him.

POLONIUS 'Tis most true,

          And he beseeched me to entreat your Majesties

          To hear and see the matter.

RISING QUICKLY, THEY START. BUT HE SPEAKS QUIETLY, THEY RELAX ● QN X TO 3/4 4

← XING TO   3/4 7:00 ROS X TO L OF GUI

QUEEN TURNS XES AWAY TO 1/2 4:00 . POL XES DOWN ONTO 3 AT 10:00

BOTH X US ON STAGE OF KING BOWING TO BOTH KING AND QUEEN AS THEY
X UP : EXIT UR

XING TO QUEEN , MEET 1/2 7:00

SNAPS FINGERS IMPATIENTLY TRYING TO REMEMBER NAME THEN GETS IT ● XING
WITH QUEEN TO 8:00 / ↙ ON

        XING US TO FACE OPH FROM R OF HER · KING XES TO 3:00
    TURNS ON STAGE

    ─⊕─ QUEEN

NYM ─⊕─   ─⊕─ SLING ↑
    ─⊕─ MAR
FRAN ─⊕─ ─⊕─ BAR ↑
    EXIT OF QUEEN

        OPH CURTSEYS · QUEEN TURNS AND EXITS UR   SOLDIERS CLICK AS SHE
        PASSES . MAR PUSHES DOORS OPEN FOR QUEEN.
        SIGNALS SOLDIERS OUT UR. THEY WHEEL AND EXIT
        XING TO OPH INDICATING DR ● OPH XES VIA L OF HIM TO 1/2 8:00 · ● CONTINUE
        X TO 1/2 12:00
                        ●TURNING TO OPH WHO STOPS AT 3/4 9:00
        XES BACK TOWARD POL

        TURNING TO KING

64

CLAUDIUS　　With all my heart, and it doth much content me
　　　　　　　　To hear him so inclined..
　　　　　　　　Good gentlemen give him a further edge,
　　　　　　　　And drive his purpose into these delights.
ROSENCRANTZ　　We shall my lord.

　　　　　　　　　　　　　　　(Exeunt Rosencrantz and Guildenstern.

CLAUDIUS　　Sweet Gertrude leave us too
　　　　　　　　For we have closely sent for Hamlet hither,
　　　　　　　　That he, as 'twere by accident, may here
　　　　　　　　Affront Ophelia.
　　　　　　　　Her father and myself, lawful espials,
　　　　　　　　Will so bestow ourselves, that seeing, unseen,
　　　　　　　　We may of their encounter frankly judge,
　　　　　　　　And gather by him as he is behaved,
　　　　　　　　If't be th' affliction of his love or no
　　　　　　　　That thus he suffers for.
GERTRUDE　　I shall obey you.
　　　　　　　　And for your part Ophelia, I do wish
　　　　　　　　That your godd beauties be the happy cause
　　　　　　　　Of Hamlet's wildness; so shall I hope your virtues
　　　　　　　　Will bring him to his wonted way again,
　　　　　　　　To both your honours.
OPHELIA　　Madam, I wish it may
　　　　　　　　　　　　　　　(Exit Gertrude.
POLONIUS　　Ophelia, walk you here. --Gracious, so please you,
　　　　　　　　We will bestow ourselves. -- Read on this book,
　　　　　　　　That show of such an exercise may colour
　　　　　　　　Your loneliness. We are oft to blame in this;

THROWS PRAYER BOOK TO OPHELIA • OPH XES WITH IT OUT. TUN R.

(X INTO BELOW L OUT L DOOR

LOOKING DS AT 2:00

XING OUT OF L BEL . HAMLET ENT AND DOOR• KING XES INTO BEL VIA DS OF POL WHO HOLDS CURTAIN OPEN FOR HIM. AFTER KING PASSES POL FOLLOWS HIM INTO BEL

HAMLET XES IN SLOWLY TO ½ 3:00 FACING DL SPEAKS AT ½ 10:00

65

POLONIUS   'Tis too much proved, that with devotion's visage

                And pious action we do sugar o'er

                The devil himself.

CLAUDIUS(aside) O 'tis too true.

                How smart a lash that speech doth give my conscience.

                The harlot's cheek, beautied with plast'ring art,

                Is not more ungly to the thing that helps it

                Than is my deed to my most painted word.

                O heavy burden!

POLONIUS   I hear him coming, let's withdraw my lord.

                                (Exeunt Claudius & Polonius.

                Enter Hamlet.

HAMLET   To be, or not to be, that is the question--

                Whether 'tis nobler in the mind to suffer

                The slings and arrows of outrageous fortune,

                Or to take arms against a sea of troubles,

                And by opposing end them. To die, to sleep--

                No more; and by a sleep to say we end

                The heart-ache, and the thousand natural shocks

                That flesh is heir to; 'tis a consummation

                Devoutly to be wished. To die, to sleep---

                To sleep, perchance to dream, ay there's the rub,

                For in that sleep of death what dreams may come

                When we have shuffled off this mortal coil,

                Must give us pause; there's the respect

                That makes calamity of so long life.

                For who would bear the whips and scorns of time,

OPH STARTS IN TUN R

    OPH ENTERS TUN R READING, XING SLOWLY, TURNS TO R AT O
    HAMLET XES SLOWLY TO $\frac{3}{4}$ 8:00. OPH STOPS AT 8:00 ON O

    XING ONTO 3 HAND EXTENDED, HAVING REMOVED BRACELET
    BACKS THEN TURNS TO FACE L AT $\frac{1}{2}$ 7:30

HAMLET Th' oppressor's wrong, the proud man's contumely,

The pangs of despised love, the law's delay,

The insolence of office, and the spurns

That patient merit of th' unworthy takes,

When he himself might his quietus make

With a bare bodkin? Who would fardels bear,

To grunt and sweat under a weary life,

But that the dread of something after death,

The undiscovered country, from whose bourn

No traveler returns, puzzles the will,

And makes us rather bear those ills we have,

Than fly to others that we know not of?

Thus conscience does make cowards of us all,

And thus the native hue of resolution

Is sicklied o'er with the pale cast of thought,

And enterprises of great pitch and moment

With this regard their currents turn awry,

And lose the name of action. Soft you now,

The fair Ophelia. --Nymph, in thy orisons

Be all my sins remembered.

OPHELIA Good my lord,

How does your honour for this many a day?

HAMLET I humbly thank you, well, well, well.

OPHELIA My lord, I have remembrances of yours

That I have longed long to re-deliver.

I pray you now receive them.

HAMLET No, not I, I never gave you aught.

STEPPING UP TO 4 · KING UP TO ½ 9'.00 FACING DOWN TO HAMLET FROM U/R
OF HIM   L HAND EXTENDED·

CURVING UP TO ¾ 15'.00   AND TURNING BACK TO HER
OPH COUNTERS SLIGHTLY

POL HAND SEEN OPENING SPLIT IN L BEL CURTAINS

TURNING AWAY TO FACE L

KING TO BENCH, SITS DOWN STAGE ON IT FACING DL

KING TO STAND BEFORE HER TAKES HEAD IN HIS HANDS SHE BURIES
HER FACE AGAINST HIM WITH A SOB, HUGGING HIM AROUND THE WAIST
THEN HE TAKES HER FACE IN HIS HANDS KNEELING BEFORE HER.

67

OPHELIA   My honoured lord. You know right well you did,
           And with them words of so sweet breath composed
           As made the things more rich. Their perfume lost,
           Take these again, for to the noble mind
           Rich gifts wax poor when givers prove unkind,
           There my lord.

HAMLET   Ha, ha, are you honest?

OPHELIA   My lord!

HAMLET   Are you fair?

OPHELIA   What means your lordship?

HAMLET   That if you be honest and fair, your honesty should
           admit no discourse to your beauty.

OPHELIA   Could beauty, my lord, have better commerce than with
           honesty?

HAMLET   Ay truly, for the power of beauty will sooner transform
           honesty from what it is to a bawd, than the force of
           honesty can translate beauty into his likeness. This
           was sometimes a paradox, but now the time gives it
           proof. I did love you once

OPHELIA   Indeed my lord you made me believe so.

HAMLET   You should not have believed me, for virtue cannot so
           inoculate our old stock, but we shall relish of it.
           I loved you not.

OPHELIA   I was the more deceived.

HAMLET   Get thee to a nunnery, why wouldst thou be a breeder
           of sinners? I am myself indifferent honest, but yet
           I could accuse me of such things that it were better

TURNING CC' AND XING AWAY FROM OPH. STOPS JUST OFF EDGE OF BENCH
PLATFORM, OPH KEEPS HOLDING ONTO HIS R HAND, WHEN HE STOPS SHE LETS
IT GO, RISES. AS HE TURNS POL'S HAND DISAPPEARS FROM BETWEEN R SECTION
OF CURTAINS

XING US AND ⌐ TO 11:00 AS IF TO EXIT

STARTING OUT UR

IN PLACE

STOPPING AT TOP OF EAR, ...

X BACK TO FACE OPH AT 3/4 10:00
OPH RUN TO HIM ARMS UP. HE GRABS HER WRISTS AND HURLS HER
TO 1/2 4:00

XING QUICKLY UR

XING TO 1/2 6:00

IXING. QUICKLY BACK TO FACE HER FROM C. SHE COUNTERS INTO
CROTCH

OPH RISES XES TOWARD HIM

XING UP 11:00, STOPS

RUNS TO R BELOW

THROWING OPEN R BEL CURTAINS

XING OUT OF BEL R ● EXITS AND DOOR

68

HAMLET   my mother had not borne me. I am very proud,
revengeful, ambitious, with more offences at my beck,
than I have thoughts to put them in, imagination to
give them shape, or time to act them in. What should
such fellows as I do crawling between earth and heaven?
We are arrant knaves all, believe none of us. Go thy
ways to a nunnery. Where's your father?

OPHELIA   At home my lord.

HAMLET   Let the doors be shut upon him, that he may play the
fool no where but in's own house. Farewell.

OPHELIA   O help him, you sweet heavens.

HAMLET   If thou dost marry, I'll give thee this plague for thy
dowry be thou as chaste as ice, as pure as snow, thou
shalt not escape calumny. Get thee to a nunnery; go,
farewell. Or if thou wilt needs marry, marry a fool,
for wise men know well enough what monsters you make
of them. To a nunnery go, and quickly too. Farewell.

OPHELIA   O heavenly powers, restore him.

HAMLET   I have heard of your paintings too well enough. God
hath given you one face, and you make yourselves
another; you jig and amble, and you lisp, you nickname
God's creatures, and make your wantonness your ignorance.   OPHELIA: My Lord.
Go to, I'll no more on't; it hath made me mad. I say
we will have no more marriages. Those that are married
already, all but one shall live, the rest shall keep
as they are. To a nunnery go.
                          (Exit.

OPHELIA   O what a noble mind is here o'erthrown!

GOING TO ENGLAND = GOING FOR A RIDE

AT C PLAT LOOKING UR

LOOKING C

MOVING TO US BENCH
SINKING TO KNEES BEFORE US BENCH FACING US, HEAD IN HANDS ON SEAT

OUT OF R BEL TO 11:00 LOOKING OFF UR : POL HOLD AT R IN BEL
KING IS PLEASED, DERISIVE OF POL'S THEORY ● LOOKS BACK AT POL LAUGHS THEN
XES DOWN TO OPH

STOPPING R OF OPH PATTING HER HEAD ABSENTLY THEN XING ON ⌣ TO 4:00

(POL XES TO OPH STANDS DL OF HER
              to ḃu ou3

POL REACTS,

69

OPHELIA   The courtier's, soldier's,scholar's, eye, tongue, sword,

Th' expectancy and rose of the fair state,

The glass of fashion, and the mould of form,

Th' observed of all observers, quite, quite down.

And I of ladies most deject and wretched,

That sucked the honey of his musicked vows,

Now see that noble and most sovereign reason,

Like sweet bells jangled, out of tune and harsh;

That unmatched form and feature of blown youth

Blasted with ecstasy. O woe is me.

T' have seen what I have seen, see what I see.

      Enter Claudius and Polonius.

CLAULIUS   Love? His affections do not that way tend;

Nor what he spake, though it lacked form a little,

Was not like madness. There's something in his soul

O'er which his melancholy sits on brood;

And I do ~~doubt~~ fear the hatch and the disclose

Will be some danger; which for to prevent,

I have in quick determination

Thus set it down--he shall with speed to England,

(For the demand of our neglected tribute)

Haply the seas, and countries different,

With variable objects, shall expel

This something-settled matter in his heart,

Whereon his brains still beating puts him thus

From fashion of himself. What think you on't?

WARN

L #13

WAVING BACKHANDED WITH R HAND, DISMISSING OPH WITHOUT LOOKING AT HER.
OPH RISES STARTS US

OPH STOPS UL OF POL TURNS BACK GIVES HIM BOOK, KING XES UP TO 3:3
OPH EXITS UR, THEN POL XES TO C FOR NEXT LINE.

✓ POL XES OUT R BEL L DOOR

STARTING DELIBERATE CROSS. EXITS AUDREI DOOR AT END OF LINE. STARTS
SPEAKING AT C

ON WORD CUE—PLAY K TUNING UP VOICE WITH 2 "DO MI SOL DO'S". ENTERS THRU R BEL CURTAINS XES TO 3/4 10:30
HAS SCRIPT HOLDS UNTIL BANK IS SET THEN XES TO SIT ON L END OF IT, LEGS US. AT SAME TIME RP #1, THEN PRO EN
UR, FOLLOWED BY MOODY (CARRYING FOOT OF BANK) AND POSHEK (CARRYING HEAD). MOODY AND POSHEK SET BANK THEN 3
TURN L. #2 (FROM DR OF SKENE) AND PRO (FROM DL) HELP SPREAD GRASS MAT. #2 THEN SITS ON FLOOR DR OF S
COMBING OUT WIG ON BLOCK WITH WHICH SHE ENTERED. PRO TAKES OUT PROP SWORD XES DS TO SIT ON H AT 4:00 F
MT, AT SAME TIME LUC THEN RP #1 ENTER THRU L CURTAINS. LUC HAS PAPER AFTER PLAY K'S TUNE UP HE RECITES "THE C
RAVEN BELLOWS FOR REVENGE" 3 TIMES. XES DOWN TO 2:30. RP #1 HAS RECORDER XES TO 2:00 ON 3

(HAMLET ENTERS THRU R CURTAINS JUST IN TIME TO CUT LUC OFF AFTER HIS THIRD "CROAKING RAVEN"

(RP I AT 2:00 ON 3 PLAYS NOTE. PLAY Q ENTERS FROM CURTAINS FIXES MAT US OF BANK

(XING R A FEW IN SILENCE THEN TURNS BACK TO LUC LUC HAS BEEN SAWING

X UP TO FACE PK, PAT HIM ON SHOULDERS ● TURN BACK TO LUC

HAMLET XES DR TO 8:00 ~ LUC XES) TO ABOVE BANK PAYING HAMLET NO HEED. PLAY Q XES
↵ BANK TO SIT AT R, LEGS DS, SEWING ON PLAY K'S L SHOULDER

OPENING

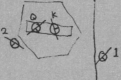

FOOTMEN ENTER TURN L, TO SET THRONES. DL
THEN EXIT UR. PRO IS FORCED TO RISE XES ~
TO 6:00 SITS ON H

70

POLONIUS   It shal do well. But yet do I believe,

The origin and commencement of his grief

Sprung from neglected love. -- How now Ophelia?

You need not tell us what Lord Hamlet said;

We heard it all -- My lord, do as you please,

But if you hold it fit, after the play,

Let his queen mother all alone entreat him

To show his grief; let her be round with him,

And I'll be placed, so please you, in the ear

Of all their conference, If she find him not,

To England send him; or confine him where

Your wisdom best shall think.

CLAUDIUS   It shall be so   L#13.

Madness in great ones must not unwatched go.

                                        (Exeunt.

(9) III, SCENE TWO

                    The same, Enter Hamlet and three Players.

HAMLET   Speak the speech I pray you as I pronounced it to you,

trippingly on the tongue; but if you mouth it as many

of our players do, I had as lief the town crier spoke THRONES

my lines. Nor do not saw the air too much with your

hand thus, but use all gently; for in the very torrent,

tempest, and as I may say, whirlwind of your passion,

you must acquire and beget a temperance that may give

it smoothness. O it offends me to the soul, to hear

a robustious periwig-pated fellow tear a passion to

tatters, to very rags, to split the ears of the

groundlings, who for the most part are capable of

nothing but inexplicable dumb shows and noise. I would

XES DL TO ASSIST IN THRONE SETTING. PRO IS FORCED TO MOVE
TO 6:00 SIT ON 4

HE IS ABOUT TO LAUNCH INTO DISCOURSE, STOPPED BY NUDGE FROM PLAY Q.

XING UP AGAIN TO DR OF SKENE, PLAY K TURNS TO FACE HAMLET; PLAY Q RISES SITS L OF HIM TO
CONTINUE WORK
(RP #1 PLAY PHRASE THEN SIT

  XES INTO SKENE, ABOVE #2, FOOT UP, LEANING ON BANK

   #1 SHAKES SPIT OUT OF RECORDER

  RP #1 RISES XES TO ABOVE BANK, PEERING NEAR SIGHTEDLY AT HAMLET

   SENSING THEIR ANTAGONISM, BACKING A LITTLE APOLIGETICALLY

MOODY THEN POSHEK ENTER UR. MOODY HAS ONE CHAIR, SET IT AT 10:00 ON 3. POSHEK
HAS 2 CHAIRS XES STRAIGHT DS SET THEM AT 7:00 ON 1. MOODY YES OUT UR, POSHEK
XES ↑ INO THEN OUT UR

X TO THRONES   , PLAY K AND Q REVERSE POSITIONS AGAIN TO ORIGINAL POSITIONS

  X TO PLAT

MOODY ENTER AND DOOR SET UR CHANDELIER

  PLAY K AND Q CHANGE POSITIONS AGAIN

    TURNING XING TO C

  PRO LAUGHS, HAMLET XES TO ABOVE C THEN TURNS BACK TO PK
  PRO TURNS DS

71

HAMLET   have such a fellow whipped for o'erdoing Termagant;
          it out-Herods Herod, pray you avoid it.

FIRST PLAYER I warrant your honour.

HAMLET   Be not too tame neither, but let your own discretion
          be your tutor. Suit the action to the word, the word
          to the action, with this special observance, that you
          o'erstep not the modesty of nature. For anything
          so o'erdone is from the purpose of playing, whose end
          both at the first, and now, was and is, to hold as 'twere
          the mirror up to nature; to show virtue her own feature,
          scorn her own image and the very age and body of the
          time his form and pressure. Now this overdone, or come
          tardy off, though it makes the unskilful laugh, cannot
          but make the judicious grieve; the censure of the which
          one must in your allowance o'erweigh a whole theatre of
          others. O there be players that I have seen play, and
          heard others praise, and that highly-not to speak it
          profanely--that neither having th' accent of Christians,
          nor the gait of Christian, pagan, nor man, have so
          strutted and bellowed, that I have thought some of
          nature's journeymen had made men, and not made them well,
          they imitated humanity so abominably.

FIRST PLAYER I hope we have reformed that indifferently with us sir.

HAMLET   O reform it altogether; and let those that play your
          clowns speak no more than is set down for them, for
          there be of them that will themselves laugh, to set on
          some quantity of barren spectators to laugh too, though

<u>X DS TO ABOVE PRO</u>

<u>POL, ROS AND GUI ENTER UR.</u> ● HAMLET STARTS US, SEES <u>POL</u> XES BACK TO <u>PRO.</u>

PRO EXIT VIA J THROWS + L

<u>PLAYERS RISE AND X OUT BELOW PLAY</u> K WAGS FINGER AT <u>PRO.</u> HAMLET XES TO C AS POL, <u>ROS</u> AND <u>GUI</u> XING IN ... <u>GUI</u> WIDE R AND FOLLOWING POL ROS WIDE L THEY STOP AT 11:00, AT SAME TIME MOODY AND POSHEK ENTER ANDREI DOOR EACH WITH CANDELABRA X ACROSS TOP OF STAGE, SET UL AND DL CANDELABRA EXIT TUN L

<u>HOR ENTERS TUN R XES TO 1 AND 2 AT 7:32</u>

<u>POL XES AND EXITS INTO BELOW.</u> HAMLET TURNS SEES HOR AND STARTS TO X TOWARD HIM. ROS AND GUI FOLLOW HIM. AFTER A FEW STEPS HE STOPS AND TURNS BACK TO THEM

<u>THEY X OUT R BELOW. DRAW CURTAINS BEHIND THEM</u>

<u>TURNING BACK TO HOR</u> XING TO HIM

<u>ONTO 4 AND 3 AT 7:30</u>

HAND ON HIS SHOULDERS

<u>HAMLET XES TO ABOVE KINGS THRONE</u>

<u>HOR</u> X TO HIM

72

HAMLET   in the mean time some necessary question of the play

be then to be considered; that's villainous, and shows

a most pitiful ambition in the fool that uses it. Go

make you ready.

                    (Exeunt Players.

          Enter Polonius, Rosencrantz, and Guildenstern.

How now my lord, will the King hear this piece of work?

POLONIUS   And the Queen too, and that presently.

HAMLET   Bid the players make haste.   (Exit Polonius.

Will you two help to hasten them?

ROSENCRANTZ &
GUILDENSTERN ⎧AY my lord.
ROSENCRANTZ   ⎨Yes, my lord, (Exeunt Rosencrantz and Guildenstern.

HAMLET   What ho, Horatio!
                 Enter Horatio

HORATIO   Here sweet lord, at your service.

HAMLET   Horatio, thou art e'en as just a man

As e'er my conversation coped withal.

HORATIO   O my dear lord.

HAMLET   Nay, do not think I flatter,

For what advancement may I hope from thee

That no revenue hast buy thy good spirits

To feed and clothe thee? Why should the poor be flattered?

No, let the candied tongue lick absurd pomp,

And crook the pregnant hinges of the knee

Where thrift may follow fawning. Dost thou hear

Since my dear soul was mistress of her choice,

And could of men distinguish, her election

Hath sealed thee for herself, for thou hast been

XING AWAY FROM HIM to ~~OTHER~~ R OF SKENE

STOPPING TURNS, HOR XES IN TO BELOW SKENE

XING BACK TO HOR

LOOKING DL

CXING TO ¾ 9'00

X TO HIM

HAMLET X US, HOR TO R BELOW BENCH

73

HAMLET   As one in suffering all that suffers nothing,

A man that Fortune's buffets and rewards

Hast ta'en with equal thanks; and blessed are those

Whose blood and judgement are so well comingled ~~comeoled~~,

That they are not a pipe for Fortune's finger

To sound what stop she please. Give me that man

That is not passion's slave, and I will wear him

In my heart's core, ay in my heart of hearts

As I do thee. Something too much of this

There is a play to-night before the King;

One scene of it comes near the circumstance

Which I have told thee of my father's death.

I prithee when thou seest that act afoot,

Even with the very comment of thy soul

Observe my uncle. If his occulted guilt

Do not itself unkennel in one speech,

It is a damned ghost that we have seen,

And my imaginations are as foul

As Vulcan's stithy. Give him heedful note,

For I mine eyes will rivet to his face,

And after we will both our judgements join

In censure of his seeming.

HORATIO   Well my lord;

If 'a steal aught the whilst this play is playing,

And 'scape detecting, I will pay the theft.   m#5

          (Trumpets and kettle-drums within.

HAMLET   They're coming to the play. I must be idle.

WARN

m#5

COURT LED BY KING AND QUEEN ENTER UR. QUEEN IS ONSTAGE OF KING
OPH AND POL FOLLOW. HOR XES TO BELOW DS BENCH. HAMLET XES UP TO MEET
KING AND QUEEN ATC OPH → SIT DS BENCH; POL TO ½ 3:00, RP 1 + 2 SET UP; #2 AT 2
#1 ABOVE HER

(VOLT, VANA AND CORN, TO UR GROUP
MACL AND REY AND MAR TO DL
DOTY TO DR. BACK TO DL
BAR AND FRAN AT UR DOOR)

HAMLET ESCORTS QUEEN TO HER CHAIR AT 4:00.

TAKING QUEEN TO PLACE, KING FOLLOWS TO HIS CHAIR

BEFORE HIS CHAIR, SITS AFTER LINE

XING R ● SEEING POL AT ½ 3:00, XING TOWARD HIM

POL XES TO BEHIND KING AND QUEEN · ROS AND GUI ENTER FROM BELOW R
HAMLET XES UP TOWARD THEM 2, THEY ARE CLOSING CURTAINS. POL XES ⟩ TO BEHIND
                                                       KING AND QUEEN ON 3
ROS AND GUI X TO PLACES · ROS TO UR · GUI DL
HAMLET XES DS

XING TO OPHELIA

   BEHIND KINGS CHAIR

SITTING ON 4 PARALLEL WITH EDGE OF STAGE HIS HEAD CROSS WISE
IN OPHS LAP

    POL XES↶ TO THEM ON 3

74

HAMLET   Get you a place.

(10)   The state is set to one side. Enter to a Danish
            march Claudius, Gertrude, Polonius, Ophelia,
            Rosencrantz, Guildenstern, Lords and Guards with
            torches. Flourish. Claudius and Gertrude take
            their place on their left Polonius and Ophelia;
            Lords on the other side.

[T]

CLAUDIUS   How fares our cousin Hamlet?

HAMLET   Excellent i' faith, of the chameleon's dish; I eat the
            air, promise-crammed, you cannot feed capons so.

CLAUDIUS   I have nothing with this answer, Hamlet; these words
            are not mine.

HAMLET   No, nor mine now. (To Polonius) My lord, you played
            once i' th' university, you say?

POLONIUS   That I did my lord, and was accounted a good actor.

HAMLET   What did you enact?

POLONIUS   I did enact Julius Caesar, I was killed i' th'
            Capitol; Brutus killed me.

WARN
L #14

HAMLET   It was a brute part of him to kill so capital a calf
            there. Be the players ready?

ROSENCRANTZ Ay my lord, they stay upon your patience.

GERTRUDE   Come hither my dear Hamlet, sit by me.

HAMLET   No good mother, here's metal more attractive.

POLONIUS(to Claudius) O ho, do you mark that?

HAMLET   Lady, shall I lie in your lap?
                                    (Sits at Ophelia's feet.

OPHELIA   No my lord.

HAMLET   I mean, my head upon your lap.

OPHELIA   Ay my lord.

HAMLET   Do you think I meant country matters?

OPHELIA   I think nothing, my lord.

POL IS NOW AT 7:00 ON 2 , OPH DOES NOT LOOK AT HAMLET

SITTING UP

SEEING POL RISING ● XING ONTO 4 TO ½ 9:00, QUEEN LAUGHS WITH KING

ALL SILENT

RISE X TO HIM , TRIES TO PULL HIM BACK, HOLDS R ARM

RP 1+2 HAVING XED TO PLACES - #2 SITTING ON 4 AT 2:00 #1 ABOVE HER
START PLAYING, OPH TAKE HAMLET BY ARM 'SHH'ING HIM . POL MOVE IN TO ASSIST. HAMLET
XES ◡ TO OFF DS BENCH TO FINISH LINE, HOR XES UP TO HELP

OPH XES TO SIT ON US BENCH . POL XES ℃ BENCH TO STAND AT 9:00 ON O

PANTO BEGINS WITH MUSIC ON 'SUIT OF SABLES'. PLAY K AND Q ENT FROM BELOW L
X ONTO DS PLATFORM   . STAND AWAY FROM EACH OTHER THEN EMBRACE
THEN PLAY Q KNEELS BEFORE HIM, KISS HEM AS HE SINK ONTO BANK.
↑ KING LIES: DOWN, QUEEN XES ↶ HIM TO ABOVE HIM THEN BACKS TO
EXIT IN BELOW C A ROLL OF DRUMS AND LUC ENTERS WHEN HE DOES SO
HAMLET MOVES QUICKLY TO BELOW BENCH SITTING ON 4, WATCHING INTENTLY
LUC XES QUICKLY TO C, TURNS US AND XES TO R OF SLEEPING KING, RE-
MOVES CROWN KISSES IT, PUTS IT ON, X TO UR OF PK, GIVE POISON, RUN TO CROUCH ON 3
AT 7:30. HAM START X ℃ BENCH TO ABOVE IT, PQ ENT BEL R X TO DR OF KING, 'TAKE', EXTEND ARM, LUC RUN TO BEHIND
CATCH WRISTS, STEP TO R OF HER, 'TAKE' IN HORROR, LUC DRAWS HER TO HIM AND THEY X OUT R BEL HIS ARM
AROUND HER
      WHEN LUC STARTS TO POISON ROS : 'OHH'. SHHED BY HOR ET AL

HAMLET ON 4 AND 3 ABOVE BENCH ● XING TO R BEL, CHECK BEHIND CURTAINS THEN
           RETURN TO ABOVE BENCH.
   PRO ENTERS. XES DS BOWS TO KING AND QUEEN THEN XES AROUND
BOWS TO DR THEN TO BENCH   THEN WAITS AT UR OF C FOR THE BACK CHAT
      TO STOP

75

HAMLET   That's a fair thought to lie between maids' legs.

OPHELIA   What is, my lord?

HAMLET   Nothing.

OPHELIA   You are merry my lord.

HAMLET   Who, I?

OPHELIA   Ay my lord.

HAMLET   O God, your only jig-maker. What should a man do but be

merry, for look you how cheerfully. my mother looks, and

my father died within's two hours.

OPHELIA   Nay, 'tis twice two months, my lord.

HAMLET   So long? Nay then let the devil wear black, for I'll have

a suit of sables. ᵐ⁶ O heavens, die two months ago, and not ⌐14

forgotten yet? Then there's hope a great man's memory may

outlive his life half a year, but by'r Lady 'a must build.

BACKLIN: Quiet, please.

churches then, or else shall 'a suffer not thinking on,

with the hobby-horse, whose epitath is, for o, for o,

the hobby-horse is forgot.

Trumpets sound. The Dumb Show is discovered in the inner
stage, and is there acted. Enter a King and a Queen very
lovingly, the Queen embracing him, and he her. She kneels,
and makes show of protestation unto him. He takes her up,
and declines his head upon her neck; he lays him down a bank
of flowers; she seeing him asleep, leaves him. Anon comes in
another man, takes off his crown, kisses it, pours poison in
the sleeper's ears, and leaves him. The Queen returns, finds
the King dead, makes passionate action; the poisoner with some
three or four come in again, seem to condole her; the dead body
is carried away; the poisoner wooes the Queen with gifts, she
seems harsh awhile, but in the end accepts his love. Bow Pk jbut
(The curtains close.

OPHELIA   What means this, my lord?

HAMLET   Marry this is miching mallecho; it means mischief.

OPHELIA   Felike this show imports the argument of the play.

Enter Prologue through the curtains.

FLIPS UP OPHELIA'S SKIRT, POL XES TO BETWEEN THEM

RISES XES TO DS OF BENCH SITS, POL FOLLOWS SITS ABOVE HER BENCH C

(ACTORS ON BENCH KEEP CHANGING POSITIONS)

APPLAUSE · RUNS OFF INTO BELOW

KING ⌐v ON STAGE LAUGHING

CONTINUING K
SITTING BELOW OPH ON 4

ENTERING FROM BELOW LEADING PLAY Q BY HAND. SHE CIRCLES HIM   Q at L of KING
CW AS THEY X DOWN. PQ L OF PK ON ENTRANCE. LETS HER GO WHEN SHE
IS DL OF HIM.

STOPPING, HAVING FINISHED CIRCLE ON L OF KG. THEY STAND BELOW SKENE

TAKING R HANDS

                    his
HAND TO BROW

INTERLACING FINGERS UNDER CHIN

76

HAMLET   We shall know by this fellow. The players cannot keep
            counsel, they'll tell all.

OPHELIA   Will 'a tell us what this show meant?

HAMLET   Ay, or any show that you will show him. Be not you
            ashamed to show, he'll not shame to tell you what it means

OPHELIA   You are naught, you are naught—I'll mark the play.

                    PROLOGUE
                    For us and for our tragedy,

                    Here stooping to your clemency,

                    We beg your hearing patiently
                                            (Exit.

HAMLET   Is this a prologue, or the posy of a ring?

OPHELIA   'Tis brief, my lord.

HAMLET   As woman's love

            Enter two Players, King and Queen.

PLAYER KING Full thirty times hath Phoebus' cart gone round Neptune's
            salt wash, and Tellus' orbed ground. And thirty dozen
            moons with borrowed sheen About the world have times
            twelve thirties been

            Since love our hearts, and Hymen did our hands

            Unite comutual in most sacred bands

PLAYER QUEEN So many journeys may the sun and moon
            Make us again count o'er ere love be done.

            But woe is me, you are so sick of late,

            So far from cheer, and from your former state,

            That I distrust you. Yet though I distrust,

            Discomfort you my lord it nothing must.

            For women's fear and love hold quantity;

HANDS TO HEART

TURNING OUT THEN BACK

A FOREBEARING HAND TO HIS LIPS

XING DOWN TO 7:00, HAND CLUTCHING BREASTS

TURN X US TO 11:00 THEN TURN TO PLAY K - GENL MOVE STARTS ON PART OF CROWD

RISING XING DN TO O THEN ↳ TO BEHIND KING AND QUEEN
AT R RAIL OF L TUN.

(COURTIERS WATCH KING AND QUEEN FOR REACTION)
GUI AND MACL STARTING XING ↙ SLOWLY TO DR

(ON 'VALIDITY' ROS XES TO BEHIND MISKA ON BENCH)
(ALL COURTIERS DS AND DL MOVE SLOWLY TO DR)

PLAY Q AT 11:00 CLOSE TO UR COURTIERS FLIPS TRAIN AROUND TRYING TO GET ATTENTION
BACK
        GENERAL WHISPERING AMONG COURTIERS   grow to crescendo BACK IN XES
        ONTO H UR
    SEEING HOUSE GOING THEN COMING ON STRONGER

77

PLAYER QUEEN   ~~In neither aught, or in extremity.~~

~~Now what my love is, proof hath made you know,~~

~~And as my love is sized, my fear is so.~~

Where love is great, the littlest doubts are fear;

Where little fears grow great, great love grows there.

PLAYER KING   Faith I must leave thee love, and shortly too,

My operant powers their functions leave to do,

And thou shalt live in this fair world behind,

Honoured, beloved, and haply one as kind

For husband shalt thou--

PLAYER QUEEN   O confound the rest,

Such love must needs be treason in my breast.

In second husband let me be accursed;

None wed the second but who killed the first.

HAMLET   That's wormwood, wormwood.

PLAYER QUEEN   The instances that second marriage move

Are base respects of thrift, but none of love.

A second time I kill my husband dead,

When second husband kisses me in bed.

PLAYER KING   I do believe you think what now you speak,

But waht we do determine, oft we break.

Purpose is but the slave to memory,

Of violent birth, but poor validity,

Which now like fruit unripe sticks on the tree,

But fall unshaken when the mellow be.

~~Most necessary 'tis that we forget~~

~~To pay ourselves what to ourselves is debt.~~

~~What to ourselves in passion we propose,~~

(WHISPERING STOPS   'PLAY Q XES TO HIM - 3 FEET AWAY
AFTER FLIPPING HER TRAIN TOWARDS UR COURTIERS

WITH A SLOW RAISE OF HER US ARM
(MUSIC STARTS)
   HAMLET STARTS SLOWLY UP TO BEHIND KING AND QUEEN

78

PLAYER KING   ~~The passion ending, doth the purpose lose~~.

~~The violence of either grief or joy~~

~~Their own enactures with themselves destroy~~.

~~Where joy most revels, grief doth most lament~~;

~~Grief joys, joy grieves, on slender accident~~.

~~This world is not for aye, not 'tis not strange~~

~~That even our loves should with our fortunes chang~~e;

~~For 'tis a question left us yet to prove,~~

~~Whether love lead fortune, or else fortune~~ love.

~~The great man down, you mark his favourite flies~~,

~~The poor advanced makes friends of enemies~~,

~~And hitherto doth love on fortune tend~~;

~~For who not needs shall never lack a friend~~,

~~And who in want a hollow friend doth try~~,

~~Di~~rectly sea~~sons him his enemy~~.

●But [orderly] to end where I begun,

Our wills and fates do so contrary run,

That our devices still are overthrown;

Our thoughts are ours, their ends none of our own.

So think thou wilt no second husband wed,

But die thy thoughts when thy first lord is [dead]

PLAYER QUEEN   ●Nor earth to me give food, nor heaven light,

●Sport and repose lock from me day and night,

~~To desperation turn my trust and hope~~,

~~An anchor's cheer in prison be my scope~~,

~~Each opposite that blanks the face of joy~~

~~Meet what I would have well, and it destr~~oy.

RUNNING TO   BEHIND QUEEN ● QUEEN: STARTS, CROWD REACTS
HAMLET XES BACK TO 1+2

GETTING ONTO SKENE, THEN LYING DOWN, PLAY Q X UP TO BEHIND HIM.

(CROWD NOW GATHERED DR - DOTY, BACK, GUI, MACL; HOR AND MAR)

PLAY Q XES C ____ TO ABOVE PLAY K HEAD, TAKING BRIEF CHECK OF
HOUSE WHEN SHE IS US
  EXIT INTO BELOW BACKING

SUDDENLY BETWEEN KING AND QUEEN LEANING ON THRONES

KING BETWEEN THEM TDC

X TO R,   LUC LOOK FROM BEL

TURN BACK AT 4/29'00 ● LAUGHS, THEN KING LAUGHS THEN HAMLET TURN
TALK TO MISKA ON BENCH
  XING TO UL OF HOPKINS, KING LOOKS AT REY AT 5.30 ON 1&2

XING TDC

XING DOWN TO 6:00 ONTO 3 AND L ● DRUM ROLL LUC IN FAST TO 4/6:00
HOLDS UP POISON FOR KING AND QUEEN THEN TURNS SLOWLY C SHOWING IT
  (CROWD MOVE ON DRUM ROLL)

POL RISES XES TO BETWEEN K+Q, REY ON 3 BETWEEN THEM, CONFER
ALL FAST, KING MAKES NOISE LOOKS AT HAMLET. POL X VIA ↳ BELOW THRONES

X TO BELOW BENCH ON 3

79

PLAYER QUEEN   Both here and hence pursue me lasting strife,

     If once a widow, ever I be |wife|

HAMLET   If she should break it now.

PLAYER KING   'Tis deeply sworn. Sweet, leave me here awhile;

     My spirits grow dull, and fain I would beguile

     The tedious day with sleep.

          (Sleeps.

PLAYER QUEEN   Sleep rock thy brain,

     And never come mischance between us twain

           (Exit.

HAMLET   Madam, how like you this play?

GERTRUDE   The lady doth protest too much methinks.

HAMLET   O but she'll keep her word.

CLAUDIUS   Have you heard the argument? Is there no offence is't?

HAMLET   No, no, they do but jest, poison is jest, no offence

     i' th' world.

CLAUDIUS   What do you call the play?

HAMLET   The Mouse-trap. Marry how? Tropically. This play is

     the image of a murder done in Vienna. Gonzago is the

     duke's name, his wife is Baptista; you shall see anon;

     'tis a knavish piece of work, but what of that? Your

     Majesty, and we that have free souls, it touches us not.

     Let the galled jade wince, our withers unwrung.

       Enter Player, as Lucianus

     This is one Lucianus, |nephew| to the king.

OPHELIA   You are as good as a chorus my lord.

HAMLET   I could interpret between you and your love, if I could

     see the puppets dallying.

RISING XING US TO 3 ABOVE BENCH

POL XES DN TO 1 AND 2 BEHIND KING AND QUEEN

HAMLET XES TO 3/4 3:00 FOLLOWING HER ● TURNING TO LUC

LUC IS BEGINING AT WRONG PLACE HAMLET SHRUGS XES TO DS BENCH SITS
HOR MOVES TO HIS SIDE QUICKLY, SITS. OFF STAGE, BELOW HAMLET.
(CROWD READJUST WHEN HAMLET X TO SIT - GROUP UR XES TO R OF
SKENE FOCUS ON HAMLET)

LUC X AROUND TO UR OF PLAY K

X → PK
LUC PUTS POISON TO EAR, POURS, KING MAKES AGONIZED NOISE, QUEEN RISES BACKS
US, POL TO O AND US (CROWD READJUSTS)
RISING XES TO 3/4 9:00, SPEAKING QUIETLY, KING MAKES NOISES THRU SPEECH

XING TOWARD HIM

KING RISES XES TO HAMLET AS IF TO STRIKE HIM

RUN TO SPOT DC HELD BY FOOTMAN, TAKES HIM TO FOCUS IT ON KING FROM
5:30

XING TO SKENE. PLAYERS EXIT INTO BEL

DODGING AROUND IN SPOTLIGHT, GROUP UR XES DOWN TO C ● TURNING XING THRU
CROWD AND OUT UR. CROWD SCURRIES ABOUT EXITS VARIOUSLY, NOISELY - HURRIEDLY
HAMLET XES AFTER CROWD EXITING UR THEN AROUND THRU BELOW OUT L AND DOWN TO HOR
FOOT HEN SHINE SPOTS INTO   BACK HISTERICS
AUDIENCE   SLING AND NYMAN STRIKE CHANDELIERS TURN L
          DURING EXIT - MAR AND REY STRIKE THRONES OUT R TUNNEL THEN RE-ENTER
                  EXIT UR, ROGO STRIKES UR CHAND OUT AND DOOR
                  GUI GETS CUSHIONS ON BENCH OUT AND DOOR
                  BAR, ROS, VOLT, CORN XOUT UR RE-ENT WITH WOLF SKIN
                  SET AND EXIT

(HAVING XED SLOWLY UP TO SKENE DURING HUBUB, NOW STANDING ON IT FACING DR

80

OPHELIA   You are keen my lord, you are keen.

HAMLET   It would cost you a ~~graning~~ _groaning_ to take off mine edge.

OPHELIA   Still better, and worse.

HAMLET   So you mis-take your husbands. Begin, murderer; pox,
            leave thy damnable faces, and begin. Come, the _The croaking raven,_
            croaking raven doth bellow for revenge".

LUCIANUS   Thoughts black, hands apt, drugs fit, and time agreeing.
            Confederate season, else no creature seeing;
            Thou mixture rank, of midnight weeds collected,
            With Hecate's ban thrice blasted, thrice infected,
            Thy natural magic and dire property
            On wholesome life usurps immediately
                              (Pours the poison in his ears.

HAMLET   A poisons him i' th' garden for his estate. His name's
            Gonzago, the story is extant, and written in very choice
            Italian. You shall see anon how the murderer gets the
            love of Gonzago's wife.

OPHELIA   The King rises

HAMLET   What, frightened with false fire!   L-14A

GERTRUDE   How fares my lord?

POLONIUS   Give o'er the play!

CLAUDIUS   Give me some light away!

ALL   Lights, lights, lights!

                        (Exeunt all but Hamlet and Horatio.
                    FUR RUG SET ON BENCH   L#15
HAMLET   Why let the strucken deer go weep,
                The hart ungalled play,
            For some must watch while some must sleep,
                Thus runs the world away.

RUNNING DOWN TO HOR WHO STANDS ON 3 AT 6:00 - TAKES OFF COAT AND TIE.
GIVES BOTH TO HOR.

RUN TO HOR   PLAYERS ENTER TIMOROUSLY TO GET GEAR. PRO AND LUC STRIKE
BANK RP 1 + 2 SIDLE DOWN TO INSTRUMENTS AND START BACK TO BELOW WITH
THEM

RUNNING US TOWARD UR DOORS

THROWING OPEN UR DOORS, SHOUTING OFF
TURNING BACK TO HOR WHISPERING

RUNNING BACK TO HOR

RUNNING TOWARD RP#1 AND #2 WHO HAVE INSTRUMENTS AND ARE MOVING UP
3 AT 2:00. THEY HELP AND RUN INTO BELOW FROM L
(TURNING BACK TO HOR FROM BELOW SKENE
TURNS, RUNS INTO BELOW FROM L. YELLS FROM PLAYERS. HAMLET RE-ENT R
BELOW WITH DRUM RUNS TO 4:30 ON 3, PUTS DOWN DRUM, VNEELS ABOVE
IT. PLAYERS ENT AFTER HIM. ROS AND GUI AT SAME TIME, RUNNING THRU PLAYERS
TO HAMLET [DIAGRAM]   ENTER

←

YELLING OVER DRUM BEATS MADE BY HAMLET

HAMLET HITS DRUM ONCE HARD

81

HAMLET   Would not this, sir, and a forest of feathers, if the
          rest of my fortunes turn Turk with me, with two
          Provincial roses on my razed shoes, get me a fellowship
          in a cry of players, sir?

HORATIO   Half a share.

HAMLET   A whole one, I.
               For thou dost know, o Damon dear,
          This realm dismantled was
               Of Jove himself, and now reigns here
          A very, very - peacock.

HORATIO   You might have rhymed.

HAMLET   O good Horatio, I'll take the ghost's word for a
          thousand pound. Didst perceive?

HORATIO   Very well, my lord.

HAMLET   Upon the talk of poisoning^

HORATIO   I did very well note him.

HAMLET   Ah ha! Come, some music! Come, the recorders'
               For if the King like not the comedy,
          Why then belike--he likes it not, perdy
          Come, some music!

                    Enter Rosencrantz and Guildenstern

JILDENSTERN   Good my lord, vouchsafe me a word with you.

HAMLET   Sir, a whole history.

JILDENSTERN   The King, sir--

HAMLET   Ay sir, what of him?

JILDENSTERN   Is in his retirement marvellous distempered.

HAMLET   With drink sir?

BEATING TATOO ON DRUM WITH FINGERS

RISING PICKING UP DRUM, THROW IT TO GUI

X VIA ABOVE GUI TO SKENE. GUI TURNS THROWS DRUM TO HOR AT WHICH
TIME #2 GRABS IT FROM HOR AT 6:00 ON 3, SHE O AT 4:00 THEN XES SLOWLY UP
GUI XES FAST TO UL OF SKENE ROS XES OVER TO C HOR X TO
4 AND 3 BELOW BENCH. WHEN HAMLET MOVED TO SKENE PK MOVED TO UR ENT
AND PG XES TO JOIN HIM THERE. PRO AND LUC X TO 3:00 1 AND 2 WHEN HAMLET
XES UP

HAMLET SITS

X UP/2

RISING, XES TO EDGE OF BENCH PLATFORM

GUILDENSTERN	No my lord, with choler.
HAMLET	Your wisdom should show itself more richer to signify this to the doctor;'for, for me to put him to his purgation would perhaps plunge him into more choler
GUILDENSTERN	Good my lord, put your discourse into some frame, and start not so wildly from my affair.
HAMLET	I am tame sir, pronounce.
GUILDENSTERN	The Queen your mother in most great affliction of spirit, hath sent me to you.
HAMLET	You are welcome.
GUILDENSTERN	Nay good my lord, this courtesy is not of the right breed. If it shall please you to make me a wholesome answer, I will do your mother's commandment; if not, your pardon and my return shall be the end of my business.
HAMLET	Sir, I cannot.
ROSENCRANTZ	What, my lord?
HAMLET	Make you a wholesome answer; my wit's diseased. But sir, such answer as I can make,you shall command, or rather as you say, my mother; therefore no more, but to the matter My mother, you say--
ROSENCRANTZ	Then thus she says, your behaviour hath struck her into amazement and admiration.
HAMLET	O wonderful son that can so stonish a mother! But is there no sequel at the heels of this mother's admiration? Impart.
ROSENCRANTZ	She desires to speak with you in her closet ere you go to bed.

LUC ⊕1
⊗ ⊕2
⊗PRO

HAMLET BECKONS ROS IN . PLAYERS FORM GROUP 3:00 ON 2 . ROS XES
TO HAMLET WARILY,
BOTH HANDS TO HIS SHOULDERS

SEE PLAYERS X TO THEM. #1 & #2 FLEE ⤴ INTO BELOW L

TAKES RECORDER FROM PRO TURNS L TO FACE GUI TAKING DAGGER FROM
LUC. PRO   MOVE TO R BELOW ● HAMLET TURNS TO GUI SHEPARDS HIM TO 3:00
GUI XES ACROSS BELOW HIM, ROS THEN XES SLOW TO 2 AND 3 AT 5:00. HOR XES
TO 3/4 9:00. LUC XES INTO C BELOW

6/6 PRO X R → L OF PQ, LUC X TO L OF DL POLE, #1 IN C BEL, #2 IN L BEL

83

HAMLET   We shall obey, were she ten times our mother.

             Have you any further trade with us?

ROSENCRANTZ   My lord, you once did love me.

HAMLET   And do still, by these pickers and stealers.

ROSENCRANTZ   Good my lord, what is your cause of distemper?

             You do surely bar the door upon your own liberty,

             if you deny your griefs to your friend.

HAMLET   Sir, I lack advancement.

ROSENCRANTZ   How can that be, when you have the voice of the King

             himself for your succession in Denmark?

HAMLET   Ay sir, but while the grass grows--the proverb is

             something musty.

                    Enter players with recorders

             O the recorders--let me see one.--To withdraw with

             you--why do you go about to recover the wind of me,

             as if you would drive me into a toil?

GUILDENSTERN O my lord, if my duty be too bold, my love is too

             unmannerly.

HAMLET   I do not well understand that. Will you play upon

             this pipe?

GUILDENSTERN My lord, I cannot.

HAMLET   I pray you.

GUILDENSTERN Believe me, I cannot.

HAMLET   I do beseech you.

GUILDENSTERN I know no touch of it my lord.

HAMLET   It is as easy as lying; govern these ventages with your

             fingers and thumb, give it breath with your mouth, and

HAMLET BACKS TO C - LUC #1 + #2 PEER OUT FROM L BELOW

GUI XES TO R OF ROS • HOR SITS DS BENCH ·2 +1 at 4:00

HAMLET XES TOWARD THEM THEY BACK DOWN STEPS. PRO RUNS TO PK
AND PQ

(POL ENTERS UR, PUSHES THRU PLAYERS

(TURN SEE POL XING TOWARD HIM   #1 AND LUC COME OUT OF L BELOW TO L OF SKENE

TURNING XING TO 7:30 · POL FOLLOWS TO UL OF HIM. WHEN HAMLET AND POL
SET DS ROS AND GUI X 1 + 2 AT 3:00
POL ENT THEN PRO X THRU BELOW TO 4 AND 3 AT 1:30, LUC UL OF HIM ON 3 AND 2

TURN TO HOR WHO IS BELOW BENCH PLAT

TURN BACK TO POL ●. RUNNING OUT UR   PQ, PK OUT UR

HAMLET	it will discourse most eloquent music. Look you, these are the stops.
GUILDENSTERN	But these cannot I command to any utterance of harmony; I have not the skill.
HAMLET	Why look you now how unworthy a thing you make of me. You would play upon me, you would seem to know my stops, you would pluck out the heart of my mystery, you would sound me from my lowest note to the top of my compass; and there is such music, excellent voice in this little organ, yet cannot you make it speak. Sblood do you think I am easier to be played on than a pipe? Call me what instrument you will, though you can fret me, you cannot play upon me.

Enter Polonius

God bless you sir.

POLONIUS	My lord, the Queen would speak with you, and presently.
HAMLET	Do you see yonder cloud that's almost in shape of a camel?
POLONIUS	By th' mass and 'tis, like a camel indeed.
HAMLET	Methinks it is like a weasel.
POLONIUS	It is backed like a weasel.
HAMLET	Or like a whale?
POLONIUS	Very like a whale.
HAMLET	Then will I come to my mother by and by. (Aside) They fool me to the top of my bent. -I will come by and by
POLONIUS	I will say so.

WARN
L #16

(Exeunt Polonius, Rosencrantz & Guildenstern.

KING QUICKLY TO #1 RETURNING RECORDER ● TO ROS AND GUI AS HE
XES TO #1 ● ROS AND GUI RACE⤷ BELOW HAMLET AND OUT UR, #1 AND LUC
INTO L BELOW. HOR TURNS XES OUT TUN R
  X Ⓞ DS AND BACK TO C

MAKES UNDERHAND STABBING MOTION, CHECKS,

TURN X ⌐ AND OUT AND DOOR. AT SAME TIME GUI PROPELLED FORWARD BY
KING PASSES UR WINDOW. XES ONTO ABOVE THEN TO L DOOR, LOOKS OUT IT, THEN TURNS BACK
TO FACE R DOOR, NODDING TO INDICATE COAST IS CLEAR FOR KING WHO APPEARS IN R DOOR
JUST AS HAMLET FINISHES COUPLET. GUI TURNS IN CIRCLE IN ABOVE ON WAY TO L ON ENTERING
'FRIGHTENED RAT'

  AS HE ENTERS R ABOVE, KING TO DC. ROS FOLLOWS HOLDING JUST IN
  DOOR WITH ROBE OVER ARMS

  GUI XES TO UL OF KING WHO FACES DS REMOVES HIS COAT AND STRIKES
  IT TO US STAND. RETURNS TO REMOVE RIBBON AND MEDAL, STRIKE THEM TO STAND

  MEETS ROS ABOVE KING GETTING PART OF ROBE, NOW PUTS ON L
  SLEEVE, CROUCHING TO DO SO. ROS PUTS KING INTO R ARM

  KNEELS TO TIE BELT, R END GIVEN BY ROS,

85

HAMLET   By and by is easily said. Leave me friends.

       (Exeunt Horatio and Players.

      Tis now the very witching time of night,

      When churchyards yawn, and hell itself breathes out

      Contagion to this world. Now could I drink hot blood,

      And do such bitter business as the day

      Would quake to look on Soft, now to my mother

      O heart, lose not thy nature, let not ever

      The soul of Nero enter this firm bosom.

      Let me be cruel, not unnatural,

      I will speak daggers to her, but use none;

      My tongue and soul in this be hypocrites   L#16

      How in my words somever she be shent,

      To give them seals never my soul consent.

                          (Exit.

III SCENE THREE

      The same. Enter Claudius, Rosencrantz & Guildenstern.

CLAUDIUS   I like him not, nor stands it safe with us

      To let his madness range therefore prepare you;

      I your commission will forthwith dispatch,

      And he to England shall along with you.

      The terms of our estate may not endure

      Hazard so near us as doth hourly grow

      Out of his braves. [lunacies]

GUILDENSTERN   We will ourselves provide,

      Most holy and religious fear it is

      To keep those many many bodies safe

      That live and feed upon your majesty

BUTTONING KING INTO ROBE

GUI RISES

PAUSE, KING XES TO SIT IN CHAIR, ARM OVER BACK FACING DL, GUI XES TO L
ABOVE DOOR

X TO KING'S R

LEANS CLOSE TO KING'S EAR, KING PUTS HANDS TO EAR

BACKING R 2

RISES, DOS BACKS 2

BOW EXIT R, THEN GUI TO HIS PLACE BOW, EXIT, HAVING TAKEN , MEDAL
RIBBON AND COAT FROM STAND,

ENTERING THRU L ABOVE DOOR AS GUI BOWS, XES TO UR OF KING'

86

ROSENCRANTZ The single and peculiar life is bound,

With all the strength and armour of the mind,

To keep itself from noyance, but much more

That spirit, upon whose weal depends and rests

The lives of many. The cess of majesty

Dies not alone; but like a gulf doth draw

What's near it with it. It is a massy wheel

Fixed on the summit of the highest mount,

To whose huge spokes ten thousand lesser things

Are mortised and adjoined; which when it falls,

Each small annexment, petty consequence,

Attends the boist'rous ruin. Never alone

Did the king sigh, but with a general groan.

CLAUDIUS Arm you I pray you to this speedy voyage,

For we will fetters put about this fear

Which now goes too free-footed.

ROSENCRANTZ We will haste us.
                    (Exeunt Rosencrantz & Guildenstern.
                     Enter Polonius.

POLONIUS My lord, he's going to his mother's closet.

Behind the arras I'll convey myself

To hear the process. I'll warrant she'll tax him home,

And as you said, and wisely was it said,

'Tis meet that some more audience than a mother.

Since nature makes them partial, should o'erhear

The speech of vantage. Fare you well my liege,

I'll call upon you ere you go to bed.

And tell you what I know.

BOW, EXIT L., KING X'S TO R DOOR THEN TURNS ↻ TO FACE DS ATC.

87

CLAUDIUS   Thanks dear my lord.

                   (Exit Polonius.

            O my offence is rank, it smells to heaven;

            It has the primal eldest curse upon't,

            A brother's murder. Pray can I not,

            Though inclination be as sharp as will.

            My stronger guilt defeats my strong intent,

            And like a man to double business bound,

            I stand in pause where I shall first begin,

            And both neglect. What if this curséd hand

            Were thicker than itself with brother's blood,

            Is there not rain enough in the sweet heavens

            To wash it white as snow? Whereto serves mercy

            But to confront the visage of offence?

            And what's in prayer but this twofold force,

            To be forestalled ere we come to fall,

            Or pardoned being down? Then I'll look up;

            My fault is past. But o what form of prayer

            Can serve my turn? Forgive me my foul murder?

            That cannot be since I am still possessed

            Of those effects for which I did the murder,

            My crown, mine own ambition, and my Queen.

            May one be pardoned and retain th' offence?

            In the corrupted currents of this world,

            Offence's gilded hand may shove by justice,

            And oft 'tis seen the wicked prize itself

            Buys out the law. But 'tis not so above;

            There is no shuffling, there the action lies

KNEEL AT R OF CHAIR , CROSS SELF

COVERS EARS WITH HANDS . HAMLET ENTER R AS IF XING TO L, STOP
INSIDE DOOR

WITH R HAND STARTING UNDERHAND THRUST, CHECKS

88

CLAUDIUS   In his true nature, and we ourselves compelled
            Even to the teeth and forehead of our faults
            To give in evidence. What then? What rests?
            Try what repentance can—what can it not?
            Yet what can it, when one cannot repent?
            O wretched state, o bosom black as death,
            O liméd soul, that struggling to be free,
            Art more engaged! Help angels, make assay.
            Bow stubborn knees, and heart with strings of steel.
            Be soft as sinews of the new-born babe.
            All may be well.   (Kneels.

                    Enter Hamlet

HAMLET   Now might I do it pat, now 'a is a-praying;
            And now I'll do't—and so 'a goes to heaven;
            And so am I revenged. That would be scanned.
            A villain kills my father, and for that,
            I his sole son do this same villain send
            To heaven.
            Why this is hire and salary, not revenge.
            'A took my father grossly full of bread,
            With all his crimes broad blown, as flush as May,   WARN
            And how his audit stands who knows save heaven--
            But in our circumstance and course of thought,   L #17
            'Tis heavy with him; and then am I revenged,
            To take him in the purging of his soul,
            When he is fit and seasoned for his passage?
            No.
            Up sword, and know thou a more horrid hent,

KING TOWARD L DOOR, STOP ON PLAT

EXIT L ABOVE

QUEEN AND'S DOOR , POL FOLLOWS , QUEEN CIRCLES⟩ TO 8:00
POL STARTS LINE AS HE XES PAST UR DOOR, POL XES IN TO ½ 9:00

QUEEN STOPS TURNS TO POL AT 8:00, POL X TO 12 BELOW CLOSING CURTAINS
BEHIND HIM
QUEEN X TO BENCH PLAT, POL APPEARS IN C BEL, CLOSES CURTAINS AFTER QUEEN'S
ADMONITION

QUEEN X ONTO BENCH PLAT · POL INTO BELOW

ENTER AND DOOR X TO ¾ 10:00 DAGGER IN HAND. STARTS SPEAKING
AS HE PASSES UR ENTRANCE, QUEEN STANDS BEFORE DS BENCH

89

HAMLET   When he is drunk, asleep, or in his rage,

Or in th' incestous pleasure of his bed,

At gaming, swearing, or about some act

That has no relish of salvation in't--

Then trip him that his heels may kick at heaven,

And that his soul may be as damned and black

As hell whereto it goes. My mother stays.

This physic but prolongs thy sickly days

(Exit.

CLAUDIUS(Rising) My words fly up, my thoughts remain below   L#17

Words without thoughts never to heaven go.

(Exit.

(12) III SCENE FOUR

Gertrude's closet. Enter Gertrude and Polonius.

POLONIUS   A will come straight. Look you lay home to him,

Tell him his pranks have been too broad to bear with,

And that your Grace hath screened and stood between

Much heat and him. I'll silence me even here. Mother

Pray you be round with him.

HAMLET   Mother, ~~mother, mother~~!
(within)

                                      HAMLET { Mother

GERTRUDE   I'll warrant you, fear me not (Withdraw,

I hear him coming.

HAMLET   mother

    Polonius hides behind the arras. Enter Hamlet.

HAMLET   Now mother, what's the matter?

GERTRUDE   Hamlet, thou hast thy father much offended.

HAMLET   Mother, you have my father much offended.

GERTRUDE   Come, come, you anawer with an idle tongue.

HAMLET   Go, go, you question with a wicked tongue.

GERTURDE   Why how now Hamlet!

'SHOW MUMMY THE BLOODSTAINED HANDS'

STARTS X VIA BELOW HAMLET TO BELOW. HAMLET GRABS HER L WRIST
WITH HIS L. HAND AND SWINGS HER BACK ONTO BENCH

HAMLET HAS POINT OF DAGGER UP, STILL GRASPG WRIST

LEANING BELOW HIM TO CALL

RUNS TO R BELOW, QUEEN RISES ● STABS UNDERHAND THRU R BELOW   DS OF
POL GRABS SWORD IN R HAND. L IS SEEN GRASPING DR POLE

— X TO 4'00 + ½
HAMLET HOLDING SWORD INTO POL TALKS OVER R SHOULDER
QUEEN TURNS QUICKLY TO FACE HAMLET
   XING DOWN TO ½ 8'00

PULLS OUT DAGGER, SWINGING TO ½ 10'00 — TO LET BODY FALL FROM BEHIND
ARRAS, QUEEN MAKING NOISE XES   OVER TO BENCH PLAT

XING QUICLY TO KNEEL DL OF BODY, PUTS SWORD DOWN ON 1st STEP OF
SKENE

RISES WITH BLOOD-STAINED HANDS, PALMS OUT, AS IF SHOWING THEM TO QUEEN
WHO NOW ON BENCH PLAT BACKS WITH A HORRIFIED GASP AGAINST IDC BENCH
HAMLET XES TO 11'00   HAMLET QUELLS QUEEN AT THE TOP OF HER RETCHING, GASPING
                      BENT

90

HAMLET   What's the matter now?

GERTRUDE   Have you forgot me?

HAMLET   No by the rood, not so.

You are the Queen, your husband's brother's wife,

And would it were not so, you are my mother.

GERTRUDE   Nay, then I'll set those to you than can speak.

HAMLET   Come, come, and sit you down, you shall not budge.

You go not till I set you up a glass

Where you may see the inmost part of you.

GERTRUDE   What wilt thou do, thou wilt not murder me?

Help, help, ho!

POLONIUS
(behind)   What ho, help, help, help!

HAMLET
(draws)   How now! A rat? Dead for a ducat, dead!
                    (Makes a pass through the arras.

POLONIUS
(behind)   O I am slain.

GERTRUDE   O me, what hast thou done?

HAMLET   Nay I know not, is it the King?

GERTRUDE   Oh what a rash and bloody deed is this!

HAMLET   A bloody deed, almost as bad, good mother,

As kill a king, and marry with his brother.

GERTRUDE   As kill a king?

HAMLET   Ay lady, it was my word.
                (Lifts up the arras, and discovers Polonius.

Thou wretched, rash, intruding fool, farewell.

I look thee for thy better, take thy fortune;

Thou find'st to be too busy is some danger.

Leave wringing of your hands; peace, sit you down,

And let me wring your heart, for so I shall,

QUEEN SITS ON DS BENCH, HAMLET XES TO UL OF BENCH PLAT

X TO DL OF BENCH PLAT.

KING TO UL OF QUEEN TAKING PICTURE FROM POCKET ● TOUCHING QUEENS LOCKET.
(L HAND HIS PICTURE - R HAND HER LOCKET)

SITTING ABOVE QUEEN HOLDING PICTURE FOR HER IN L HAND

HAMLET	If it be made of penetrable stuff,
	If damned custom have not brazed it so,
	That it be proof and bulwark against sense.
GERTRUDE	What have I done, that thou dar'st wag thy tongue
	In noise so rude against me?
HAMLET	Such an act
	That blurs the grace and blush of modesty,
	Calls virtue hypocrite, takes off the rose
	From the fair forehead of an innocent love,
	And sets a blister there, makes marriage vows
	As false as dicers' oaths, o such a ~~deed~~ act
	As from the body of contraction plucks
	The very soul, and sweet religion makes
	A rhapsody of words. ~~Heaven's face does glow~~
	~~O'er this solidity and compound mass~~
	~~With heated visage, as against the doom;~~
	~~Is thought-sick at the act.~~
GERTRUDE	Ay me, what act,
	That raars so loud, and thunders in the index?
HAMLET	Look here upon this picture, and on this,
	The counterfeit presentment of two brothers.
	See what a grace was seated on this brow,
	Hyperion's curls, the front of Jove himself,
	An eyelike Mars, to threaten and command,
	A station like the herald Mercury,
	New lighted on a heaven-kissing hill,
	A combination and a form indeed,
	Where every god did seem to set his seal

TAKING HER LOCKET

RISING

THE PICTURE IN HIS HAND, HER LOCKET ● QUEEN TURNS AWAY US

XING TO DL OF HER ON BENCH PLAT

HAMLET To give the world assurance of a man.

    This was your husband, look you now what follows.

    Here is your husband like amildewed ear,

    Blasting his wholesome brother. Have you eyes,

    Could you on this fair mountain leave to feed

    And batten on this moor? Ha, have you eyes?

    You cannot call it love, for at your age

    The heyday in the blood is tame, it's humble,

    And waits upon the judgement; and what judgement

    Would step from [this] to [this] ~~Sense sure you have,~~

    ~~Else could you not have motion; but sure that sense~~

    ~~Is apoplexed, for madness would not err,~~ On cry

    ~~Nor sense to eestasy was ne'er so thralled~~

    ~~But it reserved some quantity of choice~~

    ~~To serve in such a difference~~. What devil was't

    That thus hath cozened you at hoodman-blind?

    ~~Eyes without feeling, feeling without sight,~~

    ~~Ears without hands or eyes, smelling sans all,~~

    ~~Or but a siely part of one true sense~~

    ~~Could not so mope~~. O shame, where is thy blush?

    Rebellious hell,

    If thou canst mutine in a matron's bones,

    To flaming youth let virtue be as wax

    And melt in her own fire. ~~Proclaim no shame~~

    ~~When the compulsive ardour gives the charge,~~

    ~~Since frost itself as actively doth burn,~~

    ~~And reason pandars will~~.

GERTRUDE O Hamlet speak no more

HAMLET BACKS TO 3/4 9:00 REPLACES PIX

KING TO 3/4 9:00

RISING

QUEEN, XES ↓ TO 3 AND THEN, SHE XES WAILING ↩ ON 3, HAMLET ABOVE
AND R OF HER ON 4 AS SHE XES. GHOST STARTS IN AND DOOR

FALLING TO KNEES ON 3

QUEEN HAS XED TO 15:00 ON 3 HAMLET UR OF HER ON 4, ARMS RAISED
AS IF TO STRIKE, SUDDENLY TURNS CW ARMS RAISED NOW AS IF TO WARD
OFF BLOWS. GHOST IS AT 3/3 6:00, GHOST LOOKS AT QUEEN THROUGHOUT, !

KNEELS FACING R

KING TO DL OF GHOST

GH
⊕
⊕ QN

⊕
HT

93

GERTRUDE   Thou turn'st mine eyes into my very soul,

And there I see such black and grainéd spots

As will not leave their tinct.

HAMLET   Nay but to live

In the rank sweat of an enseamed bed,

Stewed in corruption, honeying, and making love

Over the nasty sty-

GERTRUDE   O speak to me no more.

These words like daggers enter in my ears;

No more sweet Hamlet.

HAMLET   A murderer and a villain,

A slave that is not twentieth part the tithe

Of your precedent lord, a vice of kings,

A cutpurse of the empire and the rule,

That from a shelf the precious diadem stole

And put it in his pocket.

GERTRUDE   No more.

HAMLET   A king of shreds and patches-

Enter Ghost.

Save me and hover o'er me with your wings,

You heavenly guards. What would your gracious figure?

GERTRUDE   Alas he's mad.

HAMLET   Do you not come your tardy son to chide,

That lapsed in time and passion lets go by

Th' important acting of your dread command?

O say.

GHOST   Do not forget, this visitation

REACHING TOWARD HER WITH R HAND, STILL LOOKING AT GHOST

XING ✓ TO R OF HAMLET, TAKING HIS HEAD IN HER HANDS

PUTTING HER CHEEK TO HIS. QUEEN DS, HAMLET STILL WATCHES GHOST

XING TO IN FRONT OF GHOST TURNING BACK THEN XES TO L OF GHOST

QUEEN XES US VIA R OF GHOST LOOKING ABOUT THEN ON ∩ AND TO
JUST DL OF GHOST ALMOST TOUCHING HIM

TURN AWAY DS. QUEEN US NOW STARTS BACK TO DL OF GHOST

LOOKING 'THROUGH' GHOST
● GHOST TURNS XES SLOWLY TO EXIT AND DOOR.

QUEEN STARTS 'O'X UR ● HAMLET RISES

QUEEN STOPS AT C, REACTS TURNING AWAY, XES L TO BELOW SKENE

94

GHOST   Is but to whet thy almost blunted purpose.

But look, amazement on thy mother sits:

O step between her and her fighting soul--

Conceit in weakest bodies strongest works --

Speak to her Hamlet.

HAMLET   How is it with you lady?

GERTRUDE   Alas how is't with you,

-That you do bend your eye on vacancy,

And with th' incorporal air do hold discourse?

Forth at your eyes your spirits wildly peep,

And as the sleeping soldiers in th' alarm,

Your bedded hair like life in excrements

Start up and stand an end. O gentle son,

Upon the heat and flame of thy distemper

Sprinkle cool patience. Whereon do you look?

HAMLET   On him, on him. Look you how pale he glares,

His form and cause conjoined, preaching to stones,

Would make them capable. -Do not look upon me,

Lest with this piteous action you convert

My stern effects; then what I have to do

Will want true colour, tears perchance for blood.

GERTRUDE   To whom do you speak this?

HAMLET   Do you see nothing there?

GERTRUDE   Nothing at all, yet all that is I see.

HAMLET   Nor did you nothing hear?

GERTRUDE   No, nothing but ourselves.

HAMLET   Why look you there, look how it steals away,

My father in his habit as he lived-

XING UP TO 11:00

HAMLET LOOK, FREEZES

TURN SEE POL START, X TO ½ 3:00

X TO QUEEN TAKES HER HAND, PUTS IT ON HIS CHEST (HER R HAND)
THEY MEET BELOW SLEEVE, QUEEN BACKS SLIGHTLY AS HAMLET ADVANCES ON HER

QUEEN XES ← OIA BELOW HAMLET TO SIT ON DS BENCH , MAKES CIRCLING X ∽

XES IN TO UL OF BENCH PLAT

/XES TO HER KNEELS BEFORE HER EMBRACE

EMBRACE. THEN HAMLET RISES

95

HAMLET   Look where he goes, even now at the portal.

                                         (Exit Ghost.

GERTRUDE   This is the very coinage of your brain

           This bodiless creatin ecstasy

           Is very cunning in

HAMLET   Ecstasy?

           My pulse as yours doth temperately keep time,

           And makes as healthful music. It is not madness

           That I have uttered; bring me to the test,

           And I the matter will re-word, which madness

           Would gambol from. Mother, for love of grace,

           Lay not that flattering unction to your soul,

           That not your trespass, but my madness speaks.

           It will but skin and film the ulcerous place,

           Whilst rank corruption mining all within

           Infects unseen. Confess yourself to heaven,

           Repent what's past, avoid what is to come,

           And do not spread the compost on the weeds

           To make them ranker. Forgive me this my virtue,

           For in the fatness of these pursy times

           Virtue itself of vice must pardon beg,

           Yea curb and woo for leave to do him good.

GERTRUDE   O Hamlet thou hast cleft my heart in twain.

HAMLET   O throw away the worser part of it,

           And live the purer with the other half.

           Good night, but go not to my uncle's bed,

           Assume a virtue if you have it not.

           That monster custom, who all sense doth eat

QN TAKES HIS RIGHT HAND&PRESSES IT TO HER CHEEK THEN HAMLET TURNS
STARTS TO X, STOPS SEEING POL, STILL ON PLAY

TURNING BACK TO QUEEN

QUEEN RISES VES TO HAMLET AS IF TO EMBRACE HIM. HE STOPS HER, GRABBING
WRISTS

- X TO   UR OF POL, STARTS TO KNEEL

RISES, VES SLOWLY DOWN TO ¾ 9:00

QUEEN SITS, CROTCH

QUEEN STARTS

96

HAMLET ~~Of habits evil, is angel yet in this,~~
~~That to the use of actions fair and good~~
~~He likewise gives a frock or livery~~
~~That aptly is put on.~~ Refrain to-night,
And that shall lend a kind of easiness
To the next abstinence, the next more easy;
For use almost can change the stamp of nature,
And either (house) the devil, or throw him out
With wondrous potency. Once more good night,
And when you are desirous to be blessed,
I'll blessing beg of you. For this same lord,
I do repent; but heaven hath pleased it so
To punish me with this, and this with me,
That I must be their scourge and minister.
I will bestow him, and will answer well .
The death I gave him. So again good night.
I must be cruel only to be kind.
Thus bad begins, and worse remains behind.
~~One word more good lady.~~

GERTRUDE What shall I do?

HAMLET Not this by no means that I bid you do:
Let the bloat King tempt you again to bed,
Pinch wanton on your cheek, call you his mouse,
And let him for a pair of reechy kisses,
Or paddling in your neck with his damned fingers,
Make you to ravel all this matter out
That I essentially am not in madness,
But mad in craft. 'Twere good you let him know,

XING SLOWLY DOWN TO DL OF BENCH PLAT

XING TO SIT DS OF QUEEN

GESTURING WIDE, QUEEN LAUGHS THROUGHOUT THIS PART OF SPEECH.

EMBRACE, HIS R ARM ABOUT HER, HAMLET OFF-STAGE

RISING XING L↩ TO ½ 9:00

QUEEN STARTS TO SPEAK. HAMLET RAISES A FOREBEARING HAND AND CONTINUES

TURNS, SEES POL ● XING UP TO R OF POL ↓ THEN QUEEN RISES KES TU
L OF POL

SEEING HER, STOPPING HER WITH GESTURE, QUEEN STARTS BACKING
AWAY TOWARD ½ 3:00

TAKING POL'S ARMS

97

HAMLET   For who that's but a queen, fair, sober, wise,

Would from a paddock, from a bat, a gib,

Such dear concernings hide, who would do so?

No, in despite of sense and secrecy,

Unpeg the basket on the house's top,

Let the birds fly, and like the famous ape,

To try conclusions in the basket creep,

And break your own neck down.

GERTRUDE   Be thou assured, if words be made of breath

And breath of life, I have no life to breathe

What thou hast said to me.

HAMLET   I must to England, you know that.

GERTRUDE   Alack, I had forgot. 'Tis so concluded on.

HAMLET   There's letters sealed, and my two schoolfellows,

Whom I will trust as I will adders fanged,

They bear the mandate; they must sweep my way,

And marshal me to knavery. Let it work,

For 'tis the sport to have the enginer

Hoist with his own petar; and't shall go hard

But I will delve one yard below their mines,

And blow them at the moon. O 'tis most sweet

When in one line two crafts directly meet.

This man shall set me packing.

I'll lug the guts into the neighbour room.

Mother, good night, indeed. this counsellor

Is now most still, most secret, and most grave,

Who was in life a foolish prating knave.

Come sir, to draw toward an end with you.

WARN

LI7A

DRAGGING POL OUT UR. QUEEN XES SOBBING TO FALL OVER END OF DS BENCH
HAMLET CLOSES DOORS AFTER SELF AFTER HE HAS CLEARED WITH BODY.

ENTERS AND DOOR WHEN UR DOORS CLOSE FOLLOWED BY ROS R AND GUI (L). XES
TO UL OF QUEEN, ROS TO UL OF PLAT, GUI TO ½ 4:00 ; TOUCHES QUEEN WHO RISES, RECOVERS
THEN KING SPEAKS.

  ROS AND GUI
  BACK, BOW, X AND EXIT AND DOOR AT FAST WALK

   X TO HIM EMBRACE ● PULL AWAY X VIA DS OF KING   TO ½ 3:00

   X TO DR OF SKENE

KING   X TO DAGGER AT UR OF SKENE. STARTS NEXT LINE AS HE PICKS IT UP. QUEEN
COUNTERS DOWN TO ¾ 3:30

   X TO ½ 11:00

98

HAMLET   ◆Good night mother.

                              (Exeunt severally; Hamlet dragging
                               Polonius.

*12 cont'd
ACT FOUR SCENE ONE ⓘElsinore. The Castle. Enter Claudius,
                       Gertrude, Rosencrantz, and Guildenstern.

T

CLAUDIUS   ◆There's matter in these sighs, these profound heaves◆

            You must translate, 'tis fit we understand them.

            Where is your son?

GERTRUDE   ┆Bestow this place on us a little while◆

                              (Exeunt Rosencrantz & Guildenstern.

            ◆Ah mine own lord, │what│ have I seen to-night!   L17A

CLAUDIUS   What, Gertrude? How does Hamlet?

GERTRUDE   ◆Mad as the sea and the wind when both contend

            Which is the mightier.◆ In his lawless fit,

            Behind the arras hearing something stir,

            Whips out his rapier, cries, a rat, a rat,

            And in this brainish apprehension kills

            The unseen good old man◆

CLAUDIUS   Ô heavy deed!

            It had been so with us had we been there.

            ◆His liberty is full of threats to all;

            To you yourself, to us, to every one.

            Alas, how shall this bloody deed be answered?

            It will be laid to us, whose providence

            Should have kept short, restrained, and out of haunt

            This mad young man; but so much was our love,

            We would not understand what was most fit,

            But like the owner of a foul disease,

            To keep it from divulging, let it feed

X IN 2, TO ½ 4:00

HAND EXTENDED, QUEEN BACKS SLIGHTLY.

QUEEN TURNS AWAY, KING XES TO 7/4 9:00 ● ROS AND GUI ENTER AND DOOR. GUI TO
10:30, ROS TO 11:30

LOOKING AT QUEEN

'FOR THE PRESS'

THEY STAND ROOTED ● ROS X TO GUI SLAPS ARM THEN THEY X, AND EXIT AND DOOR
(BOW)

X TO ¼ 10:00 L HAND OUT,

HAND OUT ● QUEEN TURNS XES OUT TUUL

TURN X TO UR ● EXIT UR DOORS

BLACKOUT — ROGO ENTER TUN R, THROW RUG TO OFF-STAGE, GATHER IT UP, EXIT
AND DOOR, JUST AFTER HAMLET ENTERS

99

CLAUDIUS   Even on the pith of life. Where is he gone?

GERTRUDE   To draw apart the body he hath killed,

O'er whom his very madness, like some ore

Among a mineral of metals base,

Shows itself pure; a weep for what is done.

CLAUDIUS   O Gertrude, come away

The sun no sooner shall the mountains touch,

But we will ship him hence, and this vile deed

We must with all our majesty and skill

Both countenance and excuse. Ho Guildenstern!

Enter Rosencrantz and Guildenstern.

Friends both, go join you with some further aid.

Hamlet in madness hath Polonius slain,

And from his mother's closet hath he dragged him.

Go seek him out, speak fair, and bring the body

Into the chapel, I pray you haste in this.

(Exeunt Rosencrantz and Guildenstern.

Come Gertrude, we'll call up our wisest friends;

And let them know both what we mean to do

And what's untimely done; (so haply slander.--)

Whose whisper o'er the world's diameter,

As level as the cannon to his ~~blank~~ mark,

Transports his poisoned shot--may miss our name,

And hit the woundless air. O come away

My soul is full of discord and dismay

(Exeunt.

SCENE TWO The same. Enter Hamlet.

HAMLET ~~Safely stowed.~~

COUNT 2

HAVING WAITED 3 COUNTS FROM BLACKOUT. CALLING FROM OFF ABOVE L

HAVING ENTERED HOUSE IN BLACKOUT, NOW ¼ DOWN HOUSE L AISLE
CALLING SOFTLY THEN CONTINUING SLOW ADVANCE TO STAGE

HAVING ENTERED HOUSE IN BLACKOUT, NOW ¼ DOWN HOUSE C AISLE
CALLING SOFTLY THEN CONTINUING SLOW ADVANCE TO STAGE

ENTERING AND DOOR RUNNING TO ½ 6:00

CALLING FROM R TUNNEL

AS ABOVE

                         ROSENCRANTZ
_____Lord Hamlet.

                         VON MENDE
_____Lord Hamlet.

                         STANLEY
_____Lord Hamlet.

                         HAMLET
_____Safely stowed.

                         GUILDENSTERN
_____Hamlet.

                         HAMLET
       But soft, what noise?

                         GUILDENSTERN
_____ Lord Hamlet.

                         HAMLET
       Who calls on Hamlet?

ROS ENTERS TURNING ON FLASHLIGHT

DS ON ABOVE, FOCUSING FLASH ON HAMLET

TURN TO ROS

X US TO 1/29:00, GUI ENTERS SLOWLY DN R XING TO BEHIND HAMLET

HAMLET, HAVING BACKED A STEP COLLIDES WITH GUI, HAMLET STARTS BACKS AWAY A FEW L,
GUI TURNS ON FLASH, SHINES IT IN HAMLETS EYES

ROGO ENTERS AND DOOR, ADVANCES SLOWLY ACROSS STAGE

X TO 4:00

ROGO XES TO R OF BEL, ROS TALKS SHARPLY, HAMLET FREEZES AT EDGE

TURNS TO GUI XES TOWARD HIM. ROGO XES OUT OF BEL AT L.

X TO DL OFC

ROS TURNS OUT FLASHLIGHT - PICKS UP ARMCHAIR AND STRIKES IT OUT ABOVE L

100

ROSENCRANTZ &
GUILDENSTERN (within) Hamlet, Lord Hamlet!

HAMLET But soft, what noise? Who calls on Hamlet?

Enter Rosencrantz and Guildenstern.

     O here they come.

ROSENCRANTZ What have you done my lord with the dead body?

HAMLET Compounded it with dust whereto 'tis kin.

ROSENCRANTZ Tell us whre 'tis that we may take it thence,

     And bear it to the chapel.

HAMLET Do not believe it.

ROSENCRANTZ Believe what?

HAMLET That I can keep your counsel, and not mine own.

     Besides, to be demanded of a sponge, what replication

     should be made by the son of a king?

ROSENCRANTZ Take you me for a sponge my lord?

HAMLET Ay sir, that soaks up the King's countenance, his rewards,

     his authorities. But such officers do the King best service

     in the end; he keeps them like an ape *does an apple* in the corner of his

     jaw first mouthed to be last swallowed. When he needs

     what you have gleaned, it is but squeezing you, and,

     sponge, you shall be dry again.

ROSENCRANTZ I understand you not my lord.

HAMLET I am glad of it; a knavish speech sleeps in a foolish ear.

ROSENCRANTZ My lord, you must tell us where the body is, and go with

     us to the King.

HAMLET The body is with the King, but the King is not with the

     body. The King is a thing--

GUILDENSTERN A thing my lord?

L #19A

ACTORS IN HOUSE START TOWARD STAGE. HAMLET XES TO DL STOPPED BY NYMAN WHO XES
TO I AT 4:30. HAMLET TURNS XES TO DR TO BE MET BY SLING WHO ENTERS TUN R XES TO
I AT 7:30. HAMLET XES UL MET BY ROGO. ALL TURN ON FLASHLIGHTS AS THEY MOVE TO
BLOCK HAMLETS ADVANCE. THEN HE TURNS AT C SEEING ALL WAYS BLOCKED. ALL MOVE SLOWLY
TOWARD HIM TO FORM TIGHT CIRCLE DIAGRAM

    STARTS TO X UR THEN TURNS
    PUSHING NYMAN INTO SLINGSBY THEN RUNNING OUT TUN L. ALL RUN AFTER HIM

(ENT UR KING, REY, MAR, BAR, VOLT, CORN, PETERS, FORS, MOODY RANGE ACROSS C
STAGE. RRO⌐⌐⌐ HOLD INSIDE UR DOORS. DIAGRAM KING HOLDS DISPATCH.

ROS ENTERS PANTING TUN R XES TO I AND 2 AT 7:30

REY REACHES FOR PISTOL

CALLING OUT TUN R ● HAMLET ENT TUN R FORCED ON BY GUI WHO HAS
LOCK ON HIS R ARM. HAMLET LAUGHING, GASPING FORCED TO 6:00 ON 3. GUI
THEN X TO 5:00 ON O. HAMLET SITS ON 4. HAMLET AND GUI ARE FOLLOWED
BY NYM WHO HOLDS AT L OF R TUN OPENING. HAMLET NURSES A WRENCHED R
SHOULDER

TURNING ∪ TO FACE KING

101

HAMLET   Of nothing. Bring me to him. Hide fox, and all after.
                                                     (exeunt.

SCENE THREE The same. Enter Claudius, attended.

CLAUDIUS   I have sent to seek him, and to find the body.

How dangerous is it that this man goes loose,

Yet must not we put the strong law on him.

He's loved of the distracted multitude,

Who like not in their judgement, but their eyes,

And where 'tis so, th' offender's scourge is weighed.

But never the offence. To bear all smooth and even,

This sudden sending him away must seem

Deliberate pause. Diseases desperate grown

By desperate appliance are relieved

Or not at all.
                    Enter Rosencrantz.

How now, what hath befallen?

ROSENCRANTZ   Where the dead body is bestowed, my lord,

We cannot get from him.

CLAUDIUS   But where is he?

ROSENCRANTZ   Without, my lord, guarded, to know your pleasure.

CLAUDIUS   Bring him before us.

ROSENCRANTZ   Ho Guildentstern, bring in the lord.

                   Enter Hamlet and Guildenstern.

CLAUDIUS   Now Hamlet, where's Polónius?

HAMLET   At supper.

CLAUDIUS   At supper? Where?

HAMLET   Not where he eats, but where 'a is eaten; a certain

convocation of politic worms are e'en at him. Your

worm is your only emperor for diet; we fat all

RISING STANDING AT 6:30 ON 3

ROS WILTS ON 2, MAR CATCHES HIM, EASES HIM DOWN

TO NYM ● NYM XES US UR BETWEEN VOLT AND PETERS

TO NYM AS HE XES. NYM STOPS BETWEEN VOLT AND PETERS ● XES ON,
AND OUT L BEL.
KING AND ALL COURTIERS MOVE DS TO ABOVE HAMLET

GIVE DISPATCH TO REY, HAMLET SEES IT

REY HANDS DISPATCH TO ROS WHO HAS REVIVED AND XED UP TO 4 AND 3 AT 7:30

HAMLET creatures else to fat us, and we fat ourselves for
maggots. your fat king and your lean beggar is but
variable service, two dishes, but to one table--
that's the end.

CLAUDIUS Alas, alas!

HAMLET A man may fish with the worm that hath eat of a king,
and eat of the fish that hath fed of that worm.

CLAUDIUS What dost thou mean by this?

HAMLET Nothing but to show you how a king may go a progress
through the guts of a beggar.

CLAUDIUS Where is Polonius?

HAMLET In heaven. Send thither to see; if your messenger find
him not there, seek him i' th' other place yourself.
But' if indeed you find him not within this month, you
shall nose him as you go up the stairs into the lobby.

CLAUDIUS (to attendants) Go seek him there!

HAMLET A will stay till you come.

(Exeunt attendants.

WARN
L #21,22
22A
m #8

CLAUDIUS Hamlet, this deed, for thine especial safety--
Which we do tender, as we dearly grieve
For that which thou hast done--must send thee hence
With fiery quickness. Therefore prepare thyself.
The bark is ready, and the wind at help.
The associates tend, and every thing is bent
For England.

HAMLET For England?

CLAUDIUS Ay Hamlet.

HAMLET Good.

CLAUDIUS So as it if thou knew'st our purposes.

KING TO R OF KING KISSES CHEEK THEN XES ON US . GROUPING OPENS WHEN
HAMLET XES UP. PETERS BACKS TO ABOVE REY ON 3

STOPPING AT ½ 9:00 TURNING BACK

X BACK IN 2

TURNS XES, EXITS UR

TO ROS AND GUI THEY X TO HIM

ROS AND GUI X OUT UR, REST OF LINE TO COURTIERS

PETERS, FORS , BAR , MOODY, MAR   OUT NEAREST EXIT

VOLT EXIT UR, PROSHEK EXIT BEHIND HIM, CORN OUT TUNL, REY OUT JUNR

X ⤵ TO CROTCH, THEN FACE L

KING ⤴ TO EXIT AND DOOR

FIRST SOLDIER CARRIES FIELD PHONE OVER SHOULDER , 2ND CARRIES CLIPBOARD
PHONE IS SET ON DL RAIL

SOLDIERS 1 AND 2 ENT ABOVE X TO DL SET FIELD PHONE. CAPT ENTER, HOLD AT
ABOVE R DOOR. FORT ENT. CAPT TO ATTENTION, SALUTE. FORT XES TO DS IN BEL, PUTS FOOT
UP ON RAIL

CCAPT XES TO IU FRONT OF R DOOR, CLICKS

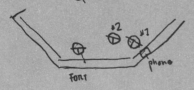

103

HAMLET   I see a cherub that sees them. But come, for England.
Farewell dear mother.

CLAUDIUS   Thy loving father, Hamlet.

HAMLET   My mother--father and mother is man and wife,
man and wife is one flesh; and so my mother
Come, for England.   (Exit.

                                                                      L*21

CLAUDIUS   Follow him at foot, tempt him with speed aboard,
Delay it not. I'll have him hence to-night.
Away, for every thing is sealed and done
That else leans on th' affair; pray you make haste.

                (Exeunt Rosencrantz and Guildenstern.

And England, if my love thou hold'st at aught--
As my great power thereof may give thee sense,
Since yet thy cicatrice looks raw and red
After the Danish sword, and thy free awe
Pays homage to us--thou mayst coldly set
Our sovereign process, which imports at full,
By letters congruing to that effect,
The present death of Hamlet. Do it, England,
For like the hectic in my blood he rages,
And thou must cure me. Till I know 'tis done,   L*22
Howe'er my haps, my joys were ne'er begun.   m*8
                                    (Exit.

(15) IV SCENE FOUR A plain near Elsinore. Enter Fortinbras with
                      his army led by Captain.

FORTINBRAS   Go captain, from me greet the Danish King;
Tell him, that by his licence Fortinbras
Craves the conveyance of a promised march
Over his kingdom. You know the rendezvous.

CAPT SALUTES XES VIA ABOVE FORT TO EXIT L ABOVE

ORDER TO# 1 AND 2 ● L OF UR DOORS OPENS, GUI ENTERS XES SLOWLY TOWARD TUNL,
THEN HAMLET ENTER FOLLOWED BY ROS HAMLET XES TO ¾ 11:00, LOOKS ABOUT. ROS HOLDS
UR OF HIM, THEN L BEL CURTAINS ARE THRUST ASIDE BY CAPT WHO STARTS X BRISKLY TO
DR

TO CAPT, WHO STOPS AT ¼ 4:00, GUI HOLDS AT 4:00 3 AND 2. FORT TAKES CLIPBOARD
FROM #2 LOOKS AT IT FACING L

XING DS 2

HAMLET TURNS TO LOOK UP AT FORT.

XING IN TO R OF C

XING DL AS IF TO LEAVE TUN L

HAMLET STOPS ½ 4:00

SLAPS SWAGGER STICK INTO FREE HAND XES AND EXITS VIA AISLE L OF
R TUN, HAMLET FOLLOWS SLOWLY ¾ 7:30 FORT RETURNS CLIPBOARD TO #2
THEN TAKES BINOCULARS LOOKS DR.

104

FORTINBRAS   If that his Majesty would aught with us,

                   We shall express our duty in his eye,

                   And let him know so.

CAPTAIN   I will do't my lord.

FORTINBRAS   Go softly on.

                       (Exeunt all but Captain.
             Enter Hamlet, Rosencrantz, Guildenstern and others.

HAMLET   Good sir, whose powers are these?

CAPTAIN   They are of Norway sir.

HAMLET   How purposed sir I pray you?

CAPTAIN   Against some part of Poland.

HAMLET   Who commands them sir?

CAPTAIN   The nephew to old Norway, Fortinbras.

HAMLET   Goes it against the main of Poland sir,

                   Or for some frontier?

CAPTAIN   Truly to speak, and with no addition

                   We go to gain a little patch of ground

                   That hath in it no profit but the name.

                   To pay five ducats, five, I would not farm it;

                   Nor will it yield to Norway or the Pole.

                   A ranker rate, should it be sold in fee.

HAMLET   Why then the Polack never will defend it.

CAPTAIN   Yes, it is already garrisoned.

HAMLET   Two thousand souls, and twenty thousand ducats,

                   Will not debate the question of this straw.

                   This is the imposthume of much wealth and peace.

                   That inward breaks, and shows no cause without

                   Why the man dies. I humbly thank you sir.

CAPTAIN   God buy you sir.   (Exit.

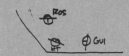

PAUSE WHILE ROS AND GUI X IN TO HAMLET SLOWLY

ROS XES ⌢ HAMLET AND HE AND ROS X SLOWLY OUT TURN L, DOWN STEPS IN
UNISON, LOOKING BACK. HAMLET FOLLOWS TO ½·4'; THEN TURNS TO LOOK US
IN EXIT ROS XES FIRST. GUI STARTS WHEN ROS IS ON LINE ABOVE HIM. 10 X 310 STEPS
ROS LOOK OVER R, GUI OVER L SHOULDER WATCHING HAMLET

TURNING ⌢ LOOKING AT FORT AS HE DOES SO.
X ⌢ TO BENCH. STANDS ON IT AT CROTCH

FORT PUTS DOWN GLASSES, LOOKS OVER CLIPBOARD FACING L

ROSENCRANTZ   Wilt 't please you go my lord?

  HAMLET   I'll be with you straight, go a little before.

                     (Exeunt all but Hamlet.

How all occasions do inform against me,

And spur my dull revenge! What is a man,

If his chief good and market of his time

Be but to sleep and feed? A beast, no more.

Sure he that made us with such large discourse,

Looking before and after, gave us not

That capability and godlike reason

To fust in us unused. Now whether it be

Bestial oblivion, or some craven scruple

Of thinking too precisely on th' event--

A thought which quartered hath but one part wisdom,

And ever three parts coward--I do not know

Why yet I live to say, this thing's to do,

Sith I have cause, and will, and strength, and means

To do't. Examples gross as earth exhort me.

Witness this army of such mass and charge,

Led by a delicate and tender Prince;

Whose spirit with divine ambition puffed

Makes mouths at the invisible event,

Exposing what is mortal, and unsure,

To all that fortune, death, and danger dare,

Even for an eggshell. Rightly to be great,

Is not to stir without great argument,

But greatly to find quarrel in a straw

When honour's at the stake. How stand I then

[handwritten: WARN L #23, HOUSE + L #24 M #9]

ONE FOOT DOWN OFF BENCH

LOOKING TOWARD 8:30

OTHER FOOT OFF BENCH, TURNS LOOKS AT FORT WHO RAISES GLASSES SCANNING
HORIZON
TURNS YES SLOWLY ACROSS TO DOWN LEFT AND OUT TURN L, AT SAME TIME
FORT LOOKS IN HALF CIRCLE WITH GLASSES FROM L TO R

HAMLET   That have a father killed, a mother stained

Excitements of my reason, and my blood,

And let all sleep, while to my shame I see

The imminent death of twenty thousand men,

That for a fantasy and trick of fame

Go to their graves like beds; fight for a plot

Whereon the numbers cannot try the cause,

Which is not tomb enough and continent enough

To hide the slain. O from this time forth,

My thoughts be bloody, [or] be nothing worth.

L#23
m#9

COUNT 5
INTERMISSION

HSE + L#24

RED LITES OUT

(106-47)

ACT III - <u>CHECK LIST</u>

chair struck
stand struck
above doors open
below doors closed
UR doors closed
Andrei door open

MUSICIANS READY
STARTERS READY

<u>WARN</u>

HOUSE
L #25
m #9A

ENTRANCE FOR SCENE 16

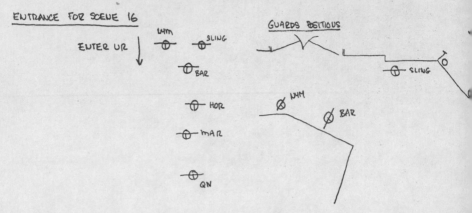

DOORS OPEN AT END OF FANFARE, QUEEN ENTERS UR XING BRISKLY ↘ TO 6:00. SHE IS FOLLOWED BY MAR WHO IS FOLLOWED BY HOR AND GUARDS.

(STOPS AT ½ 11:00 ● LOOKS TO HOR THEN XES TO C HOR XES U\X THRU BELOW TO 2:00

QUEEN TURNS XES UP TO 2:30

HOUSE READY ◾ _____ HOUSE

HOUSE OUT ◾ _____ L#25, m#9A

ACT IV, SCENE FIVE (16)

GERTRUDE   ❡I will not speak with her.

MARCELLUS   ❡She is importunate, indeed distract.❡
            Her mood will needs be pitied.

GERTRUDE   What would she have?

MARCELLUS   She speaks much of her father,❡says she hears
            There's tricks in the world, and hems, and beats
            her heart,
            Spurns enviously at straws, speaks things in doubt
            That carry but half sense. Her speech is nothing,
            Yet the unshaped use of it doth move
            The hearers to collection; they aim at it,
            And botch the words up fit to their own thoughts,
            Which as her winks, and nods, and gestures yield them,
            Indeed would make one think there might be thought,

JUST ABOVE QUEEN AT 4:00

MAR CLICK HEELS EXIT UR. BAR X DS TO 9:00 OAND I. QUEEN XES WEARILY
TO BEFORE CROTCH. HOR CHEATS DOWN TO 3:00 ON 3

ENT UR RUNS TO ½ 12:00. MAR FOLLOWS TO 11:00. LINE TO HOR

SITTING DS IN CROTCH

OPH SMILES XES TO ABOVE QUEEN SITS, STARTS SONG. AT SAME TIME MAR XES
TO ABOVE HOR AND BAR XES DOWN TO 7:30 ON O

REACHES OUT TO TOUCH OPH

PULLS OUT OF RANGE

QUEEN RISES XES TO ½ 12:00

OPH TURNS TO LOOK AT "GRAVE" ACROSS STAGE, CENTERED AT ½ 6:00 ● RISES
XES TO KNEEL AT ¼ 6:00 FACING DS

(INDICATING HEAD AND FOOT (R) ON LINES ● DOORS OPEN UR · KING ENTERS KING SLOWLY
TOWARD OPH.

X TO R OF OPH TRYING TO TOUCH HER

PULLING AWAY

KING ENTERS UR, XES TO 11:00

SEEING KING
TURNING KING TO ½ 10:00, ● XES SLOWLY DOWN TO UR OF OPH · ON XES ON
TO CROTCH

(107)

MARCELLUS
~~GENTLEMAN~~   Though nothing sure, yet much unhappily.

HORATIO   'Twere good she were spoken with, for she may strew

Dangerous conjectures in ill-breeding minds.

GERTRUDE   Let her come in.   (Exit Gentleman.
(aside)
To my sick soul, as sin's true nature is,

Each toy seems prologue to some great amiss.

So full of artless jealously is guilt,

It spills itself, in fearing to be split.

Enter Gentleman with Ophelia.

OPHELIA   Where is the beauteous Majesty or Denmark?

GERTRUDE   How now Ophelia?

OPHELIA(sings)   How should I your true-love know

From another one?

By his cockle hat and staff,

And his sandal shoon.

GERTRUDE   Alas sweet lady, what imports this song?

OPHELIA   Say you? Nay, pray you mark,   (Sings.

He is dead and gone lady,

He is dead and gone,

At his head a grass-green turf,

St his heels a stone.

~~O ho~~!

GERTRUDE   Nay but Ophelia--

OPHELIA   Pray you mark.   (Sings.

White his shroud as the mountain snow--

Enter Claudius

GERTRUDE   Alas look here my lord.

OPHELIA(sings)   Larded all with sweet flowers,

LYING ON STOMACH ON 'GRAVE' ARMS OUT TO SIDE

AT ABOVE C

TURNING OVER

ONTO KNEES, QUEEN X TO 3/4 9:00

KING REACHES TO HELP HER UP, SHE MOVES OUT OF RANGE SKITTERING DL ON FLOOR
THEN RISES STARTS OUT DL. BAR RUNS TO 6:00 IN 0. HOR & MAR X DS 2

STOPPING ON 1 TURNING BACK TO KING ● RUNNING BACK TO L OF KING

HAND TO KING'S L EAR, WHISPERS RUDELY THEN STARTS CC AROUND KING SINGING
SUGGESTIVELY, SLIPPING HER L ARM AROUND KINGS WAIST AS SHE DOES SO HER PULLS
IT AWAY. HOR XES TO BAR AT 6:00 ON 0 AD LIBS THEN XES TO 7:00 ON 0

QUEEN XES TO CROTCH, OPH XES SING DOWN TO 3/4 7:00

TURNING BACK TO KING, RAISING SKIRT THEN XING UL

SEEING MAR AT 2:30 ON 4 KING TO R OF HIM

TRYING TO GROPE MAR WHO FIGHTS HER OFF

REPULSED TURNING DR

AT ABOVE CENTER

WITH RIGHT FIST THEN LEFT FLAILING HER STOMACH, MOANING AFTER EACH HIT THEN
HALF SQUATTING, ROCKING MOANING SOFTLY FOR A COUPLE OF BEATS, THEN SHE STRAIGHTENS
UP FOR LINE LOOKING DR ● RUNS FAST DR TOWARD R TUN. HOR TO 1 AND 2 AT 7:30
BAR TO R OF HIM, STOP HER, PUSH HER BACK ONTO 4, MAR ONTO 4 AND DIZZ, NYM DOWN
TO 9:00 ON 0. AD LIBS BY ALL AS OPH STARTS RUN

(NOW ON 4 SCREAMING THE SONG BAWDILY AT HOR AND BAR, THEN BACKING TO 3/4 6:00 INCLUDING
KING AND MAR

MOVING ON TO 1/2 4:30

108

OPHELIA (SINGS) Which bewept to the grave did not go

With true-love showers.

CLAUDIUS   How do you pretty lady?

OPHELIA   Well, God dild you. They say the owl was a baker's

daughter. Lord, we know what we are but know not what

we may be. God be at your table.

CLAUDIUS   Conceit upon her father.

OPHELIA   Pray let's have no words of this but wehn they ask you

what it means, say you this   (Sings.

To-morrow is Saint Valentine's day,

All in the morning betime.

Am. I a maid at your window,

To be your Valentine.

Then up he rose, and donned his clothes,

And dupped the chamber door,

Let in the maid, that out a maid,

Never departed more.

CLAUDIUS Pretty Ophelia.

OPHELIA Indeed without an oath I'll make an end on't (Sings.

By Gis and by Saint Charity,

Alack and fie for shame,

Young men will do't if they come to't,

By cock, they are to blame,

Quoth she, before you tumbled me,

You promised me to wed.

He answers,

So would I' a done by yonder sun,

An thou hadst not come to my bed.

LINE TO MAR

STANDING AT ½ 4:00 - AT L OF "GRAVE" LOOKING DOWN AT IT, ● KNEELING CLAWING AT GRAVE.

RISING SLOWLY, AKWARDLY

WITH A SNAP OF THE FINGERS - TO HOR

INSINUATINGLY TO KING THEN MAR AS SHE XES UP BETWEEN THEM ●RUNNING OUT UR MAKING A GRAB FOR SLING'S COCK ON THE WAY OUT. BAR XES ↳ to 6:00 INO

HOR XES US VIA BETWEEN KING AND QUEEN EXITS BELL MAR AND BAR FOLLOW, SLING AND WH FOLLOW OPN OUT UR.

QUEEN AND KING X TOWARD ONE ANOTHER EMBRACE AT ½ 9:00 ● PUTTING QUEEN FROM HIM

QUEEN TURNS AWAY XES OUT O 3 AT 8:00 AND STARTS SLOW X ↳ TO UL CORNER

KING XES TO CROR-H, SITS

QUEEN NOW AT UL CORNER ON 3, TURNS BACK TO KING

109

CLAUDIUS   How long hath she been thus?

OPHELIA   I hope all will be well. We must be patient, but I
           cannot choose but weep to think they would lay him i'
           th' cold ground. My brother shall know of it, and so
           I thank you for your good counsel. Come, my coach.
           Good night ladies, good night, sweet ladies, good night
           good night.   (Exit.

CLAUDIUS   Follow her close; give her good watch I pray you.
                              (Exeunt Horatio and Gentleman
           O this is the poison of deep grief, it springs
           All from her father's death. And now behold,
           O Gertrude, Gertrude--   WARN
           When sorrows come, they come not single spies, S#4,5,5A
           But in battalions. First her father slain,   5B
           Next your son gone, and he most violent author
           Of his own just remove, the people muddied.
           Thick and unwholesome in their thoughts and whispers,
           For good Polonius' death. And we have done but greenly
           In hugger-mugger to inter him. Poor Ophelia
           Divided from herself and her fair judgement,
           Without the which we are pictures, or mere beasts.
           Last, and as much containings as all these,
           Her brother is in secret come from France,
           Feeds on his wonder, keeps himself in clouds,
           And wants not buzzers to infect his ear
           With pestilent speeches of his father's death;
           Wherein necessity, of matter beggared,
           Will nothing stick our person to arraign

HANDS TO EARS

XING ONTO 4

RISING, XING TO 3/4 9:00

BAR OPENS UR DOORS HOLDS AT R OF THEM

RUNNING IN FROM UR XING TO 1/2 10:00. BAR SHUTS DOORS BEHIND HIM, HOLDS THEM SHUT
FACING ON-STAGE

KING AND QUEEN X SLOWLY INTO BELOW LISTENING TO MAR   ⟍○ Ⓠ ○ KG ○╱

MAR AND BAR X OUT UR LEAVING DOORS OPEN

APPEARING US IN UR ENTRANCE, FACING L, TALKING TO ACTORS OFF.

110

CLAUDIUS   In ear and ear. O my dear Gertrude, this ·

Like to a murdering-piece in many places

Gives me superflous death.   (Noise within.   S# 4

GERTRUDE   Alack, what noise is this?

CLAUDIUS   Attend!

                    Enter Gentleman.

Where are my Switzers? Let them guard the door.

What is the matter?

MARCELLUS
~~GENTLEMAN~~   Save-yourself my lord.

The ocean overpeering of his list

Eats not the flats with more impitious haste

Than young Laertes in a riotous head

O'erbears your officers. The rabble call him lord,   S# 5

~~And as the world were now but to begin,~~

~~Antiquity forgot, custom not known,~~ d

~~The ratifiers and props of every word,~~

They cry, choose we! Laertes shall be king.

Caps,hands, and tongues applaud it to the clouds,

Laertes shall be king, Laertes king?
                                (Noise within.

GERTRUDE   How cheerfully on the false trail they cry!   S# 5A

O this is counter, you false Danish dogs.
                    END OF GLASS CRASH   S# 5B
                Enter Laertes and other Danes, armed.

CLAUDIUS   The doors are broke.

LAERTES   Where is this King? Sirs, stand you all without.

DANES   No let's come in.

LAERTES   I pray you give me leave.

DANES   We will, we will.

Qu push out to R

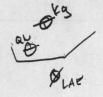

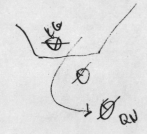

111

LAERTES   I thank you. Keep the door. (Exeunt Danes.) O thou

vile King,

Give me my father.

GERTRUDE   Calmly, good Laertes.

LAERTES   That drop of blood that's calm proclaims me bastard,

Cries cuckold to my father, brands the harlot

Even here between the chaste and unsmirchéd brow

Of my true mother.

CLAUDIUS   What is the cause, Laertes,

That thy rebellion looks so giant-like?

Let him go Gertrude, do not fear our person.

There's such divinity doth hedge a king,

That treason can but peep to what it would,

Acts little of his will. Tell me Laertes,

Why thou art thus incensed--let him go Gertrude--

Speak man?

LAERTES   Where is my father?

CLAUDIUS   Dead.

GERTRUDE   But not by him.

CLAUDIUS   Let him demand his fill.

LAERTES   How came he dead? I'll not be juggled with.

To hell allegiance, vows to the blackest devil,

Conscience and grace to the profoundest pit!

I dare __damnation__. To this point I stand,

That both the worlds I give to negligence,

Let comes what comes, only I'll be revenged

Most throughly for my father.

CLAUDIUS   Who shall stay you?

112

LAERTES   My will, not all the world's.

And for my means, I'll husband them so well,

They shall go far with little.

CLAUDIUS   Good Laertes,

If you desire to know the certainty

Of your dear father, is't writ in your revenge,

That, swoopstake, you will draw both friend and foe,·

Winner and loser?

LAERTES   None but his enemies.

CLAUDIUS   Will you know them then?

LAERTES   To his good friends thus wide, I'll ope my arms,

And like the kind life-rendering pelican,

Repast them with my blood.

CLAUDIUS   Why now you speak

Like a good child, and a true gentleman,

That I am guiltless of your father's death,

And am most sensibly in grief for it,

It shall as level to your judgement 'pear

As day does to your eye.

DANES (within)   LET HER come in!

LAERTES   How now, what noise is that?   Enter Ophelia.

O heat, dry up my brains, tears seven times salt

Burn out the sense and virtue af mine eye,

By heaven thy madness shall be paid with weight,

Till our scale turn the beam. O rose of May,

Dear maid, kind sister, sweet Ophelia—

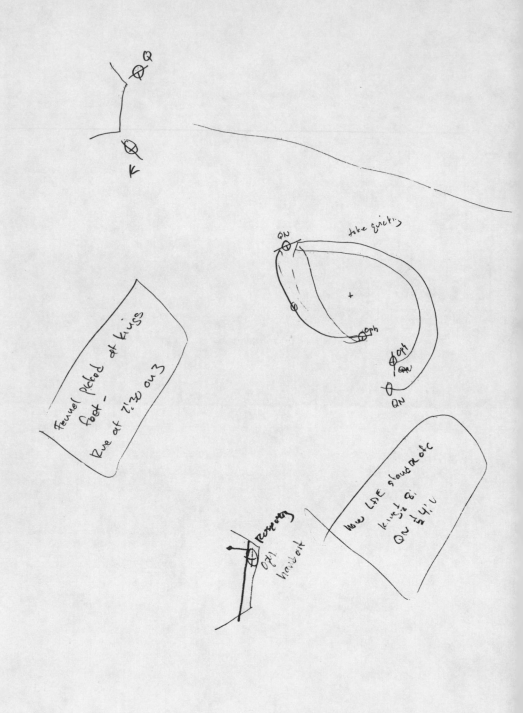

113

LAERTES   O heavens, is't possible a young maid's wits

Should be as mortal as an old man's life?

Nature is fine in love, and where 'tis fine,

It sends some precious instance of itself

After the thing it loves.

OPHELIA(sings)   They bore him barefaced on the bier;

Hey non nonny, nonny, hey nonny,

And on his grave rained many a tear--

Fare you well my dove.

LAERTES   Hadst thou thy wits, and didst persuade revenge,

It could not move thus.

OPHELIA   You must sing, adown, adown, an you call him adown-a.

O how the wheel becomes it! It is the false steward

that stole his master's daughter.

LAERTES   This nothing's more than matter.

OPHELIA(To
LAERTES   There's rosemary that's for remembrance--pray you love,

remember--and there is pansies, that's for thoughts.

LAERTES   A document in madness, thoughts and remembrance fitted.

OPHELIA(to
CLAUDIUS)   There's fennel for you, and columbines. (To Gertrude)

There's rue for you, and here's some for me; we may call

it herb of grace a Sundays--o you must wear your rue with

a difference. There's a daisy. I would give you some

violets, but they withered all when my father died--they

say 'a made a good end.

(Sings.

For bonny sweet Robin is all my joy!

LAERTES   Thought and affliction, passion, hell itself,

KG

QN

114

LAERTES   She turns to favour and to prettiness.

OPHELIA(Sings)   And will 'a not come again?

           And will 'a not come again?

           No, no, he is dead,

           Go to thy death-bed,

           He never will come again.

           His beard was as white as snow,

           All flaxen was his poll.

           He is gone, he is gone,

           And we cast away moan.

           God a mercy on his soul

     And of all Christian sould I pray God. God buy you.

                                          (Exit.

LAERTES   Do you see this, O God?

CLAUDIUS   Laertes, I must commune with your grief,

           Or you deny me right, Go but apart.

           Make choice of whom your wisest friends you will,

           And they shall hear and judge 'twixt you and me.

           If by direct or by collateral hand

           They find us touched, we will our kingdom give,

           Our crown, our life, and all that we call ours

           To you in satisfaction; but if not,

           Be you content to lend your patience to us,

           And we shall jointly labour with your soul

           To give it due content.

LAERTES   Let this be so.

           His means of death, his obscure burial,

           No trophy, sword, nor hatchment o'er bones,

WARN

L 27,27A

LOBBY
FLASH

L 27

2

1

Horz

Stewleyhold leaving
in door

115

LAERTES   No noble rite, nor formal ostentation,

               Cry to be heard as 'twere from heaven to earth,

               That I must call't in question.

CLAUDIUS   So you shall;

               And where th' offence is, let the great axe fall.

               ~~I pray you go with me.~~   (Exuent.

                   17
          IV SCENE SIX The same. Enter Horatio and Servant

HORATIO   What are they that would speak with me?

SERVANT   Seafaring men sir, they say they have letters for you.

HORATIO   Let them come in.   (Exit servant.

               ~~I do not know from what part of the world~~

               ~~I should be greeted, if not from Lord Hamlet~~

                   Enter Sailors

FIRST SAILOR   God bless you sir.

HORATIO   Let him bless thee too.

FIRST SAILOR   'A shall sir an't plese him. There's a letter for you

               sir, it came from th' ambassador that was bound for

               England, if your name be Horatio, as I am let know it is.

HORATIO (reads) Horatio, when thou shalt have overlooked this, give

               these fellows some means to the King, they have letters

               for him. Ere we were two days old at sea, a pirate of

               very warlike appointment gave us chase. Finding ouselves

               too slow of sail, we put on a compelled valour, and in the

               grapple I boarded them, on the instant they got clear of

               our ship, so I alone became their prisoner. They have

               dealt with me like thieves of mercy, but they knew what

               they did, I am to do a good turn for them. Let the King

ENT L BEL, LAE 1ST, THEN KING. X OUT THRU C. LAE XES TO '/4 12:00. KING
FOLLOWS TO UR OF HIM,

*XING DL 2

X BACK TO L OF KING

116

~~LAERTES~~ have the letters I have sent, and repair thou to me with

as much speed as thou wouldest fly death. I have words

to speak in thine ear will make thee dumb, yet are they

much too light for the bore of the matter. These good

fellows will bring thee where I am. Rosencrantz and

Guildenstern hold their course for England, of them I

have much to tell thee. Farewell.

He that thou knowest thine, Hamlet.

Come I will give you way for these your letters,

And do't the speedier that you may direct me   L27B

To him from whom you brought them.   (Exuent.

SCENE SEVEN The same. Enter Claudius and Laertes.

CLAUDIUS Now must your conscience my acquittance seal,

And you must put me in your heart for friend,

Sith you have heard, and with a knowing ear,

That he which hath your noble father slain

Pursued my life.

LAERTES It well appears. But tell me

Why you proceeded not against these feats,

So crimeful and so capital in nature,

As by your safety, greatness, wisdom, all things else,

You mainly were stirred up.

CLAUDIUS O for two speaial reasons,

Which may to you perhaps, seem much unsinewed.

But yet to me th' are strong. The Queen his mother

Lives almost by his looks, and for myself--

My virtue or my plague, be it either which--

117

CLAUDIUS   She is so conjunctive to my life and soul.

That as the star moves not but in his sphere,

I could not but by her. The other motive,

Why to a public count I might not go,

Is the great love the general gender bear him;

LAERTES   And so have I a noble father lost,

A sister driven into desperate terms,

Whose worth, if praises may go back again,

Stood challenger on mount of all the age

For her perfections. But my revenge will come

CLAUDIUS   Break not your sleeps for that you must not think

That we are made of stuff so flat and dull,

That we can let our beard be shook with danger,

And think it pastime. You shortly shall hear more.

I loved your father, and we love ourself

And that I hope will teach you to imagine--

                    Enter Messenger.

How now, what news?

MESSENGER   Letters my lord, from Hamlet.

These to your Majesty; these to the Queen

CLAUDIUS   From Hamlet? Who brought them?

MESSENGER   Sailors my lord they say, I saw them not;

They were given me by Claudio, he received them

Of him that brought them.

CLAUDIUS   Laertes, you shall hear the Leave us (Exit Messenger.

(reads) High and mighty, "you shall know I am set naked

on your kingdom. To-morrow shall I beg leave to see your

kingly eyes, when I shall, first asking your pardon

118

CLAUDIUS   thereunto, recount the occasion of my sudden and more

strange return.
                    Hamlet.

What should this mean? Are all the rest come back?

Or is it some abuse, and no such thing?

LAERTES   Know you the hand?

CLAUDIUS   "Tis Hamlet's character. Naked?

And in a postscript here he says, alone.

Can you devise me?

LAERTES   I am lost in it my lord. But let him come;

It warms the very sickness in my heart

That I shall live and tell him to his teeth,

Thus didest thou.

                    Enter Queen.

CLAUDIUS   How now sweet Queen?

GERTRUDE   One woe doth tread upon another's heel.

So fast they follow; your sister's drowned., Laertes.

LAERTES   Drowned! O where?

GERTRUDE   There is a willow grows askant the brook,

That shows his hoar in the glassy stream;

Therewith fantastic garlands did she make

Of crowflowers, nettles, daisies, and long purples

That liberal shepherds give a grosser name,

But our cold maids do dead men's fingers call them.

There on the pendent boughs her coronet weeds

Clamb'ring to hang, an envious silver broke,

When down her weedy trophies and herself

Fell in the weeping brook. Her clothes spread wide,

And mermaid-like awhile they bore her up,

2 planks set across grave, us by #1, ds by #2 during verse

A pickaxe and a spade, a spade

For and a shrouding sheet

A bit of clay for to be made ⟶ #2 out to DL of grave
starts on R foot

For such a guest is meet.

119

WARN L#28,29

GERTRUDE   Which time she chanted snatches of old tunes,

As one incapable of her own distress,   WARN

Or like a creature native and indued   BRAVE-UR

Unto that element; but long it could not be

Till that her garments, heavy with their drink,

Pulled the poor wretch from her melodious lay

To muddy death.

LAERTES   Alas, then she is drowned?

GERTRUDE   Drowned, drowned.

LAERTES   Too much of water hast thou poor Ophelia,

And therefore I forbid my tears; but yet

It is our trick, nature her custom holds,

Let shame say what it will; when these are gone,

The woman will be out. Adieu my lord.

I have a speech of fire that fain would blaze,

But that this folly drowns it (Exit.

CLAUDIUS   Let's follow, Gertrude.   L#28

How much I had to do to calm his rage!

Now fear I this will give it start again,

Therefore let's follow. BLACKOUT (Exeunt.   UR↓ GRAVE

COUNT 2   L#29

ACT FIVE SCENE ONE Elsinore. A churchyard. Enter Sexton and
Gravedigger, to an open grave.

SEXTON   Is she to be buried in Christian burial, when she

wilfully seeks her own salvation?

GRAVEDIGGER   I tell thee she is, therefore make her grave straight.

The crowner hath sat on her, and finds it Christian

burial.

SEXTON   How can that be, unless she drowned herself in her own
defence?

cup and bottle

GRAVEDIGGER   Why 'tis found so.

SEXTON   It must be se offendendo, it cannot be else. For here

lies the point, if I drown myself wittingly, it argues

an act, and an act hath three branches; it is to act,

to do, to perform; argal she drowned herself wittingly.

GRAVEDIGGER   *+ swing legs C to sit facing us lean on l hand*
Nay, but hear you goodman delver--

SEXTON   *now swing*   *illustrating with lunch, putting them on ds plank*
Give me leave. Here lies the water--good. Here stands *cup*

the man--good. If the man go to this *bottle* water and drown

himself, it is, will he, nill he, he goes, mark you that.

But if the water come to him, and drown him, he drowns

not himself; argal, he that is not guilty of his own

death, shortens not his own life.— *putting lunch stuff away into sack*
                                                    into ds sack

GRAVEDIGGER   But is this law?

SEXTON   Ay marry is't, crowner's quest law.

GRAVEDIGGER   *swing legs ds*
Will you ha' the truth an't? If this had not been a

gentlewoman, she should have been buried out a Christian

burial.

SEXTON   *hiking self up to sit grave L*   *rising ix across us plank to R of gr.*
Why there thou sayst, and the more pity that great folk

*2 undo
1 sleeves*
should have countenance in this world to drown or hang

themselves, more than their even-Christen. *x ac* *hold bag open 2 reaches* ·Come my *put shovel in it*
——— 2nd   *us*
spade, there is no ancient gentlemen but gardeners,   *sack*

ditchers, and grave-makers. they hold up Adam's

profession.—   (Enters the grave.
                    L 2 c.
GRAVEDIGGER   (Was he a gentlemam?

SEXTON   'A the first that ever bore arms. *+ sack at us of gr.*

GRAVEDIGGER   *rising 2 L Lat*
Why he had none.

SEXTON   What, art a heathen? How dost thou understand the

Scripture? The Scripture says Adam digged. Could he
                              us plank
dig without arms? I'll put another question to thee;

121

SEXTON: if thou answerest me not to the purpose, confess

thyself--

GRAVEDIGGER: Go to.

SEXTON: What is he that builds stronger than either the mason,

the shipwright or the carpenter?'

GRAVEDIGGER: The gallows-maker, for that frame outlives thousand

tenants.

SEXTON: I like thy wit well in good faith; the gallows does well

but how does it well? It does well to those that do ill

now thou dost ill to say the gallows is built stronger

than the church; argal, the gallows may do well to thee.

To't again, come.

GRAVEDIGGER: Who builds stronger than a mason, a shipwright, or a

carpenter?

SEXTON: Ay, tell me that and unyoke.

GRAVEDIGGER: Marry now I can tell.

SEXTON: To't.

GRAVEDIGGER: Mass I cannot tell.

Enter Hamlet and Horatio and stay retired.
TUNNEL.

SEXTON: Cudgel thy brains no more about it, for your dull ass

will not mend his pace with beating; and when you are

asked this question next, say a grave-maker, the houses

he makes lasts till doomsday. Go, get thee to Yaughan,

fetch me a stoop of liquor.

(He digs and sings. Exit Gravedigger.

In youth when I did love, did love,

Methought it was very sweet,

~~To contract o the time for a my behove,~~

122

SEXTON(singing)   ~~O methought there a was nothing-a meet~~.

HAMLET   Has this fellow no feeling of his business, that 'a

sings in grave-making?

HORATIO   Custom hath made it in him a property of easiness.

HAMLET   ¶ 'Tis e'en so, the hand of little employment hath the

daintier sense.

SEXTON(sings)   But age with his stealing steps

Hath clawed me in his clutch, ─skull to DL cor of grave

And hath shipped me ~~intil the land~~,

~~As if I had never been such.~~

                    (~~Throws up a skull~~,

HAMLET   That skull had a tongue in it, and could sing once.

How the knave jowls it to the ground, as if 'twere Cain's

jawbone, that did the first murder. This might be the

pate of a politician, which this ass now o'er-reaches;

one that would circumvent God, might it not?

HORATIO   It might my lord.

HAMLET   Or of a courtier, which could say, good morrow sweet

lord, how dost thou sweet lord? This might be my lord

such-a-one, that praised my lord such-a-one's horse,

when 'a meant to beg it, might it not?

HORATIO   Ay my lord.

HAMLET   Why e'en so, and now my Lady Worm's; chapless, and

knocked about the mazzard with a sexton's spade; here's

fine revolution an we had the trick to see't. ─bones out DC Did these

bones cost no more the breeding, but to play at loggats

with them? Mine ache to think on't.

SEXTON (Sings)   A pickaxe and a spade, a spade,

For and-a shrouding sheet, ─skull to DR cor

123

SEXTON (Singing)   ~~O a pit of clay for to be made~~

~~For such a guest is meet.~~

~~(Throws another skull across the stag~~e.

HAMLET   There's another--why may not that be the skull of a

lawyer? Where be his quiddities now, his quillities, his

cases, his tenures, and his tricks? Why does he suffer

this rude knave now to knock him about the sconce with

a dirty shovel, and will not tell him of his action of

battery? (Picks up skull) ~~Hum! This fellow might be~~

~~in's time a great buyer of land, with his statues, his~~

~~recognizances, his fines, his double vouchers, his~~

~~recoveries. Is this the fine of his fines, and the~~

~~recovery of his recoveries, to have his fine pate full of~~

~~fine dirt? Will his vouchers vouch him no more of his~~

~~purchases, and double ones too, than the lenght and~~

~~breadth of a pair of indentures? The very conveyance~~s

~~of his lands will scarcely lie in this box; and must th'~~

~~inherito~~r himself ~~have no more, ha~~?

HORATIO   ~~Not a jot more my lord.~~

HAMLET   ~~Is not parchment made of sheep-skins~~?

HORATIO   ~~Ay my lord, and of calves' skins too.~~

HAMLET   ~~They are sheep and calves which seek out assurance in that.~~

I will speak to this fellow. (~~They come forwar~~d) Whose

grave's this sirrah?

SEXTON   Mine sir.   (Sings.

~~O a pit of clay for to be made~~

~~For such a guest is meet.~~

HAMLET   I think it be thine indeed, for thou liest in't.

124

SEXTON   You lie out on/t sir, and therefore 'tis not yours;

          For my part I do not lie in't, yet it is mine.

HAMLET   Thou dost lie in't, to be in't and say it is thine.

          Tis for the dead, not for the quick; therefore thou liest

SEXTON   'Tis a quick lie sir, 'twill away again from me to you.

HAMLET   What man dost thou dig it for?

SEXTON   For no man sir.

HAMLET   What woman then?

SEXTON   For none neither.

HAMLET   Who is to be buried in't?

SEXTON   One that was a woman sir, but rest her soul she's dead. ↓grave

HAMLET   ⌐HOR→ 4/5 at 21.30 · HT xes ⌒ grave to HOR
          How absolute the knave is! We must speak by the card,

          ·collects skulls and⌐
          ·s puts them into⌐   or equivocation will undo us. By the Lord, Horatio, this
          ·s at end grave⌐

          three years I have took note of it--the age is grown so

          picked, that the toe of the peasant comes so near the
                                                     x→L of Gr. Hor x→7½ l.00
          heel of the courtier he galls his kibe. ⌐How long hast

          thou been grave-maker?
          ⌐sit on us plank
SEXTON   Of all the days 'i th' year I came to;t that day that

          our last King Hamlet overcame Fortinbras.

HAMLET   How long is that since?

SEXTON   Cannot you tell that? Every fool can tell that; it was
                                        ⌐HT b us of gr.⌐
          that very day that young Hamlet--was born--he that is

          mad and sent into England.

HAMLET   Ay marry, why was he sent into England?

SEXTON   Why because 'a was mad. 'A shall recover his wits there,

          or if 'a do not, 'tis no great matter there.

HAMLET   Why?

SEXTON   'Twill not be seen in him there, there the men are

          as mad as he.

125

HAMLET   How came he mad?

SEXTON   Very strangely they say.

HAMLET   How strangely?

SEXTON   Faith e'en with losing his wits.

HAMLET   Upon what ground?

SEXTON   Why here in Denmark. I have been sexton here man and
boy for thirty years.

HAMLET   How long will a man lie i' th' earth ere he rot?

SEXTON   Faith if 'a be not rotten before 'a die, as we have many
pocky corses nowadays that will scarce hold the laying
in, 'a will last you some eight year, or nine year.
A tanner will last you nine year.

HAMLET   Why he more than another?

SEXTON   Why sir, his hide is so tanned with his trade that 'a
will keep out water a great while; and your water is a
sore decayer of your whoreson dead body. Here's a
skull now hath lien you i' th' earth three and twenty
years.

HAMLET   Whose was it?

SEXTON   A whoreson mad fellow's it was, whose do you think it was?

HAMLET   Nay I know not.

SEXTON   A pestilence on him for a mad rogue, 'a poured a flagon
of Rhenish on my head once; this same skull sir, was sir,
Yorick's skull, the King's jester.

HAMLET   This?

SEXTON   E'en that.

HAMLET   Let me see. (Takes the skull) Alas poor Yorick! I knew
him Horatio, 'a fellow of infinite jest, of most excellent

126

HAMLET   fancy; he hath borne me on his back a thousand times,
and now how abhorred in my imagination it is--my gorge
rises at it. Here hung those lips that I have kissed I
know not how oft. Where be your gibes now? Your gambols,
your songs, your flashes of merriment, that were wont to
set the table on a roar? Not one now to mock your own
grinning? Quite chop-fallen? Now-get you to my lady's
chamber, and tell her, let her paint an inch thick, to this
favour she must come. Make her laugh at that . Prithee
Horatio tell me one thing.

HORATIO   What's that my lord?

HAMLET   Dost thou think Alexander looked a this fashion i' th'
earth?

HORATIO   E'en so.

HAMLET   And smelt so? Pah! (Puts down the skull.

HORATIO   E'en so my lord.

HAMLET   To what base uses we may return, Horatio! Why may not
imagination trace the noble dust of Alexander, till 'a
find it stopping a bunghole?

HORATIO   'Twere to consider too curiously to consider so.

HAMLET   No faith, not a jot, but to follow him thither with
modesty enough, and likelihood to lead it; as thus--
Alexander died, Alesander was buried, Alexander returneth
to dust, the dust is earth, of earth we make loam, and
why of that loam whereto he was converted might not they
stop a beer barrel?
          Imperious Caesar, dead and turned to clay,
         Might stop a hole, to keep the wind away.

X to HOR, MEET 10:30

stoops put on bed by edge
cath down on usher.

XES INTO BEL R THEN TO L DOOR, HOR FOLLOWS, XES TO R OF HIM

PRIEST, UNDERTAKERS, LAERTES, KING AND QUEEN FOLLOWED BY COURTIERS ENTER
TUN L. DURING ENTRANCE GD'S ENTER. #1 FROM AND DOOR WITH DIRT. #2 FROM TUN R
THEY X TO BEFORE BENCH PLAT. PRIEST XES (* TO PLACE AT ABOVE GRAVE. #2 HAS STOUPS OF
WINE. DIAGRAM

SHUTTING PRAYER BOOK

a̅ ɡ̅s

HAMLET   O that the earth which kept the world in awe   maʒ

            Should patch a wall t' expel the winter's flaw!

            But soft, but soft awhile--here comes the King,

            The Queen, the courtiers. *bk toward below? how Proud.*

X Ht   ~~Enter Claudius, Gertrude, Laertes, in funeral procession~~

X   ~~following the corpse of Ophelia, then Priest and Lords~~.

            Who is this they follow?

            And with such maimed rites? This doth betoken,

            The corse they follow did with desperate hand

            Fordo it own life. 'Twas of some estate.

            Couch we awhile and mark.

                                (Retires with Horatio.

Laertes   What ceremony else?

HAMLET   That is Laertes, A very noble youth. ~~Mark~~.

LAERTES   What ceremony else?

PRIEST   Her obsequies have been as far enlarged

            As we have warranty. Her death was doubtful,

            And but that great command o'ersways the order,

            She should in ground unsanctified have lodged

            Till the last trumpet. For charitable prayers,

            Shards, flints, and pebbles should be thrown on her;

            Yet here she is allowed her virgin crants,

            Her maiden strewments, and the bringing home

            Of bell and burial.

LAERTES   Must there no more be done?

PRIEST   No more be done.

            We should profane the service of the dead,

            To sing a requiem and such rest to her

            As to peace-parted souls.

GD MOVE TO GRAVE, PULL OUT PLANKS (#2 DS) RETURN TO PLACE, #1 GIVES US PLANK TO
#2, UNDERTAKERS PICK UP STRAPS LOWER COFFIN, THROW STRAPS IN GRAVE THEN MOVE
AWAY (DIAGRAM)

UNDERTAKERS NOW MOVE AWAY
                DUR pole   HOR ↑ → R
HAMLET XES TO R IN BELOW ● #1 MOVES TO R OF PRIEST WITH EARTH

QUEEN XES TO EDGE OF GRAVE SCATTER FLOWERS

L TO R OF GRAVE

PRIEST HAVING TAKEN EARTH FROM BOX, HOLDS, HAND OVER GRAVE STARTS 'DUST THOU ART - - CUT OFF
BY LAE.
JUMPS DOWN INTO GRAVE - ALL EXCLAIM AND MOVE (DIAGRAM)

HAMLET XES OUT OF R BELOW TO 11:00, HOR FOLLOWS TO HIS L ● ALL MOVE
(DIAGRAM)

RUNS TO UR OF GRAVE

LEAPS DOWN INTO GRAVE - GEN'L NOISE AND CONFUSION
PRIEST TO 1st PANEL L

128

LAERTES   Lay her i' th' earth

And from her fair and unpolluted flesh

May violets spring, I tell thee churlish priest,

A minist'ring angel shall my sister be

When thou liest howling.

HAMLET   What, the fair Ophelia!

GERTRUDE   Sweets to the sweet. Farewell. (Scatters flowers.

I hoped thou shouldst have been my Hamlet's wife.

I thought thy bride-bed to have decked, sweet maid,

And not have strewed thy grave.

LAERTES   O treble woe

Fall ten times treble on that cursed head

Whose wicked deed thy most ingenious sense

Deprived thee of. Hold off the earth awhile,

Till I have caught her once more in mine arms.

                      (Leaps in the grave.

Now pile your dust upon the quick and dead,

Till of this flat a mountain you have made

T' o'ertop old Pelion or the skyish head

Of blue Olympus.

HAMLET(comes forward)
    What is he whose grief

Bears such an emphasis, whose phrase of sorrow

Conjures the wandering stars, and makes them stand

Like wonder-wounded hearers? This is I,

Hamlet the Dane.   (Leaps in the grave.

LAERTES   The devil take thy soul

                   (Grapples with him.

HAMLET   Thou pray'st not well

X TO BELOW GRAVE, THIS LINE AND 3 FOLLOWING LOST IN HUB BUB. GOING
MAR AND SLING WHO GIVES UMB TO PETERS RUSH IN PULL LAE OUT OF GRAVE AND
TO 3/4 9:00, AT SAME TIME CORN, BAR LINE AND STAN RUSH TO HAMLET PULL HIM OUT
TO 2:00 FROM 12 OF GRAVE (STAN GIVES HIS UMB TO VON M). WHEN THEY ARE BEING PULLED
BACK, REY X TO ABOVE GRAVE V(A L OF IT, KING TO UR OF GRAVE VIA R OF IT, VON M X TO
PETERS AND RETURN TO PLACE. GD X ↳ TO BELOW BENCH

X TO DL OF GRAVE

BOTH GROUPS MOVE IN TO SIDES OF GRAVE, FORCED BY HAMLET AND LAE

QUEEN X TO BACK

PULLING FREE KNEELING, BAR XES ⌐ TO BELOW HIM

HAMLET PULLED TO 4:00 ON 3 BY CORN AND BAR, LAE IS PULLED BACK ONTO
PLAT THEN LEFT TO SIT CROTCH, PANTING, GOING AND SLING X⌐ TO BEHIND US BENCH
MAR TO BEHIND DS BENCH.

HAMLET: ~~I prithee take thy fingers from my throat,~~

~~For though I am not splenitive and rash,~~

~~Yet have I in me something dangerous,~~

~~Which let thy wiseness fear,~~ hold off thy hand.

CLAUDIUS: Pluck them asunder.

GERTRUDE: Hamlet, Hamlet!

ALL: Gentlemen! Gentlemen!

HORATIO: Good my lord, be quiet!
HAMLET: Why, I will fight with him upon this theme until my eyelids
           as he is being dragged back
           no longer wag.

GERTRUDE: O my son, what theme?

HAMLET: I loved Ophelia, forty thousand brothers

           could not with all their quantity of love

           make up my sum. What wilt thou do for her?

                                                          WARN"

                                                          L#29A

CLAUDIUS: O, he is mad, Laertes.
                                                          try easier
GERTRUDE: For the love of God, forbear him.

HAMLET: 'Swounds, show me what thou't do:

           Woo't weep? woo't fight? woo't fast? woo't tear thyself?

           Woo't drink up eisel? eat a crocidile?

           I'll do it. Dost thou come here to whine?

           To outface me with leaping in her grave?

           Be buried quick with her, and so will I.

           And if thou prate of mountains, let them throw

           Millions of acres on us, till our ground,

           Singeing his pate against the burning zone,

           Make Ossa like a wart! nay, and thou'lt mouth,

           I'll rant as well as thou.

GERTRUDE: This is mere madness,

X TO ABOVE HAMLET

XR SLOWLY TO ½ 9:00

TURNING TO LOOK AT GRAVE

STARTS, XES, EXITS UR - GOING AND SLING X DOWN TO 7:30 ON O
PRIEST XES SLOWLY DOWN TO ABOVE GRAVE

                ● HOR EXIT UR

KING XES TO LAE

    X TO ½ 9:00 ● WHEN QUEEN TURNS WOUDY XES TO HER LEFT SHE TAKES HIS ARM THEY
    EXIT TUN L . ALL FOLLOW. OSR AT L OF PRIEST STARTS HIM OUT PRIEST EXIT HUFFILY DL, OSR K
SLOWLY DL , TURNS BACK TO KING WHO GIVES HIM HIGH SIGN TO LEAVE . OSR INCLINES HEAD, TURNS
OPENS UMBRELLA , EXITS TUN L

129

GERTRUDE And thus awhile the fit will work on him;

Anon as patient as the female dove

When that her golden couplets are disclosed,

His silence will sit drooping.

HAMLET Hear you sir,

What is the reason that you use me thus?

I loved you ever—but it is no matter.

Let Hercules himself do what he may,

The cat will mew, and dog will have his day. (Exit.

CLAUDIUS I pray thee good Horatio, wait upon him. (Exit Horatio.

(aside to Laertes)

Strengthen your patience in our last night's speech,

We'll put the matter to the present push.

Good Gertrude set some watch over your son.

~~This gave shall have a living monument.~~
(Exuent Gertrude, courtiers and grave-
diggers.
King detains Laertes.

LAERTES Since Hamlet is returned,—

~~As checking at his voyage, and that he means~~

~~no more to undertake it—~~Good Laertes

Will you be ruled by me?

LAERTES Ay, my good lord,

So you will not o'errule me to a peace.

CLAUDIUS To thine own peace, Laertes, I will work him

to an exploit, now ripe in my device,

Under the which he shall not choose but fall.

And for his death no wind of blame shall breathe,

but even his mother shall uncharge the practice,

and call it accident.

130

LAERTES   My lord I will be ruled.

CLAUDIUS   You have been talked of since your travel much,

and that in Hamlet's hearing, for a quality

wherein they say you shine. Your sum of parts

did not pluck such envy from him

As did that one, and that in my regard,

of the unworthiest life.

LAERTES   ~~What part is that, my Lord~~?

CLAUDIUS   ~~Very riband in the cap of youth;~~

~~Yet needful too, for youth no less becomes,~~

~~The light and careless livery that it wears,~~

~~Than settled age his sables and his weeds,~~

~~Importing health and graveness.~~ Two months since

Here was a gentleman of Normandy...

LAERTES   Upon my life, Lamond.

CLAUDIUS   The very same.

LAERTES   ~~I know him well~~.

CLAUDIUS   ~~He made confession of you~~,

and gave you such a masterly report,

For art and exercise in your defence,

And for your rapier most especial,

That he cried out, 'twould be a sight indeed,

if one could match you. | This report of his

did Hamlet so envenom his envy,

that he could nothing do but wish and beg

Your sudden coming o'er to play with him

Now out of this.

LAERTES   What out of this, my Lord?

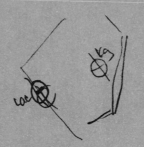

131

DIUS   Laertes, was your father dear to you?

Or are you like the painting of a sorrow,

A face without a heart?

RTES   Why ask you this?

US   Not that I think you did not love your father,

Hamlet comes back, what would you undertake

to show yourself in deed join fathers son

More than in words.

RTES   To cut his throat i' the church.

DIUS   No place indeed should murder sanctuaries.

Revenge should have no bounds. But, good Laertes,

Hamlet returned shall know you are come home

We'll put on those shall praise your excellence,

and set a double varnish on the fame

The Frenchman gave you, bring you in fine together

And wager on your heads; he being remiss

Most generous, and free from all contriving.

Will not peruse the foils, so that with ease,

Or with shuffling, you may choose

A sword unbated, and in a pass of practice

Requite him for your father.

RTES   I wil do't,

And for that purpose I'll annoint my sword.

I bought an unction of a mountebank,

So mortal, that but dip a knife in it,

Where it draws blood no cataplasm so rare,

Collected from all simples that have virtue

Under the moon, can save the thing from death

" An hour " - x with him out Turn L 1kg of LAEL

20 - Exit Aud door , HT let X → R of C

Hor → 3/4 9;
HT stay dlt trap x → 1/2 8

gve papes with L other u R

      S. firs opp Hor.

Vaud bizacu entrance

132

LAERTES   That is but scratched withal. I'll ~~touch~~ my point
     touch
     With this contagion, that if I gall him slightly,

     It may be death.

CLAUDIUS   Let's further think of this,

     Weight what convenience both of time and means

     May fit us to our shape. If this should fail,

     And that our drift look through our bad performance,

     'Twere better not assayed; therefore this project

     Should have a back or second. Let me see...

     We'll make a solemn wager on your cunnings--

     I ha't!

     When in your motion you are hot and dry,

     As make your bouts more violent to that end,

     And that he calls for drink, I'll have prepared him

     A chalice for the nonce, whereon but sipping,

     If he by chance excape your venomed stuck,

     Our purpose may hold there.

     This grave shall have a living monument.

     An hour of quiet shortly shall we see,

     Till then in patience our proceeding be.

20

✗ SCENE TWO The Castle. Enter Hamlet and Horatio.

HAMLET— So much for this sir, now shall you see the other--

     You do remember all the circumstance?

HORATIO— Remember it my lord!

HAMLET— Sir, in my heart there was a kind of fighting,

     That would not let me sleep; methought I lay

     Worse than the mutines in the bilboes. Rashly--

     And praised by rashness for it; let us know,

133

HAMLET   Our indiscretion sometimes serves us well

When our deep plots do pall, and that should ~~learn~~ us

There's a divinity that shapes our ends,

Rough-hew them, how we will--

HORATIO   That is most certain.

HAMLET   Up from my cabin,

My sea-gown scarfed about me, in the dark

Groped I to find out them, had my desire,

Fingered their packet, and in fine withdrew

To mine own room again; making so bold,

My fears forgetting manners, to unseal

Their grand commission; where I found,

      Horatio--

O royal knavery—an exact command,

Larded with many several sorts of reasons,

Importing Denmark's health, and England's too,

With ho, such bugs and goblins in my life,

That on the supervise, no leisure bated,

No not to stay the grinding of the axe,

My head should be struck off.

HORATIO   Is't possible?

HAMLET   Here's the commission; read it/at more leisure.

But wilt thou hear now how I did proceed?

HORATIO   I beseech you.

HAMLET   Being thus be-netted round with villainies--

Ere I could make a prologue to my brains,

They had begun the play--I sat me down,

Devised a new commission, ~~wrote it fair~~--

134

HAMLET   ~~I once did hold it as our statists do,~~

    ~~A baseness to write fair, and laboured much~~

    ~~How to forget that learning, but sir, now~~

    ~~It did me yeoman's service~~ wilt thou know

    Th' effect of what I wrote?

HORATIO   Ay, good my lord. x ↓ ✓

HAMLET   An earnest conjuration from the King,

    ~~As England was his faithful tributary;~~

    ~~As love between them like the palm might flourish,~~

    ~~As peace should still her wheaten garland wear~~

    ~~And stand a comma 'tween their amities,~~

    ~~And ,any such like As'es of great charge,~~

    That on the view and knowing of these contents,

    ~~Without debatement further more or less,~~

    ~~He~~ England should ~~those bearers~~ those bearers to the put ~~to sudden~~ death,

    Not shriving time allowed. "

HORATIO   ~~How was this sealed?~~

HAMLET   ~~Why even in that was heaven ordinant.~~

    ~~I had my father's signet in my purse,~~

    ~~Which was the model of that Danish seal;~~

    ~~Folded the writ up in the form of th' other,~~

    ~~Subscribed it, gave't th' impression, placed it safely,~~

    ~~The changeling never known. Now the next day~~

    ~~Was our sea-fight, and what to this was sequent~~

    ~~Thou knowest already.~~

HORATIO   So Guildenstern and Rosencrantz go to't. Hor + US

HAMLET   Why man, they did make love to this employment.

    They are not near my conscience, their defeat

135

HAMLET   Does by their own insinuation grow.

                 'Tis dangerous when the baser nature comes

                 Between the pass and fell incensed points

                 Of mighty opposites.

HORATIO   Why what a King is this!

HAMLET   Does it not, think thee, stand me now upon--

                 He that hath killed my King, and whored my mother;

                 Popped in between th' election and my hopes,

                 Thrown out his angle for my proper life,

                 And with such cozenage--is't not perfect conscicience

                 To quit him with this arm? And is't not to be <u>damned</u>

                 To let this canker of our nature come

                 In further evil?

HORATIO   It must be shortly known to him from England

                 What is the issue of the business there.

HAMLET   It will be short; the interim is mine,

                 And a man's life no more than to say, one.

                 But I am very sorry, good Horatio,

                 That to Laertes I forgot myself;

                 For by the image of my cause, I see

                 The portraiture of his; I'll court his favours.

                 But sure the bravery of his grief did put me

                 Into a towering passion.

                           Enter Osric.

HORATIO   Peace, who comes here?

OSRIC   Your lordship is right welcome back to Denmark.

HAMLET   I humbly thank you sir. (Aside to Horatio.)

                 Dost know this water-fly?--

136

HORATIO (aside)   No my good lord.

HAMLET (aside)   Thy state is the more gracious, ~~for 'tis vice to know~~
~~him. He hath much land, and fertile. Let a beast be~~
~~lord of beasts, and his crib shall stand at the king's~~
~~mess. 'Tis a chough, but as I say, spacious in the~~
~~possession of dirt.~~

OSRIC   Sweet lord, if your lordship were at leisure, I should
impart a thing to you from his Majesty.

HAMLET   I will receive it sir, with all diligence of spirit.
Put your bonnet to his right us, 'tis for the head.

OSRIC   I thank you your lordship, it is very hot.

HAMLET   No believe me, 'tis very cold, the wind is northerly

OSRIC   It is indifferent cold my lord indeed.

HAMLET   But yet methinks it is very sultry, and hot for my
complexion.

OSRIC   Exceedingly my lord, It is very sultry, as 'twere, I
cannot tell how. But my lord, his Majesty bade me
signify to you, that 'a has laid a great wager on your
head. Sir, this is the matter---

HAMLET   I beseech you remember--

(Hamlet moves him to put on his
hat)

OSRIC   Nay good my lord, for my ease in good faith. Sir here
is newly come to court Laertes; believe me an absolute
gentleman, full of most excellent differences, of very
soft society, and gret showing; indeed to speak
feelingly of him, he is the card or calendar of gentry,
for you shall find in him the continent of what part a
gentlemean would see.

nomoles

x → ½ q"

137

HAMLET   ~~Sir, his definement suffers no perdition in you, though~~
          ~~I know to divide him inventorially would dizzy 'th~~
          ~~arithmetic of memory, and yet but yaw neither, in~~
          ~~respect of his quick sail. But in the verity of~~
          ~~extolment, I take him to be a soul of great article,~~
          ~~and his infusion of such dearth and rareness, as to~~
          ~~make true diction of him,~~ ~~his semblable is his mirror,~~
          ~~and who else would trace him, his umbrage, nothing more.~~

OSRIC   ~~Your lordship speaks most infallibly of him.~~

HAMLET   The concernancy sir? ~~Why do we wrap the gentleman in~~
          ~~our more rawer breath?~~

OSRIC   ~~Sir?~~

~~TIO~~   ~~Is't not possible to understand in another tongue?~~
          ~~You will do't sir really.~~

HAMLET   What imports the nomination of this gentleman?

OSRIC   ~~Of Laertes?~~

HORATIO (Aside
to Hamlet) ~~His purse is empty already, all's golden words are spent.~~

HAMLET   ~~Of him sir.~~

OSRIC   ~~I know you are not ignorant--~~

HAMLET   ~~I would you did sir, yet in faith if you did, it would~~
          ~~not much approve me, well sir?~~

OSRIC   ~~--~~ You are not ignorant of what excellence Laertes is--

HAMLET   ~~I dare not confess that, lest I should compare with him~~
          ~~in excellence; but to know a man well, were to know~~
          ~~himself.~~

OSRIC   I mean sir for his weapon, ~~but in the imputation laid~~
          ~~on him by them, in his meed he's unfellowed.~~

138

SOUND BACK

HAMLET   What's his weapon?

OSRIC   Rapier and dagger.

HAMLET   That's two of his weapons--but well.

OSRIC   The King, sir, hath wagered with him six Barbary horses,

against the which he has imponed, as I take it, six

French rapiers and poniards, with their assigns, as girdle,

hangers, and so. Three of the carriages in faith are very

dear to fancy, very responsive to the hilts, most delicate

carriages, and of very liberal conceit

HAMLET   ~~What call you the carriages?~~

HORATIO (aside
to Hamlet) ~~I knew you must be edified by the margent ere you had done.~~

OSRIC   ~~The carriages sir, are the hangers.~~

HAMLET   ~~The phrase would be more german to the matter if we could~~

~~carry a cannon by our sides; I would it might be~~

~~hangers till then.~~ But on--six Barbary horses against

six French swords, their assigns, and three liberal-

conceited carriages; that's the French bet against the

Danish. Why is this imponed, as you call it?

OSRIC   The King, sir, hath laid sir, that in a dozen passes

between yourself and him, he shall not exceed you three

hits; he hath laid on twelve for nine; and it would come

to immediate trial, if your lordship would vouchsafe

the answer.

HAMLET   How if I answer no?

OSRIC   I mean, my lord, the opposition of your person in trial.

HAMLET   Sir, I will walk here in the hall. If it pleases his

Majesty, it is the breathing time of day with me) let

139

HAMLET   the foils be brought, the gentleman willing, and the King

hold his purpose; I will win for him and I can, if not,

I will gain nothing by my shame and the odd hits.

OSRIC   Shall I re-deliver you e'en so?

HAMLET   To this effect sir, after what flourish your nature will.

OSRIC   I commend my duty to your lordship. bow

HAMLET   Yours, yours." (Exit Osric) He does well to commend it

himself, there are no tongues else for's turn.

HORATIO   ~~This lapwing runs away with the shell on his head.~~

                    Enter Lord.

OSRIC
~~LORD~~   The King and Queen, and all are coming down.

HAMLET   ~~In~~ happy time.

LORD   ~~The Queen desires you to use some gentle entertainment~~

~~to Laertes, before you fall to play.~~

HAMLET   She ~~well instructs me.~~   (Exit Lord)

HORATIO   You will lose this wager my lord.

HAMLET   I do not think so. Since he went into France, I have

been in continual practice; I shall win at the odds.

But thou wouldst not think how ill all's here about

my heart—but it is no matter.

HORATIO   Nay good my lord—

HAMLET   It is but foolery, but it is such a kind of gain-

giving as would perhaps trouble a woman.

HORATIO   If your mind dislike any thing, obey it. I will

forestall their repair hither, and say you are not fit.

HAMLET   Not a whit, we defy augury; there is a special

providence in the fall of a sparrow. If it be now,

WARN
M#10
L#30AA

HORATIO, XES TO DS BENCH, GETS DISPATCH, STARTS UL, STOPS BELOW MACL D BOW AS
ON PASSES THEN XES TO EDGE OF BELOW, PUTS DISPATCH ON TABLE, GETS HAMLET
HELMET, JACKET AND MASK FROM BAR

Enter UR:
(MAR open doors)
MAR
Bryars (mask + jacket) ; Von Mende (hold UR for QU + ladies then X DL
Osric- (foil case)
after fanfare ends
King (CR) - Lao & jacket unbuttoned

Enter Bel L ; (MACL open doors)
BACK (R) - MACL (L)
VAN   HOP
DOTY   MISKA
        QUEEN
    Chaptman shut

Enter DR   Volt   ENt TUN L
           Corn
           Peters   SLING
           Rose   NYMAN
           Stan , Pogue
           (Tors)

140

HAMLET   'tis not to come; if it be not to come, it will be

now; if it be not now, yet it will come--the readiness

is all. Since no man of aught he leaves knows, what

is't to leave betimes? Let be.   M#10

(21) Enter servants with table, chairs of state, and
      cushions, and place foils and daggers on the
      table. Enter trumpets and drums. Then enter
      Claudius, Gertrude, Lords, Osric, and Laertes.

CLAUDIUS Come Hamlet, come and take this hand from me.

   (He puts Laertes' hand into Hamlet's. Claudius and Gertrude
                     take their states.

HAMLET   Give me your pardon sir, I have done you wrong

But pardon't as you are a gentleman.

This presence knows,

And you must needs have heard, how I am punished

With a sore distraction. What I have done

That might your nature, honour, and exception

Roughly awake, I here proclaim was madness.

Was't Hamlet wronged Laertes? Never Hamlet.

If Hamlet from himself be ta'en away,

And when he's not himself does wrong Laertes,

Then Hamlet does it now, Hamlet denies it.

Who does it then? His madness. If't be so,

Hamlet is of the faction that is wronged,

His madness is poor Hamlet's enemy.

Sir, in this audience,

Let my disclaiming from a purposed evil

Free me so far in your most generous thoughts,

That I have shot my arrow o'er the house

And hurt my brother.

141

LAERTES   I am satisfied in nature,

Whose motive in this case should stir me most

To my revenge; but in my terms of honour

I stand aloof, and will no reconcilement

Till by some elder masters of known honour

I have a voice and precedent of peace,

To keep my name ungored. But till that time

I do receive your offered love like love,

And will not wrong it.

HAMLET   I embrace it freely,

And will this brother's wager frankly play.

Give us the foils. Come on.

LAERTES   Come, one for me.

HAMLET   I'll be your foil Laertes, in mine ignorance

Your skill shall like a star i' th' darkest night

Stick fiery off indeed.

LAERTES   You mock me sir.

HAMLET   No by this hand.

CLAUDIUS   Give them the foils, young Osric. Cousin Hamlet,

You know the wager?

HAMLET   Very well, my lord.

Your Grace has laid the odds a th' weaker side.

CLAUDIUS   I do not fear it, I have seen you both;

But since he is bettered, we have therefore odds.

LAERTES   This is too heavy. Let me see another.

HAMLET   This likes me well. These foils have all a lenght?

OSRIC   Ay my good lord. (Enter servants with wine.

VOLT
Ø

BAR   LAE
Ø   Ø
                              ↓
Judging for 1st   Ø +   Ø CORN
fight   #   CORN

                                      Ø
                                      HOR

                                                  stay en gard
                    HOR   Judgement.
                    Ø

        CC
        Ø   LAE
                   Ø

              Ø
              HT   Ø
                        VOLT

              Ø
              BAR

Horatio gives glove and mask to HAMLET   V.M towel then back to Sling?
X @B to 4:00 4 + 3   Nyman x ——→ bel ——→ Hop before
                                              touch, a touch!
                                              on touch touch Forst Doty — 9:00

AFTER 2nd HOR and CORN X DN to SLING AND UM
           TO CONVERSE.

142

LAE standing 1100
HT at 4:00 344

CLAUDIUS	Set me the stoops of wine upon that table. his keg b table in below
	If Hamlet give the first or second hit,
	Or quit in answer of the third exchange,
	Let all the battlements their ordnance fire.
	The King shall drink to Hamlet's better breath,
	And in the cup an union shall he throw,
	Richer than that which four successive Kings
	In Denmark's crown have worn. Give me the cup, All'Ah'
	And let the kettle to the trumpet speak,
	The trumpet to the cannoneer without,
	The cannons to the heavens, the heaven to earth,
	Now the King drinks to Hamlet.--Come, begin;
	And you the judges bear a wary eye. x in salute; KG
HAMLET	Come on sir.
LAERTES	Come my lord. (They play. OSR beat up blades
HAMLET	One. HOR & CORN acm up
LAERTES	No.
HAMLET	Judgement.
OSRIC	A hit, a very palpable hit. reverse us.
LAERTES	Well--again.
CLAUDIUS	Stay, give me drink. Hamlet, this pearl is thine,
	Here's to thy health. applause
	(Trumpets and drums sound, and
	shot goes off within. 3 secs
	Give him the cup.
HAMLET	I'll play this bout first, set it by awhile.
	Come Another hit. What say you?
LAERTES	A touch, a touch, I do confess t
CLAUDIUS	Our son shall win.

Third Fight

    Moody & Proshek move out

    Corn press people back arms out

    after poisoning Hamlet pursue LAE into below

    LAE run out to 6:00 for final clash and fall

    All on stair crouch for Hamlet's mask removal

    Ladies to UR when fight continues after LAE out of below

    Men to DL

    Bock, Miska and Van to Queen

    Slingsby catch LAE

HOR to 4:00 buckos HAMLET when he nears edge   <

HAMLET remove mask inspects L hand. HOR climbs stairs line, HOR move to 3:00 on
3 as HAMLET advance on LAE in below

           QN has X'ed to bench, ↓

         OSr tries to interpose blade, HT beats it upwards   ←
         ; OSr X √ → DR

    on coup de grace LAE +, fall DR stA. HT to below
    HOR 5:00 on 3. HOR takes blade.   ←

143

GERTRUDE   He's fat and scant of breath. (Rises.

             Here Hamlet, take my napkin, rub thy brows. HTx→4:00

             The Queen carouses to thy fortune, Hamlet.
                                    (Takes his cup.

HAMLET   Good madam.

CLAUDIUS   Gertrude, do not drink.

GERTRUDE   I will my lord, I pray you pardon me! (Drinks.

CLAUDIUS (aside)
             It is the poisoned cup; it is too late. Qun offer cup

HAMLET   I dare not drink yet madam--by and by

GERTRUDE   Come, let me wipe thy face (HT on 3+2, QU 6̄)

LAERTES   My lord, I'll hit him now.

CLAUDIUS   I do not think't.

LAERTES (aside)
             And yet it is almost against my conscience.

HAMLET   Come, for the third Laertes, you do but dally.

             I pray you pass with your best violence;

             I am afeard you make a wanton of me.

LAERTES   Say you so, come on.
             FIGHT

OSRIC   Nothing either way

LAERTES   Have at you now!

                 (Laertes wounds Hamlet; then, in
                     scuffling, they exchange rapiers.   L #30B

CLAUDIUS   Part them, they are incensed.

HAMLET   Nay come again. He wounds Laertes. Gertrude falls.

OSRIC   Look to the Queen there. ho!

HORATIO   They bleed on both sides. How is it my lord?

OSRIC   How is't Laertes?

LAERTES   Why as a woodcock to mine own springe, Osric.

             I am justly killed with mine own treachery.

table cleared for kings death
as QN dies HOR above her on 3 ↙

thrust at King – all mime swords going in
then noise from King then "Treason" and cries
CORN ⎫
HOR ⎬ Treason
MAR ⎭

HT x→ KG – all inspire
OSR cower to kneel in crotch

Back behind bll when QN leaves → lie
; x ↷

§

HOR to L tunnel (DIAGRAM)

Slide sword along floor to Moody x to
below take bowl in R hold Claudius who
kneels   with L arm about neck make
him drink. HT stands ½ in bel R of D L pole

HT steps back Claudius↑ turns, raises his
arm as if to strike Hamlet then turns
C tipping over table upstage and falling
against it.

144

HAMLET   How does the Queen?

CLAUDIUS   She swounds to see them bleed.

GERTRUDE   No, no, the drink, the drink—o my dear Hamlet—

HAMLET   The drink, the drink! I am poisoned.

           O villainy! Ho, let the door be locked!
           Treachery! Seek it out.   (Laertes falls.

LAERTES   It is here, Hamlet. Hamlet, thou art slain.

           No medicine in the world can do thee good,

           In thee there is not half an hour of life.

           The treacherous instrument is in thy hand,

           Unbated and envenomed. The foul practice

           Hath turned itself on me, lo here I lie

           Never to rise again. Thy mother's poisoned--

           I can no more--the King, the King's to blame.

HAMLET   The point envenomed too!

           Then venom, to thy work.   (Stabs Claudius.

ALL   Treason, treason!

CLAUDIUS   O yet defend me friends, I am but hurt.

HAMLET   Here, thou incestous, murderous, damned Dane,

           Drink off this potion. Is thy union here?

           Follow my mother.   (Claudius dies.

LAERTES   He is justly served,

           It is a poison tempered by himself.

           Exchange forgiveness with me noble Hamlet.

           Mine and my father's death come not upon thee,

           Nor thine on me.   (Dies.

HAMLET   Heaven make thee free of it. I follow thee.

Hamlet falls— HOR R hand under R pit
n L hand on shoulder. As he goes
down kneel on R, squat on L leg

(145)

HAMLET   I am dead, Horatio. Wretched Queen || adieu.   *QN die*

You that look pale, and tremble at this chance,

That are but mutes or audience to this act,

Had I but time, as this fell sergeant Death

Is strict in his arrest, o I could tell you--

But let it be. Horatio, I am dead,   *HOR to him*

Thou livest; report me and my cause aright   *HT at ½ 4'.*

To the unsatisfied.

HORATIO   Never believe it;

I am more antique Roman than a Dane.

Here's yet some liquor left.

HAMLET   As th' art a man,

Give me the cup--let go, by heaven I'll ha't.   *pull it from him throw it DL*

Back leave QN   O God, Horatio, what a wounded name,
x → keulb CC at
3:30 on O

Things standing thus unknown, shall live behind me.

If thou didst ever hold me in thy heart,

Absent thee from felicity awhile,

And in this harsh world draw thy breath in pain   *L31A M#12*

To tell my story.   *Mar enter above right. Stay at door*

(March afar off, and shot within.)

What warlike noise is this?

MAR
~~OSRIC~~   Young Fortinbras, with conquest come from Poland,

~~To th' ambassadors of England gives~~

~~This warlike volley.~~

HAMLET   O I die Horatio,

The potent poison quite o'er -crows my spirit.

I cannot live to hear the news from England,

But I do prophesy th' election lights

146

HAMLET   On Fortinbras, he has my dying voice;

So tell him, with th' occurrents more and less

Which have solicited--the rest is silence.   (Dies.

HORATIO   Now cracks a noble heart. Good night sweet Prince,

And flights of angels sing thee to thy rest.   M#12A

Why does the drum come hither?

          Enter Fortinbras and English Ambassadors, with
          drum and colours, and Soldiers.

FORTINBRAS   Where is this sight?

HORATIO   What is it you would see?

If aught of woe, or wonder, cease your search.

FORTINBRAS   This quarry cries on havoc. O proud Death,

What feast is toward in thine eternal cell,

That so many princes at a shot

So bloodily hast struck?

FIRST AMBASSADOR ~~The sight is dismal,~~

~~And our affairs from England come too late.~~

~~The ears are senseless that should give us hearing,~~

~~To tell him his commandment is fulfilled,~~

~~That Rosencrantz and Guildenstern are dead.~~

~~Where should we have out thanks?~~

HORATIO   ~~Not from his mouth,~~

~~Had it th' ability of life to thank you;~~

~~He never gave commandment for their death.~~

~~But since, so jump upon this bloody question,~~

~~You from the Polack wars, and you from England,~~

~~Are here arrived,~~ give order that these bodies

High on a stage be placed to view,

And let me speak to th' yet unknowing world

Sling x ⤵ body to L of HOR who
rises. Sling takes his place and HOR
xes out to R of body

147

WARN *(handwritten)* L#32,33 34 HOUSE FUCK S#8 M#13

HORATIO	How these things came about; so shall you hear
	Of carnal, bloody, and unnatural acts,
	Of accidental judgements, casual slaughters,
	Of deaths put on by cunning, and forced cause,
	And in this upshot, purposes mistook
	Fall'n on the inventors' heads. All this can I
	Truly deliver.
FORTINBRAS	Let us haste to hear it,
	And call the noblest to the audience.
	For me, with sorrow I embrace my fortune.
	I have some rights, of memory in this kingdom,
	Which now to claim my vantage doth invite me, *unfurl banners*
HORATIO	Of that I shall have also cause to speak,
	And from his mouth whose voice will draw on more.
	But let this same be presently performed,
	Even while men's minds are wild, lest more mischance
	On plots and errors happen.
FORTINBRAS	Let four captains
	Bear Hamlet like a soldier to the stage,
	For he was likely, had he been put on,
	To have proved most royal; and for his passage,
	The soldiers' music and the rite of war
	Speak loudly for him.
	Take up the bodies--such a sight as this
	Becomes the field, but here shows much amiss. *4 paces*
	Go bid the soldiers shoot. *FIRST CANON*

(handwritten left margin notes: BAR, SING, BAR, NYM, Hamlet slowly, ...rd or with)

(handwritten right side: M 13, S#8, L#32, L#33, L#34)

```
        (A dead march.  Exuent, bearing off the dead
          bodies; after which a peal of ordnance is
          shot off.        hold b.o 5

                    end of call
                    b.o
```

HOUSE *(handwritten)*

WHAN

use for farewell
murder
peace
~~tell todo~~
bustle
bk

WARN: HOUSE LITES OUT
        LITES 1 · 2 · 2A
        MUSIC 1 · 1A
        BEL CUE LITE

	HOUSE LITES TO ½	
	HOUSE LITES	
	MUSIC 1	GO
(END MUSIC 1 - 2 COUNT)	LITE 1	
	MUSIC 1A	GO
(ON B.O.)	BEL CUE LITE	GO
(START MUSIC 1B)	LITE 2	GO

COSTUME DESIGNS

FORTINBRAS

Dark grey collar
& epaulettes.

Important Rank
gilt ensignia.

Silvery-grey
heavy face cloth
OVERCOAT

Very long.

½ belt at back.

Slot for Sword

Silver embossed
buttons —

White
gauntlets

Black boots

Sword,
scabbard,
belt &
sword slings.

Extra high
steel helmet
with spike.

High
stand &
fall collar.

Badge
on cap.

High-ranking
type cap. to
match coat.
Sun-burst &
laurel badge
(gilt.)

© Tanya Moiseiwitsch

LIFE GUARDS

Ⓐ

5 prs. of these

COLLARS EXTRA HIGH!

White lining

Boots
Black leather (not patent leather) with high polish. 1½" HEELS & ELEVATORS.

Back View of Cuirass with pouch and strap.

Detail of coat tails
Piping or narrow cord — V. dark crimson.

Brass buttons

Silver & Brass Helmet

Steel and Gilt Cuirass.

Dark cerise cocks' feathers in helmet.

Salmon face-cloth tunic

Sabre type SWORD + SCABBARD

White sword-belt + hangers.

Breeches:
to look like white buckskin (suggest ski-pant material.)
GAUNTLETS in white buckskin

© Tanya Moiseiwitsch

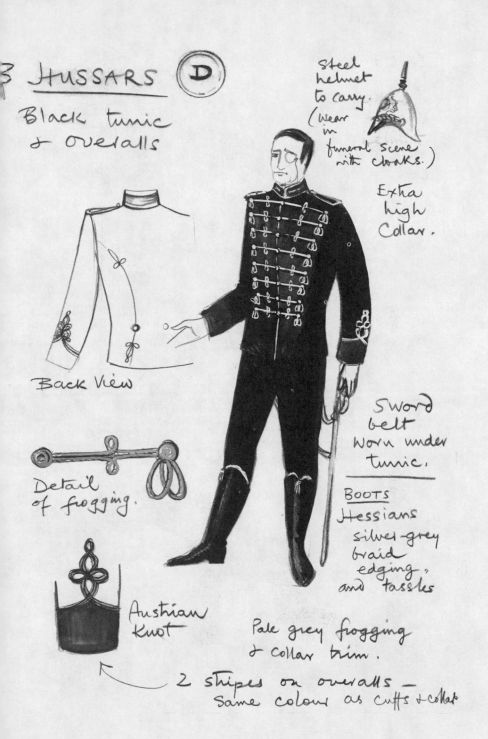

HUSSARS (D)

Black tunic & overalls

Back View

Detail of frogging.

Austrian Knot

Steel helmet to carry. (Wear in funeral scene with cloaks.)

Extra high Collar.

Sword belt worn under tunic.

BOOTS
Hessians
silver-grey braid edging, and tassels

Pale grey frogging & collar trim.

2 stripes on overalls — same colour as cuffs & collar

LAERTES'
RETURN

Trench
Coat.

Soft
felt
hat
instead
of
peaked
cap.

Pistol
in
holster.

Dark
trousers
tucked into
boots.

T.M.
1963

PHOTOGRAPHS

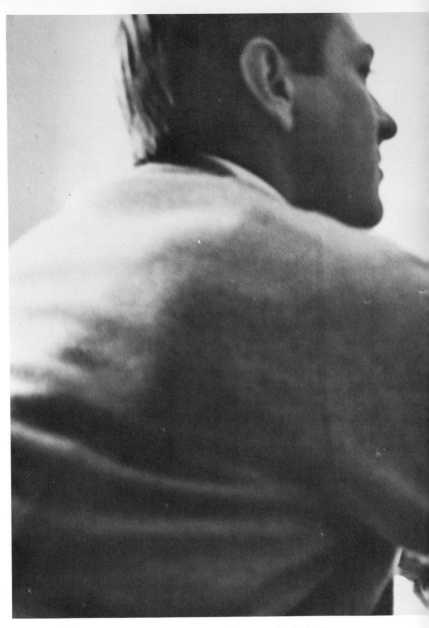

George Grizzard recites a soliloquy as Tyrone Guthrie listens.
The Minneapolis Tribune

The Mad Scene: Laertes, Ophelia, and Gertrude.
The Tyrone Guthrie Theatre

Hamlet recites part of the "Hecuba" speech for the First Player.
The Tyrone Gutrhie Theatre

The Closet Scene: Hamlet, The Ghost, and Gertrude.
The Tyrone Guthrie Theatre

The Finale: Hamlet, Gertrude, and attendants.
The Tyrone Guthrie Theatre

Hamlet advises the players to "Speak the speech . . ."
The Tyrone Guthrie Theatre

Hamlet questions **Guildenstern and Rosencrantz** about their
presence in Elsinore.
The Tyrone Guthrie Theatre

Tyrone Guthrie and Georgie Grizzard in rehearsal.
The Minneapolis Tribune

Rosencrantz tries to get the attention of the preoccupied Hamlet
as Guildenstern watches.
The Tyrone Guthrie Theatre

Rosencrantz and Guildenstern help undress Claudius after the Play Scene.
The Tyrone Guthrie Theatre

The antic Hamlet beats a drum after the Play Scene
as Rosencrantz watches.
The Tyrone Guthrie Theatre

Tyrone Guthrie watches George Grizzard execute a direction in rehearsal.
The Minneapolis Tribune ·

REVIEWS

Dan Sullivan
The Minneapolis Tribune, May 8, 1963

Compelling 'Hamlet' is Traditional

Tyrone Guthrie's production of "Hamlet" is always interesting, often compelling and sometimes great.

Some feared—you had the feeling that some almost hoped—it would be gimmicky. It isn't.

Despite the tennis rackets and umbrellas, it is in the best, nonacademic sense of the word, a traditional performance.

Guthrie has done us a very great favor by presenting "Hamlet" virtually uncut. In a little less than four hours it unfolds like a novel in a pattern of tension, relief (often comic relief) and greater tension. No minor character from Cornelius to Fortinbras is eliminated, and the result is a balanced picture of a world off-balance.

If the play seems at times incoherent and tedious, the reviewer will venture the heresy that this may be more the fault of the author than of the director.

"Hamlet" is a great poem, trapped inside a bulky melodrama, and you can't cut the melodrama without hurting the poem.

Nor, since its hero does not quite know what to make of himself, is it surprising that he leaves us a little puzzled too.

Guthrie's Hamlet is George Grizzard. It is an excellent performance, conveying best the hero's youth, his sense of fun, his basic decency, and most important, his strength.

Grizzard's Hamlet is no moony sentimentalist dripping self-pity at every pore. He is a sturdy, fine young man for the first time up against some of the ugly facts of life. That he is unable to cope with them illustrates more their power than his weakness.

Though Grizzard's rhetorical force is considerable, his performance is basically realistic. The famous soliloquies, for example, are not set pieces; they flow naturally from the mind of the man.

77

Grizzard's performance lacks the extra-dimension of greatness, but is masculine, sympathetic, consistent and very, very intelligent. It should deepen as the season progresses.

"Great" is the word for Ellen Geer's Ophelia. The girl shows backbone in her early interview with the prince ("Indeed, my lord, you made me believe so" is delivered without the customary whimper) and in the mad scene she is actually mad.

Hair in dirty disorder, gown stained with grass, she falls to her knees with a sob and claws the floor of the palace with her fingernails. She is raking her garden—or is it the grave of her father? This double image of fertility and decay is one of the finest moments in the play.

There are several others. Gertrude (Jessica Tandy) enters in her wedding finery in Act One. She looks at Hamlet; Hamlet looks back; his eyes drop; her eyes drop. This situation is revealed as it could not be on the picture frame stage.

Guthrie makes audacious use of his semi-arena stage in the play within-the-play sequence. The lords and ladies ringing the platform hush Hamlet's taunting of Ophelia: they came to see a show. The bone-white beam of a portable spotlight makes the Player Queen's "None wed the second but who killed the first" a shocking breach of social decorum. Claudius (Lee Richardson) purples as he gets the point. He lunges at his nephew and the stage—the theater, too, it seems—explodes in panic. The final duel scene also is beautifully staged.

Guthrie's invention extends to characterization. Robert Pastene's Polonius is, within his limits, a rather capable adviser. Ken Ruta's Ghost is a very substantial figure suffering very substantial pain in the next world and bitterly resents it. Rosencrantz and Guildenstern (University of Minnesota graduate students Alfred Rossi and Michael Levin) are two thoroughly modern sell-out types whose fate we do not regret.

Tanya Moiseiwitsch's splendid 20th century costumes are almost always an asset, clarifying relationships and, since they are mostly formal, illustrating the "royalty" theme as well as costumes from any era might.

The cast is well spoken; Miss Tandy and Richardson are excellent; Nicolas Coster (Laertes) and Graham Brown (Horatio) are capable. The Guthrie Theater is off to a happy start.

Herbert Whittaker
Reprinted from the *Globe and Mail,* Toronto, May 9, 1963

The familiar imprint of Sir Tyrone Guthrie's very particular genius for staging Shakespeare can henceforth be recognized and enjoyed in the middle of the United States, far from Broadway and other capitals of the world's theater. For the new and very modern building which bears his name was this week opened by a production of "Hamlet" richly detailed by his rare and unusual creativity as a stage director.

For Minneapolitans, honored by the latest attempt to establish a classic repertory theater in the English-speaking world, this "Hamlet" must have burst with almost bewildering novelty. For playgoers more experienced in the Guthrie touch, this "Hamlet" seemed less of a new production than one epitomizing the great Guthrie style.

To Canadians the theater itself marks a development of Sir Tyrone's great Stratford experiment, for it incorporates the basic philosophy and many aspects of the Ontario theater and stage in its ultra-modern building.

With the lights on, this new Tyrone Guthrie is multicolored and asymmetrical; house lights down, its projecting stage and encircling theater give much the Stratford feeling.

To Stratfordian buffs, the period selected by Sir Tyrone for this new production of "Hamlet" is even a little familiar, for Tanya Moiseiwitsch's subtle coloring and design return to the direction taken by Stratford's second play, "All's Well That Ends Well."

This is to state less a period than a mingling of periods since the turn of the century. The uniforms are splendidly Teutonic, the ladies' traveling clothes quite Edwardian, but Claudius and Gertrude are impeccable in modern evening dress, Laertes rebellious in a trenchcoat.

Director and designer like their Shakespeare in a world not so far removed from us that trousers are not yet fashionable, yet one in which their queens may wear long gowns every hour of the day. The most brilliant stroke of costuming is that which brings Gertrude on for her first appearance in an immediately recognizable wedding dress. The point of the second marriage is immediately made.

It is the first of many such touches, as if Sir Tyrone had made this production the sum of all his annotations of Shakespeare. Wit and invention hover over every scene, and one watches with a happy smile as one recognises his cleverness.

For instance, we have a Polonius who is no dodderer, but yet aware of his diplomat's tendency to waffle. Indeed, most of his famous precepts are delivered while he is busy signing official documents pertaining to the king's household. Indeed, Robert Pastene's playing of the role is one of the best things of the early part of the long evening. As his king, Lee Richardson is no deep-dyed usurper, but a handsome rather stupid gentleman conscience-stricken and rather clumsily come to intrigue.

Jessie Tandy's Gertrude is a foolish woman, perhaps, but one for whom it is possible to have considerable affection. She is regal, womanly as well as queenly, and well-spoken.

Good speech, as separate from good acting (if that can be) is not yet a matter of full accomplishment by the Minneapolis company, and the extensions of the nearly complete text employed here is hard on them—and often on their audience.

Not even George Grizzard is completely free from this handicap. His Hamlet is a young, serious idealist, capable of careful reason, less so of flights of fancy. Emotionally and intellectually, Mr. Grizzard plots his way most admirably; but he does not soar, and passion traps his spirit rather than releases it. It is an excellent thing to have the second break in the intermission come after the Fortinbras scenes, leaving us to carry the image of a Hamlet newly commited to action.

A Hamlet who does not take off into space with the wild whirlings of his spirit can do serious damage to the heart's core of the play. Still, there is a certain appropriateness to the fact that the first production at the Tyrone Guthrie Theater belongs plainly to Sir Tyrone himself.

How witty he is, and how wicked he can be. His use of spotlights in the play scene, for instance. Claudius is glaring into one when he cries out for "Lights!" and the whole auditorium is set in a dazzle by them. Or the flashlights picking out the hunted Hamlet from the long night's darkness.

And so it goes in parade of fine theatrical tricks. There are umbrellas in the graveyard, revolvers for the rebellion, tennis-rackets before it. The Ophelia of Ellen Geer pushes modernity in another direction, for her madness releases the obscenities lurking in her mad scene in startling fashion. Grizzard's blond Hamlet is matched by a dark-skinned Horatio, well-played but spoken with difficulty by Graham Brown.

Some of the actors take the verse in their stride with greater ease. Ken Ruta is expressive as the Ghost, cut off in a world of death, and he doubles the second Gravedigger with clarity. Ed Preble is a very minor canon as the principal Gravedigger but Ruth Nelson and John Cromwell have fine, full moments as Player Queen and King, and Nicolas Coster is a forthright as well as handsome rebel as Laertes.

As for all those other parts which the full-length Hamlet reveals, Guthrie has devised wonderful flourishes and tricks to explain them away, even if it means turning Rosenkrantz and Guildenstern into gangsters eventually. Alfred Rossi and Michael Levin play the roles. Clayton Corzatte finds it hard to find 20th century flourishes for Osric and Claude Woolman stays well in modern history as the helmeted Fortinbras.

It is all a great accomplishment for the Middle West audience to discover a classic repertory theater doesn't mean finding Shakespeare treated with picturesque reverence. With Sir Tyrone to set the Bard on his ear, they can sail into possession of a rare new and important theater, a citadel of theater far from Broadway.

Less Brown
Variety, May 8, 1963

The "Hamlet" that launched the new Tyrone Guthrie repertory theatre in the Twin Cities may not classify with the great productions of the play but, in its own way, is a memorable edition. Perhaps because he is working with a less than distinguished company, Guthrie has eschewed the grand Shakespearean style for an eccentric interpretation that is rewarding because he brings it off smartly, although it will surely outrage the purists for its sacrilege

This is primarily a director's show, and a bold one that seems to bid deliberately for controversy. Not only has Guthrie outfitted the tragedy in modern Ivy League dress, he has also staged it in a contemporary patrician style with strong American accents.

In this conception, it might be taking place on the New England seacoast, with Hamlet a Princeton graduate whose classmates, Rosencrantz and Guildenstern, are moving up the ladder in modern industry as junior executives.

Laertes packs a pistol, Claudius wears tophat and tails and serves sherry from a teacart, the grave digger smokes cigarets and Horatio is a Negro. Hamlet himself soliloquizes in a smoking jacket as though muttering to himself, and there are hints throughout of the Hitchcock TV mysteries, Henry James and even "Philadelphia Story."

It may not be good Shakespeare, but it is a refreshingly adventurous presentation of the Bard's most familiar work. It becomes an exciting theatrical experience, much as does any experiment that works. The poetry suffers seriously, however, and the mumbling and slurring of language opening night gave the impression of terrible accoustics, although that was dispelled in the next evening's performance of "The Miser."

George Grizzard is not a princely nor even profound Hamlet, but he does admirably by the interpretation. Lee Richardson's Claudius is skillful and polished, Robert Pastene's is a brilliantly realized later-day Polonius, and Jessica Tandy's Gertrude is properly that of a society matron.

Less successful are Ellen Geer's strident Ophelia and Graham Brown's stilted Horatio, but there are a number of commendable minor contributions, notably by Ken Ruta, John Cromwell, Clayton Corzatte and Ed Preble.

Guthrie has done little cutting of script, but keeps the four hours moving with dazzle and smoothness. Tanya Moiseiwitsch's color schemes and functional set are elements in the aesthetic effect, as are the lighting and music. The three-quarter arena theatre is handsome and has good sight lines.

Walter Kerr
New York Herald Tribune, May 9, 1963

We are accustomed to seeing all of the seats in the theater the same color, and there is no particular reason why they should look

like a crazy-quilt of jostling pastels, with yellows and blues and or-
anges contending for elbow room—except that, as it happens, they
look gayer that way.

There is no particular reason why a $2 million playhouse with
two exterior faces (one glass, one wood, both with multiple eyes) and
with an interior resembling a waxed and polished prize-ring, should
have been imagined, financed, built, and fed with actors in Minneapolis, Minn.—except that Minneapolis just decided to go ahead and
do it.

Nor is there any entirely sane reason why director Tyrone
Guthrie should have thought actor George Grizzard ready to play
"Hamlet," except that (A) Grizzard is one of the finest actors in
the country, and (B) ready or not, if he doesn't do it now, he never
will.

As of Tuesday evening, Guthrie, Grizzard, Minneapolis and
an architect with holes in his facade all said, "What have we got to
lose, except money and our reputations?" and went for broke. They
won't go broke. They'll probably go to heaven for their nerve, cheek,
faith, recklessness, impracticality and wisdom, with no more than a
month or two in purgatory for the sins they haven't bothered to
avoid.

The occasion is exciting because it just plain doesn't care
about anything except the right to work. Guthrie doesn't care about
time, in any of its possible senses. His new "Hamlet" is more than
four hours long, and seems so. It also uses candles and flashlights in
the very same castle, just as it uses rapiers in one scene and revolvers
in the next. The night-watch on the ramparts wear costumes out of
"Graustark," Hamlet returns from England in a curled-wool cap that
suggests an impending mission to Moscow, and between times we
are eaves-dropping on a patent-leather Polonius.

Does the circus-on-a-clothesline spirit do any damage to
Shakespeare? Sometimes, yes. To see Hamlet captured by a posse
carrying flashlights suggests that he has been misbehaving in a movie
theater and has been rounded up by the ushers. And there is no need
for Claudius to sneak the bullets out of the gun Laertes has been
waving around; we knew Claudius was a villain all the time.

But out of all the free invention, Guthrie gets another effect
—the effect of looking at the entire play naked, of watching its bones
dance on the grave side, or hearing what it is saying without quite
remembering that it is old.

And there are typical Guthrie improvisations that work most wonderfully. Two doors closing firmly in Hamlet's face as he means to follow his mother from the court. A buzz of spectators catching the implications of the play-within-a-play long before Claudius lets his own nerves be shown: the grapevine runs ahead of the guilty man.

John Cromwell, as the player king, threatening to quit in splendid petulance when Polonius suggests he has gone on "too long." (And ironically Cromwell is the only player king I have seen who did not seem to go on too long.) Jessica Tandy, as Gertrude, standing directly beside the ghost she cannot see, the husband she chooses not to remember; or again, Miss Tandy reporting Ophelia's death and moving away from us all, a vanishing stalk of gray, as though she were going to say nothing more as long as she lived.

There is a ghost (Ken Ruta) who whispers of poison poured in an ear, while whispering poison into Hamlet's ear. There is an Ophelia (Ellen Geer) who redeems the vocal monotony of her earlier distress with the scratched-nails groveling of her madness. Lee Richardson makes an oily tycoon-in-trouble out of Claudius; Ed Preble reads the live-and-let-die philosophy of his gravedigger perfectly; Graham Browne is an impassioned rather than a passive Horatio. But we are keeping Grizzard waiting at center stage. To him.

The first word of his performance is cautious, as though he thought he would be sent home if he did not get each line-reading right. In this mood, he offers us the intelligence of the words, but leaves his own quick actor's intelligence—his altertness, his liveliness, his swiftness of response—in the dressingroom. He is never surprised; he knows the lines too well. With the arrival of the players, though, something happens to him; one feels he has found friends. Actors are actors, after all, and why not just go ahead and be one?

By the time of the closet scene, his instincts have taken command, he is direct, abandoned, pressing—and, lo and behold, his voice has caught up with him and is penetrating, too. The scene lives in its own right—so firmly, in fact, that the "guts" of Polonius can be disposed of in a most unembarrassed fashion. Grizzard is not at present holding his gains: en route to England he has become fuzzily reflective again. It cannot be said that, over-all, this is anything like a mature, or fiery, or poetically free Hamlet. What can be said is that it was entirely worth doing.

For this is the plunge, a plunge of many kinds for many people. The theater will never get anything done if it isn't willing to take a whack at it, and here are talented and determined people whacking in all directions. The score doesn't have to come out heavily in their favor. It is the game that counts just now.

Kevin Kelly
The Boston Globe, May 9, 1963

While the Guthrie Theater must still prove itself in the rough test of time, the question lingering over the first performance was not merely contained in the Dane's soliloquy "To be or not to be."

A theater goer, separate from Minnesota's growing pains, might ask: Can Hamlet be played in context yet appear in contemporary costume, and not, like his father's ghost, becomes bodiless, a mannequin martyred on a directorial whim? Is formal dress a tailor's effort to stitch the gap between centuries by making "Hamlet," despite the flowing words, closer to our own fashionable mould of form? Is, in effect, a chic visual image of a classic a disservice, a perhaps unintended style of patronization, a guileful gimmick?

Let me cancel any such notion.

Under the scheme of Guthrie's direction, this "Hamlet" is magnificent. If it is poetically shy, it is dramatically forceful, and has the awesome sweep of tragedy, a vortex of it whirling in the exact center of its spiralled layers of psychology. In the bravura of its showmanship, the costumes become unimportant, and the play surges with passion rather than fashion.

"Hamlet," for the first time in my experience, becomes a vital encounter, not merely a wordy drama centered on a figure forever lost in his own brooding. Guthrie has charted nothing so cold and distant as a classic; he has carved a relentless memory which involves us all, and the stage becomes the personal battleground of emotion for which it was always intended.

The stage-craft is hypnotic, yet like individual tiles cemented in a large mosaic, it is part of a carefully integrated image. The theater is stabbed with light which cuts through the anguish, floods out of the swirling dark, and illuminates an atmosphere as inducive as the narrative which propels the play. The fanfare music, edged with drum rolls, is like scattered thunder echoing man's pain across a troubled universe. And through it all, there is the pulsing parade of movement which Guthrie has patterned across Tanya Moise-iwitch's altar-like stage.

It works. It carries the play beyond mere stance of poetry to a march of adventure, through the reflective moments to tragic fulfillment. Guthrie has the guts of Shakespeare in his grasp, the unrelenting exhiliration behind the play which makes it what it is, and nothing, least of all academic reverence, dissuades him from dropping guts for easy grace. In case you've missed the point, he has staged the most remarkable production of "Hamlet" the contemporary theater is likely to see.

And now, a slight reservation.

The central role is played by George Grizzard, unmistakably, I think, a giant-in-the-making, a gifted and disciplined actor with, however, a path still to cut.

He plays Hamlet very well, as an intelligent man rather than a prissy spiritual fairy hanging on the night. He is driven by desperate inner force and gradual self-awareness. He is melancholic, a scholar, gentleman, idealist, and, at last, the bloody avenger. Yet, somehow, he did not completely persuade me, as Shakespeare would have it, that he was likely, had he been put upon, ". . . to have proved most royally." Grizzard has greatness within him; at the moment he is only startling good.

Jessica Tandy is excellent as the weak-willed queen. The showdown scene between Grizzard and Miss Tandy is extraordinary.

Ellen Geer is heartbreaking as Ophelia, a young maiden orphaned into madness; Robert Pastene is noble and comic rather than merely addled as Polonius, an old man stumbling in his own prolixity; Nicholas Coster is virile and impetuous as Laertes; Graham Brown is eloquent as Horatio; Lee Richardson is unctuous and despicable as Claudius, "a vice of kings"; and the wandering Ghost of Hamlet's father, played by Ken Ruta, is a nightmare refusing to be stilled in the listener's mind or driven from sight.

John H. Harvey
St. Paul Pioneer Press, June 30, 1963

GUTHRIE'S HAMLET REVISITED

"What a playwright Shakespeare was!" exclaimed my companion.

We were just leaving the Tyrone Guthrie theater last week after a second visit to Sir Tyrone Guthrie's production of *Hamlet*.

On the face of it, that remark might seem a laughable statement of the obvious. But the exclamation expressed a vivid rediscovery of an old truth. Undimmed by all the years, *Hamlet* not only has majesty of poetry, depth and range of human insight and a sweeping sense of the awesome mysteries of this world, but a power to move and excite in purely theatrical terms.

What the Guthrie production of the tragedy does triumphantly is to bring home the fact that Shakespeare wrote both a work of intellectual and esthetic greatness and a whale of a show besides.

All of this comes sharply into focus on a second visit to the production—and that is largely because the production itself now has come into clear, steady focus.

Timing, pacing, weighing, proportioning and dramatic trajectory are superb now that all members of the company have relaxed from the tension of the early performances and have come into full rapport with their parts, with each other and with the entire work and Sir Tyrone's conception of it.

It now becomes clear that there is nothing wayward or extravagantly individualistic about the staging, however strange or even shocking some of the business and details of mounting may have seemed to some at first. They are the work of creative genius in clarifying, illuminating and vivifying the director's reading of the text. This reading is penetrating and analytical from a purely dramatic point of view and never goes beyond what is plainly implicit in Shakespeare's words.

And, as one acquaintance remarked in the lobby, "I never realized before how much the old, traditional costumes actually got in the way of what Shakespeare was saying."

George Grizzard's characterization of the title role has grown admirably since opening night. What was careful and even tentative in the earlier stages of the portrayal has been replaced by greater definition, intensity and bite. There are nuances, accents, flashes of spirit and wit that weren't there before; the sensitivity of his Hamlet is heightened and the agony cuts more deeply.

Ellen Geer's Ophelia has been strengthened, too. The high-school ingenue touches of the portrayal have been eliminated, and she stands forth as a virtuous young woman of spirit and passion. In consequence the sexual flavor of some of her mad songs and accompanying business can be understood simply as expression of natural desire frustrated.

Much the same story can be told about the other cast members in their parts, although I feel Alfred Rossi and Michael Levin need to rein in their activity as Rosencrantz and Guildenstern both in speech and gesture. They are in danger of becoming merely frantic.

To anyone who saw performances of *Hamlet* in the first week or so, my advice is: See it again. You will be gratified at the way the production has grown and matured. And I think you will find, as I did, that it is more gripping and exciting that [sic] you imagined Hamlet could ever be.

Henry Hewes, "Broadway Proscript"
Saturday Review, May 25, 1963

Northwestward Ho!

. . . For its inaugural presentation, Guthrie has chosen to challenge pretentiousness by staging an unusual and uncut *Hamlet.* In it he seems to have discovered that Shakespeare was not Bacon, not Marlowe, but Arthur Wing Pinero. For the actors not only appear in Edwardian costumes, but the play itself is performed in an acting style that resembles the effete and unabashedly impassioned manner in which actors of that period performed. While certain moments gain something from this, its total effect is a reduction in the size of the characters and in the scope of Shakespeare's play.

Claudius, as played by Lee Richardson, begins interestingly as a hyprocrite overly benign in public but abrupt and vicious in private. Over the course of the evening, however, he becomes gradually more comic, like one of those bumbling British dolts Nigel Bruce used to create so well. Robert Pastene's mannered Polonius is all fashion-conscious swagger. Graham Brown's Horatio is so inadequate as to make us suspect that Hamlet has put his confidence in the wrong man. And Ellen Geer's Ophelia is colorless when she is sane, and embarrassingly hysterical when she is mad. Of the others, only Jessica Tandy's Gertrude, with her properly terror-stricken response to Hamlet's chiding, rises to the vividness we expect from this play.

As the Prince, George Grizzard gives a disappointingly flat performance far below the sort of thing he has achieved in his roles on Broadway and with the APA repertory last season. Perhaps he and his director have concentrated too much on modulating the portrayal in a soft-spoken gliding style that presents Hamlet as a man of taste in an effete court where wisdom and justice have been replaced by artificial class-conscious decorum. Only very occasionally, such as when he tells the king that the player-usurper poisons but "in jest," does Mr. Grizzard show us flashes of his magnificent brand of sarcasm, making us wonder whether a Hamlet sustained in that vein might not have been remarkable.

The principal virtues of this *Hamlet* are shown in certain comic moments, such as the one in which Claudius, like the rest of us, cannot keep straight which is Rosencrantz and which is Guildenstern; or in romantic byplay such as the meeting between Hamlet and Ophelia when they suddenly embrace with a lush, forbidden passion; or theatrically imaginative inventions such as the use of old-fashioned spotlights on stands for the play-within-a-play scene, not only to emphasize the difference between the true and the false drama, but to blind the King suddenly and ironically when he turns smack into them and shouts, "Give me some light!" Nor can we help admiring the way Guthrie has staged Claudius's death with a spectacular backward fall against an overturning couch that seems to break his neck.

But *Hamlet* is not *Getting Gertie's Husband.* And while Guthrie's inventive, sure-handed staging, and audacity do make us see the play's events freshly, they are cumulatively self-defeating. . . .